MAXIMIZING
YOUR
EFFECTIVENESS

Also by Aubrey Malphurs

Advanced Strategic Planning
Biblical Manhood and Womanhood
Developing a Dynamic Mission for Your Ministry
Developing a Vision for Ministry in the Twenty-first Century
The Dynamics of Church Leadership
Ministry Nuts and Bolts
Planting Growing Churches for the Twenty-first Century
Pouring New Wine into Old Wineskins
Strategy 2000
Values-Driven Leadership
Vision America
Doing Church
A Contemporary Handbook for Weddings & Funerals and Other Occasions (coauthor)
Church Next (coauthor)
Being Leaders
Building Leaders (coauthor)
Leading Leaders

MAXIMIZING

YOUR

EFFECTIVENESS

HOW TO DISCOVER AND DEVELOP
YOUR DIVINE DESIGN

Second Edition

AUBREY MALPHURS
FOREWORD BY CARL GEORGE

BakerBooks
Grand Rapids, Michigan

Published by Baker Books
a division of Baker Publishing Group
P.O. Box 6287, Grand Rapids, MI 49516-6287
www.bakerbooks.com

Printed in the United States of America

Library of Congress Cataloging-in-Publication Data
Malphurs, Aubrey.
    Maximizing your effectiveness : how to discover and develop your divine design
  / Aubrey Malphurs ; foreword by Carl George.—2nd ed.
        p.   cm.
    Includes bibliographical references and index.
    ISBN 10: 0-8010-6612-3 (pbk.)
    ISBN 978-0-8010-6612-2 (pbk.)
    1. Clergy—Office. 2. Pastoral theology. I. Title.
  BV660.3.M34 2006
  253—dc22   2005032591

Appendix I, Training Venues, was first published as part of chapter 10 of Aubrey Malphurs and Will Mancini, *Building Leaders* (Grand Rapids: Baker, 2004).

To my friend Bruce L. Bugbee,
who first catalyzed my thinking
in the area of creative design.
May his tribe increase.

CONTENTS

FOREWORD

The three dominant generations of Americans who now play significant roles in the general society are all in need of guidance. The Sponsor generation must deal with the consequences of an unprecedented longevity. The Boomers are hit with the digital revolution and its resulting corporate downsizing and job dislocations. The rising Generation X faces a world in which their elders can barely cope, much less give counsel, struggling as they are to find direction themselves as they experience collapses of familiar paradigms in almost every field of endeavor. There is a widely felt cry for personal reevaluation.

Increasingly, the restless and unending search for personal meaning that characterizes much of contemporary life reaches throughout society and into the church.

An industry, the self-help publishing sector, addresses the questions: Of what am I capable? What is my potential? Why am I here? What is to become of me? Is there a meaning and purpose for my life? How do I find fulfillment? At what kinds of activities will I be good? How can I make a contribution to the lives of others? How can I make the most of my talents and opportunities?

The devout Christian adds these questions: What does God expect of me? What clues to God's call are to be found in understanding how God has made me? How can I cooperate with the Creator to bring his plans for me and the world into existence?

This book is a manual for coming to understand yourself and what you should do with yourself. It lays out a process for thinking through the questions that gives practical, straightforward guidance to those who will take the time to work patiently through it. And it makes use of the spiritual-gift discovery and personality-type identification tools that have proved to be so helpful in churches over the past two decades.

The prayerful Christian, willing to listen as well as ask, will be challenged by the awesome implications of realizing what stewardship of a life can mean, in terms of personal fulfillment as well as benefit to humankind. Dr. Malphurs's work in *Maximizing Your Effectiveness* helpfully marks a path to that realization.

Carl George

INTRODUCTION

Carol was excited about her new church and the authentic ministry it had in her life. She and her husband had grown up Baptist in south Texas where church was a way of life—where it had become deeply embedded in their bones. But he was transferred, and now they found themselves in another part of the country attending a new, intentionally different church. She was told that the rapidly growing church had been planted five years ago as a "new paradigm" church—whatever that meant. Regardless, the pastor's sermons had a profound impact on her life. She had heard the Bible preached before but not with such integrity, vulnerability, and relevance.

Most of all, she was amazed at the number of passionate people her age who were involved "up to their elbows" in one form of ministry or another. The tiny congregation in the little church back home had always insisted that the ministry was the pastor's job not theirs—that is what they paid him for! She could remember being coaxed into teaching a class of bored adolescents and hating every minute of it. When she resigned a year later, she swore she would never be abused like that again. She almost left the church. But this situation was entirely different. It seemed as if all her friends were somehow involved in significant ministry and loving every minute of it. They called it authentic ministry: they were doing what God had designed them to do. But what could she do? Where could she serve? Would it be another miserable experience? And how might she discover the answers to these and other similar questions?

Lately Tom had been having trouble falling asleep. Once he was securely under the covers, he tossed and turned much of the night. And when he did fall asleep, a passing car or the neighbor's barking dog easily awakened him. This was highly unusual. In the past, once his head hit the pillow, he remembered absolutely nothing until his faithful alarm awakened him early the next morning. But life was different now; it had taken a new twist.

Two years before, Tom had come to faith in the Savior through the ministry of Campus Crusade for Christ. Another student, who sat next to him in English 101, had periodically invited him to informal get-togethers in the dorm. Finally, when he told Tom that the attractive young lady seated behind them would be there, Tom took the bait. That night Tom heard the claims of Christ, and things had not been the same since. While he had grown up in a church, spiritual things had never made much sense until that special night when they all came together. While it had not been a deeply moving experience—he was not an emotional guy—he did feel a tear welling up in the corner of his eye as he embraced the Savior.

After that night, life quickly took on a whole new perspective. It was as if Tom had finally found what he had been looking for. A missing piece of life's puzzle had fallen into place. He quietly sensed that things would be different from here on. It was both a little frightening and exciting. One of the Crusade directors noted Tom's abilities and saw much potential for Christ. He pulled Tom alongside and began to nurture his newfound faith.

Now two years later, graduation was just around the corner, and Tom was struggling with life after college. Should he pursue what looked to be a decent future in the marketplace? He could return to his blue-collar roots and go home to run his dad's gas station for a while. Or he could pursue vocational Christian ministry. What should he do with the rest of his life, and how could he discern which was the best choice for him in his circumstances? Would he make a good businessman, station manager, or pastor? Where could he best glorify his Savior? Which pursuit would best use the gifts, talents, and abilities that God had given him? Chances were good he would not experience another good night's sleep until he resolved these questions.

Like Tom, David had his share of insomnia. But their situations were different. David was a Christian who had graduated from seminary, married his college sweetheart, and had been a pastor for the last two years—two years that he would describe as the most difficult years of his life.

When he originally applied to the seminary, the application inquired about his vocational plans. He did not have a clue. Initially, as a growing, committed Christian, he wanted to know more about the Bible and theology, so he put that down. That response must have been okay because a month later he received his acceptance in the mail. Toward the end of seminary he chose the pastoral track because one or two of his influential friends had done the same, and he was under pressure—he had to make a decision or delay the completion of his last year.

Upon graduation he and his new bride accepted a call to a small church in a sleepy little town not far from where her parents lived. That is where the nightmare began. The first year was tolerable. He spent most of his time in his study doing what he liked best: studying and preparing scholarly sermons and messages for Sunday morning, Sunday evening, and Wednesday night prayer meeting. What he did not like were the interruptions: weddings, funerals, and pastoral visitations.

In time the criticism began to mount like a tidal wave bearing down on a solitary bather on some lonely beach. The most vocal complaint related to his people skills: "Our pastor should have been a teacher, not a preacher. He loves his books more than his people!" Ouch! That hurt! But deep down in his heart, he knew they were right. He did not seem to fit. What he was doing—pastoral ministry—was not authentic. What should he do? What could he do? Had he made the wrong choice in seminary? Should he leave the church and find another church? Should he even stay in the ministry? Should he pursue doctoral studies? These questions and others recycled through his mind at bedtime and often would not allow him to fall asleep.

Carol, Tom, and David represent the future of the church of Jesus Christ in America and abroad. And it promises to be a delightful future because all, in different contexts, have a deep, God-given desire to serve their Savior in some significant ministry. But they are not sure how to go about it. Everywhere the questions are the same: How can I best serve the risen Savior either as a layperson in my church or in a vocational ministry full-time? How can I serve God authentically, that is, with the feeling that the person he has made me to be connects with what I am doing? I am convinced that believers will not experience the joy and satisfaction of authentic ministry until they are serving Christ in ministries consistent with how God designed them—with their spiritual gifts, passions, temperaments, talents, abilities, and leadership styles.

The problem lies in the answer, or better the lack of an answer. Committed Christian people desire to discover their true place in the body of Christ but are not sure how to go about it. Is the answer found in playing some kind of guessing game with God? Is serious involvement in Christian ministry a trial-and-error process? Does it involve one in a simple cast of the divine die, or is it some kind of colossal, cosmic crapshoot?

I have written this book to help serious Christians like Carol, Tom, and David find some answers to their questions and in turn to discover their places of service in Christ's body, whether part- or full-time. Ultimately what they are seeking is a ministry direction—their personal ministry direction. Life for the believer does not have to be unfulfilled, meaningless, without purpose. Instead Christ offers meaning and significance in his service. The key is discovering your personal ministry direction—your ministry niche. And the result is authentic ministry.

Our vision for ministry exists on both a personal and an institutional level. Institutional vision relates directly to the ministry of a particular Christian organization, whether church or parachurch. I wrote *Developing a Vision for Ministry in the 21st Century* to help leaders develop unique institutional visions tailor-made for the organizations in which they are involved or lead. *Maximizing Your Effectiveness: How to Discover and Develop Your Divine Design* is the companion volume designed to help individuals discover their personal ministry directions. Once Christians have determined their personal direction, they would be wise to identify with a ministry organization that has an organizational vision that aligns most closely with their personal ministry vision. This prevents ministry burnout and in time achieves a greater impact because their vision has the entire ministry organization behind it.

Several churches in America have become pioneers in developing programs to help their congregations discover their personal ministry visions. Bruce Bugbee gave birth to the well-designed Networking program for the people at Willow Creek Community Church located in northwest suburban Chicago, and it has served them well. The same is true of Pastor Rick Warren who has implemented the exciting SHAPE program at Saddleback Church in Mission Viejo, California. In addition, several ministry assessment centers now exist in various parts of the country to help those considering full-time ministry, especially church planters, determine their ministry visions. Though Willow Creek and Saddleback are large, influential churches, it is doubtful that Carol, Tom, David, and most of America will be helped by their ministries. And as helpful as professional assessment centers may be, most people, especially laypeople, will not likely seek out their valuable services.

This book is designed precisely for these people. Discovering our place in the body of Christ is a process consisting of three distinct phases that relate directly to the three parts of this book. Part 1, Discovering Your Design for Ministry, is the logical starting place. It focuses on your ministry design and answers the question, Who are you?

Part 1 consists of four chapters that will help Christians understand how God has uniquely designed them for spiritual service inside or outside the walls of the church. Chapter 1 introduces the biblical concept of divine design by showing from Scripture how God has uniquely crafted and equipped each of us for ministry within his divine purpose and plan. Chapter 2 emphasizes the importance of discovering that design, which results in knowing who you are, liking who you are, and being who you are. Chapter 3 presents the different components that make up the Christian's design, such as spiritual gifts, passion, temperament, natural talents and abilities, and leadership style. Chapter 4 presents and applies the various tools available to assist in the process of discerning your unique divine design.

Part 2, Determining Your Direction for Ministry, builds on part 1 and addresses the primary question of the book, What can I do? Once people know and understand their ministry design, the next step is to discover their ministry direction—their personal ministry mission and vision. Part 2 consists of two chapters. Chapter 5 explains the biblical concept that God has a unique, fulfilling place of ministry for each person in the body of Christ. Chapter 6 leads you through the process of determining your unique ministry niche.

Part 3, Directing Your Development for Ministry, presents the third logical step in the process. Once we know our ministry design and ministry direction, we need to answer the question of ministry development: How do I prepare for my ministry direction? What is the best plan, considering my design, to help me best accomplish my direction? Chapter 7 focuses on how to initiate your plan. Chapter 8 assists you in designing a training plan unique to your ministry, and chapter 9 helps you implement your plan.

The discovery of personal and organizational ministry direction helps Christians in general and leaders in particular determine their future place of ministry in the body of Christ. Consequently this book and its companion are for all serious Christians, whether on a lay or professional level, who desire to be called God's servants. I suspect that this describes you, or you would not have read this far. I suggest you read this book with your Christian friends and the people in your church or parachurch ministry. Be sure to discuss it with them because their insight into your life will be of great value to you. After you have read it and understand your personal direction for ministry, read *Developing a Vision for Ministry in the 21st Century* to determine your organizational vision for the ministry you are involved in or lead. Then answer the question, Am I serving in a ministry organization that best uses my ministry design and vision?

PART 1

DISCOVERING YOUR DESIGN FOR MINISTRY

The first part of this book is aimed at helping you understand that God has designed you in a wonderful, unique way for service in the body of Christ. Further, it will help you understand what your divine design is. This is a necessary prerequisite to determining your ministry direction. Who you are is as important as what you do. Design for ministry precedes direction of ministry.

The key to determining what you can do in the body of Christ is discovering who you are—your ministry identity in Christ.

1

THE CONCEPT
OF YOUR DIVINE DESIGN

Who Do You Think You Are?

Most people have a profound inner desire to accomplish something of importance with their lives during their brief stay on planet Earth. They want more than anything to lead fulfilling, productive lives that leave them with a deep sense of significance. The reality is that few, very few, will achieve it, and most do not know what it is. Consultants Ralph Mattson and Arthur Miller say, "Somewhere between 50 to 80 percent of working Americans occupy jobs wrong for them, according to published surveys."[1] They provide several examples:

> In the teaching profession, we have found that at least two-thirds are not motivated to teach, and we have been criticized for being conservative in our estimates. Examining managers and executives, we have found that only one out of three appears well-matched to his job. Many clergy are not gifted at central requirements like preaching, teaching, and evangelism. One wonders how bad it is with waitresses, doctors, bankers, electricians, and assembly workers.[2]

19

Unfortunately this is true of far too many who make up the Christian community. Many do not know who they are, why they are here, and what they are supposed to accomplish with their lives. The result is nominal Christianity. Few Christians seem fulfilled and lead what they believe to be happy, productive lives for Christ. Instead, many go through this life with a sense of having missed something, of having never realized their full potential for the kingdom of God.

Major culprits are the secular models of human behavior and a common false church model. Public schools, colleges and universities, even the media, mirror these secular concepts so that the average Christian unknowingly imbibes them on a regular basis. The result is much confusion among Christians and a misunderstanding of how God has designed them. But what are these secular models and the false church model, and more important, what does the Bible have to say about people and their design? Just who do you think you are?

Problem: Nonbiblical Models

While several models of the nature of man have surfaced over the centuries, two have affected the Christian mind in particular.[3] These two views are polar opposites that have exerted a major influence from outside the church on how people in general and Christians in particular view themselves and their roles and their potential for accomplishment in this life.[4] The third model—the false church model—has exerted a major influence within the church.

The Deterministic Model

Students of behavior who promote the deterministic or mechanistic model believe a person is born into this world as a piece of clay or a blank slate. Various forces in the environment, such as parents, teachers, peers, and the workplace, act as potters or scribes to mold and shape or write upon the person and, in essence, determine to a large extent who he or she is. The point is that persons become who they are in response to and under the primary influence of others. The behavioral perspective that undergirds this model had its origin in the middle of the twentieth century and was influenced by the work of men such as B. F. Skinner. Though modified to some degree, it continues up to the present and exerts an enormous impact on the psychological world.[5]

A major problem is that this model strips individuals of any personal responsibility for their actions. When a person sins or even commits some heinous crime against society, mechanists are quick to rally around that person and argue that he or she is not to blame for that behavior. They argue that, instead, society in general or the individual's immediate environment is to blame. The person is simply mirroring society in all its ugliness and injustice. The person must not be made to pay for the crime; rather, society is ultimately paying for its crimes against humanity.

Like so many other ideas bantered about in this world, this view of man has some merit. Little question exists that people are affected by their environment, especially by parents and peers. Scripture contains numerous exhortations that make this very point. Proverbs 22:6 encourages parents and others: "Train a child in the way he should go, and when he is old he will not turn from it." Proverbs 22:24–25 warns of our peers: "Do not make friends with a hot-tempered man, do not associate with one easily angered, or you may learn his ways and get yourself ensnared."

At the same time, Scripture does not absolve people of their crimes by shifting the blame to others. Instead, the Bible places the blame squarely on the offender. A case in point is Nathan's confrontation of David over the latter's sin against Uriah and Bathsheba (2 Sam. 12:1–10).

The primary effect this model has on the Christian, however, is that it focuses on society or environment and not on God in determining who the Christian is. The Bible teaches that God has initially designed each person in terms of his or her gifts, talents, and abilities. The mechanistic model divorces God from the process and places blame on or gives credit to parents, peers, and teachers. Consequently Christians may look to the influence of others in the process rather than to God's unique design.

The Developmental Model

Proponents of the developmental model believe people can essentially become whoever or whatever they want to be in this life. It is possible for people to develop their skills, talents, and abilities and become the kind of people they admire and want to be. Thus the emphasis is on personal development. One psychology book states it this way: "Unlike behaviorists and psychoanalysts, who believe that your behavior is determined by your environment or your unconscious needs, humanists believe that you have control of your fate and are free to become whatever you are capable of being."[6]

The New Age movement has picked up on this humanistic perspective and promoted it among its followers. They teach that because people are godlike, they have unlimited potential to be and do whatever they desire. This viewpoint was reflected by one American president who, when he accepted his party's nomination to run for the nation's highest office, said that a part of his dream for every child in this country was that someday they would be able to grow up to become whatever they wanted to be.

Numerous problems exist for this model. First, like the mechanistic model, it ignores God as part of the process. The focus is completely on man, without any reference to divine instruction. That is unacceptable for the Christian.

Second, few debate the idea that people can and should grow and develop their talents, skills, and abilities. According to Luke 2:52 the Savior did this. Yet this view fails to look at who a person is to begin with. The emphasis is on the future. Yet if man is basically good or even godlike, why does he have to become something other than who he already is?

Third, the view fails in the pragmatic realm. It does not work. Though some have been helped, things have not changed appreciably since this view became popular. In general, people continue to struggle with the same old problems of self-esteem and significance. People focus so much on who or what they want to become that they fail to discern and be satisfied with who they are. The latter is the key not the former.

Finally and most important for believers, we cannot be or become whomever we want. As the rest of this chapter will show, God has designed all of us as unique, talented, and gifted individuals who do not need to become other than who we already are. Nothing is wrong with the way God has designed us. The issue is discovering and developing who you are, not becoming who you are not.

In spite of the many problems, it is common to hear the developmental model perpetuated in the Christian community. At Christian colleges, universities, and even seminaries, sincere students who desire to serve the Savior decide what they plan to do with their lives with little regard for who God has designed them to be. As described in the introduction, a young seminarian such as David plans to be a pastor without ever asking the question, *Has God designed me with the gifts, talents, and abilities necessary to function in the pastoral role?* As Mattson and Miller point out, the problem is that far too many clergy today "are not gifted at central requirements like preaching, teaching, and evangelism."[7] Others pursue a particular kind of pastoral ministry, such as church planting or church revitalization, without realizing that different situations call for different leadership styles and abilities. In addition, no two congregations are alike. Lyle Schaller concludes, "These differences among congregations also influence the style of ministerial leadership that is appropriate for a particular congregation at a certain stage of its life. These differences have also made obsolete the old cliché, 'Every minister should be able to serve any congregation.'"[8]

The False Church Model

In addition to the two popular secular models, there exists a false church model. It teaches that in the church, the pastor, not the people, must do the work of the ministry. You can trace its roots back to Roman Catholicism where the priest (clergy) was responsible for ministering to the people (laity). In the twentieth and now the twenty-first century, I have found that the older Builder generation in the Protestant church has held and promoted this view. They believe this for several reasons. First, the pastor is the one who has been trained for ministry. Some have even been to seminary. Second, God has called the pastor to the ministry. Third, many pastors are ordained, whereas the laity is not. Fourth, that is what we pay the pastor to do.

I am convinced that this view, which is so contrary to Scripture (see Eph. 4:11–13), brought the church in the twentieth century to its knees, causing many churches to close their doors. If the employees at General Motors held this view, they would build few cars, and the company would go out of business. Hopefully we will correct this in the twenty-first century.

The Biblical Model

What does Scripture say about humankind and their design? Who are we? What role does God play in our developmental process? Both the Old and New Testaments provide a different picture of humankind from those portrayed by the deterministic and developmental models. The Bible articulates a design theology that places God's stamp on his creation. Both Testaments put God in the picture and teach that he has fashioned us with a wonderful, unique design. The biblical emphasis is not on the shaping role of the environment or our becoming someone else. Instead, the thrust of the Scriptures is on who you are as God's creative expression. So the question is not only, Who do you think you are? It's also, Who does God say you are?

The Old Testament

The Old Testament reflects a design theology. The concept of God as the master designer is displayed throughout his creation. In Psalm 19:1 David writes, "The heavens declare the glory of God; the skies proclaim the work of his hands." God is the sovereign Creator whose handiwork is evident not only in the beauty of the physical universe but in its design, from the function, precise placement, and circulation of the sun, moon, and planets (Gen. 1:14–19; Eccles. 1:5), to the circulation patterns of the winds and seas (Eccles. 1:6–7), right down to the intricate structure of a leaf.

The animal world reflects God's design. He created animal life on days five and six (Gen. 1:20–25). He divided the animal kingdom into various distinct species that reproduced "according to their kind." Each mirrors God's unique craftsmanship, as illustrated by the story "A Rabbit on the Swim Team."

Once upon a time, the animals decided they would do something meaningful to meet the problems of the new world. So they organized a school.

They adopted an activity curriculum of running, climbing, swimming, and flying. To make it easier to administer the curriculum, all the animals took all subjects.

The duck was excellent in swimming; in fact, he was better than his instructor. But he made only passing grades in flying and was very poor in running. Since he was slow in running, he had to drop swimming and stay after school to practice running. This caused his webbed feet to be so badly worn he became only average in swimming. But average was quite acceptable, so nobody worried about that—except the duck.

The rabbit started at the top of his class in running but developed a nervous twitch in his leg muscles because of so much makeup work in swimming.

The squirrel was excellent in climbing, but he encountered constant frustration in flying class because his teacher made him start from the ground up instead of from the treetop down. He developed a charley horse from overexertion, and so got only a C in climbing and a D in running.

The eagle was a problem child and was severely disciplined for being a nonconformist. In climbing classes he beat all the others to the top of the tree but insisted on using his own way to get there.[9]

The lesson is obvious. God created each animal with a unique design to accomplish a distinct purpose. He designed ducks to swim, rabbits to run, squirrels to climb, and eagles to fly.

We, too, reflect God's special design. Genesis 1:27 records the creation of man, not in the image and likeness of the animal kingdom but in the image and likeness of God. Thus we were created and designed to function as God's representatives on earth with dominion over the earth (Gen. 1:26–28; Psalm 8). God placed Adam in the garden "to work it and take care of it" (Gen. 2:15). For Adam there was a clear sense of meaning and purpose to his existence.

In several passages the Old Testament presents God as the Potter and people as the clay vessels that he molds and shapes (Job 10:8–9; Ps. 119:73; Isa. 29:16; 64:8). The primary implication of this metaphor is that God is both Creator and sovereign Lord over man. The very figure itself hints of design. Molding and shaping implies designing. As a potter molds and shapes each vessel of clay, so God in the creative act designs humankind.

This design relates to both our immaterial and material aspects. In Psalm 139:13–16 the psalmist writes, "For you created my inmost being; you knit me together in my mother's womb. I praise you because I am fearfully and wonderfully made; your works are wonderful, I know that full well. My frame was not hidden from you when I was made in the secret place. When I was woven together in the depths of the earth, your eyes saw my unformed body." In the passage David is emphasizing God's sovereignty and superintendence over the creative processes relating to reproduction, even the immaterial or spiritual as well as the physical. Yet in the midst of this graphic but figurative language—the creating, knitting, weaving, and making, and the wonder of it all—the design aspect, though by no means the emphasis, is present.

God's creative design is also reflected in our skills, talents, and abilities. In the process of constructing the tabernacle, the Lord appointed certain craftsmen, in particular Bezalel and Oholiab, to engage in their areas of expertise—making artistic designs for gold, silver, and bronze; the cutting and setting of stones; and working with wood (Exod. 31:1–5). Verse 3 says that God filled Bezalel with the Spirit and gave special skill, ability, and knowledge to execute the project. The same is found in other texts: Exodus 28:3; 35:30–36:1. They were all skilled craftsmen by divine gift. Whether these skills were a part of their initial design from birth is not clear, for the text does not indicate such. I suspect they were, and that is why they were selected to begin with. Regardless, God gave them the necessary skills and abilities or additional skills and abilities to accomplish the temple project.

Several other passages and some parallel passages in the Gospels and Epistles also suggest God's unique, personal design-stamp on people. In Jeremiah 1:4–5 the prophet writes, "The word of the Lord came to me, saying, 'Before I formed you in the womb I knew you, before you were born I set you apart; I appointed you as a prophet to the nations.'" Much the same is said of John the Baptist (Luke 1:13–17), the Messiah (Isa. 49:1–6), and Paul (Gal. 1:15). The question is whether these are unique cases that would not be true of the rest of us. The biblical teaching on predestination, foreknowledge, and the divine will indicates that God does not sit up in heaven and capriciously guess at the future (Acts 2:23; 4:27–28). God knows all about us and our designs because he has determined them beforehand. However, he chose to reveal his design in a special way to Jeremiah, Zechariah, and Paul because of their unique circumstances.

The New Testament

The New Testament reflects a design theology as well. It is communicated through the concept of the body of Christ, the parable of the talents, and the biblical teaching on spiritual gifts. In 1 Corinthians 12:12–27 and Romans 12:4–5, Paul draws an analogy between believers who make up the church, the body of Christ, and the human body. As God's design is evident in the human body, so it is in the spiritual body—made up of all who are in Christ. Spiritual gifts in the church body reflect the principle of design (1 Cor. 12:1–11, 28–31).

What does this figure imply about our designs? First, God has sovereignly made us just the way we are—God is the Architect, the Master Designer, the Potter. Whether you are an ear or an eye, 1 Corinthians 12:18 teaches, "God has arranged the parts in the body, every one of them, just as he wanted them to be." Therefore, there is no need to be upset with our place or function in the body of Christ. Instead there is much satisfaction in knowing we are ministering in accordance with God's design and purpose for our lives. The key is discovering which body part you are, then functioning according to that design.

Second, God has made us different—a hand, an ear, or an eye (1 Cor. 12:14–17). While Christians may have similar designs, no two have the same design. When it comes to making people, God is not in the cookie-cutting business—each of us is unique. Consequently Christians need to discover their different designs and places of service; they cannot do anything they want. As the story "A Rabbit on the Swim Team" illustrates, God designed ducks to swim and rabbits to run. When ducks attempt to run or rabbits try to swim, they are functioning outside their intended design, and serious problems soon develop. The same is true of people. An eye cannot serve God effectively as an ear, nor can an ear serve as an eye.

Third, while God has made us different, all of us are needed if the body is to function well (1 Cor. 12:14–17). A major problem for the church in the twenty-first century is "unemployment." Too many Christians have dropped out of church, joining the ranks of the unchurched across America. And those remaining tend to be involved as spectators. Larry Richards and his colleagues asked five thousand pastors what the greatest needs are for strengthening the church. From a twenty-five-item list, nearly 100 percent gave a first or second priority to "Getting my laypeople involved as ministering men and women."[10] I suspect that a major reason for this problem is the church's insistence on placing believers in ministry positions for which they are not designed—round pegs in square holes. In a short period of time, they burn out and drop out. Discovering our divine design is the key to implementing Ephesians 4:11–12 in the church.

Another passage in the New Testament that touches on God's divine design is the parable of the talents in Matthew 25:14–30. In this parable a master (God) decides to take a journey, leaving three servants in charge of his property. According to the ability of each one, he gives a certain amount of money ("talents") to invest. (Here the term *talents* is not to be confused with natural gifts or abilities.) One man doubles his five talents to ten and is well rewarded when the master returns (vv. 19–21). Another doubles his two and is also rewarded (vv. 22–23). However, the third accomplishes nothing with his single talent, and the master rebukes him and gives that talent to the first servant (vv. 24–28).

Several observations are important for the divine design concept. First, this parable is one of two parables following the disciples' request for Jesus to explain the destruction of the temple, the sign of his return, and the end of the age (Matt. 24:1–3). The two parables appear to address life as it will be at his return. The parable of the talents addresses how God's professed servants should use their God-given abilities for him until he returns.

Second, all the servants have differing abilities. Both the first and second are highly commended and rewarded, yet they are not the same. This holds true for Christians. All have various abilities worthy of the master's commendation and reward, yet some have more ability than others.

Third, the master understands the abilities of each servant and distributes the money accordingly. The one with the most ability is given the five talents and the one with the least is given only one talent. God also apparently distributes ministry opportunities on the basis of our abilities. God as Creator understands each person's design and does not ask us to accomplish more in life with those natural abilities than we are capable of doing. He did not give five talents to the servant who was capable of handling only one.

Fourth, the harsh treatment of the last servant involved his failure to discern who God is, which in turn led to his mishandling of the single talent. His failure was not that he was a one-talent person, for God rewarded the other two not according to their talents but their abilities. The point in verses 24 to 26 is that the man did not understand God's true character and failed to use his ability accordingly. God is not hard, harvesting where he does not sow and gathering where he has not cast seed. Based on his misunderstanding of the master's true character, the servant would not venture any risk and failed to invest his talent wisely. It is most important that Christians seek to use their God-given capabilities wisely, understanding God's true nature. Once we have discovered what those abilities are, we must understand God's provision and take risks to use those abilities to their fullest for Christ. Though God's judgment of us will not be as harsh as that of the wicked servant, who most likely was not a true believer (v. 30), service for the Savior is not to be viewed lightly.

A third portion of the New Testament that contributes to the divine design concept is the biblical teaching on spiritual gifts. Far too many in the body of Christ are not aware that this topic is in the Bible. Consequently they go through life never realizing that God has bestowed on them special abilities to make a vital contribution to his kingdom. When individual, gifted believers are not aware of their spiritual gifts and do not minister with them, the whole body of Christ is hindered in its effectiveness (1 Cor. 12:20–26). Some confuse spiritual gifts with other related areas of their design, such as the ability to work with a particular age group. Others confuse them with the fruit of the Spirit in Galatians 5:22–23.

Scriptures that relate to God's spiritual gifts are found in 1 Corinthians 12; Romans 12; Ephesians 4; and 1 Peter 4. Spiritual gifts are God-given abilities to serve him in a particular manner in his kingdom. They are God-given for they come from him (1 Cor. 12:7; Eph. 4:7–11). He bestows them sovereignly so that each Christian has at least one as a part of his or her divine design (1 Cor. 12:11). They are distributed to each individually to make a distinctive contribution to the body as a whole (v. 7).

Worksheet

1. Do you have a strong desire to live a meaningful, fulfilling life while on this earth? Do you feel an inner compulsion to accomplish something of importance with your life? Why or why not?

2. Do you believe that up to this point you have made a significant contribution to your community, church, or family? Have you gained a deep sense of significance? Why or why not?

3. Do you know who you are—how God has designed you? Do you know why you are here, and what God wants to accomplish with your life? Have you realized your full potential for the kingdom of God? Why or why not?

4. Most likely you have been exposed directly or indirectly to the ideas that your environment has exclusively shaped you into who you are (deterministic model) or that you can be or do anything you want (developmental model). You've also been taught by example that the pastor, not the people, must do the work of the ministry. Which model has most influenced you? When and where did this take place? Did this exposure come through your parents, teachers, peers, the media, your church?

5. Has your exposure to these models influenced your thinking about your own abilities to serve God? If so, explain.

6. What are some of the passages or concepts in the Bible that teach the divine design? As you read this chapter, did any other passages come to mind? If so, what are they?

7. Can you think of any arguments or reasons other than those in the Bible that imply or illustrate the divine design concept?

2

THE IMPORTANCE
OF YOUR DIVINE DESIGN

What Difference Does It Make?

There was little question in Carol's mind that God wanted her to be an attorney. She got her start in the field as a part-time clerk during her first year at law school in south Texas. And she was good at it. It did not take the firm long to realize her potential, so by the time of her graduation she was practically functioning as an attorney with two clerks and one secretary—even though she had not taken the bar exam. She loved every minute of it—the challenge, the intrigue, and the people. When her husband had a job transfer, she easily relocated and quickly adapted to a similar position in a branch firm in their new city.

Though she had completely devoted her life to Christ, Carol believed her full-time ministry was to be a good attorney. Still, she craved meaningful involvement in her church for many reasons. Its ministry had become important to her and her husband. Many exciting things were happening, convincing her that God had wonderful plans for this rapidly growing congregation. Carol was thrilled when several of her friends at work visited the church and in time embraced the Savior. Since she and her husband could not have children, they decided to invest a significant portion of their lives in ministry in the church. They had become serious Christians, intent on accomplishing authentic ministry for their Savior. They did not have a lot of discretionary time, however, so what was available needed to be invested wisely.

One item of immense importance in Carol's life was her divine design, her ministry identity. Her understanding of this would determine what Christ would accomplish through her life and ministry both at work and in the church.

The divine design concept is important in two ways for Carol, her husband, and all who are serious about serving Christ on a part-time basis in a church or in a vocational Christian ministry. The first is personal and the other is institutional.

The importance of the divine design concept for each Christian is practically unlimited. Three areas, however, stand out.

Knowing Who You Are

First, it is important that you know who you are. Initially this could pose a threat. You may fear probing your design because in the past you have taken psychological tests focused on uncovering pathological problems (sin problems). While this can prove spiritually valuable, it can also be a frightening and disconcerting experience. There is an analytical side to assessment, often associated with the field of psychological counseling, that uses tools such as the Minnesota Multiphasic Personality Inventory (MMPI) to discover emotional abnormality or dysfunctional behavior (these are problems in the area of your "flesh" or "sinful nature" described in Gal. 5:16–21). Whether you use these tools or not, it is critical to any ministry for Christ that you understand where your sin problems lie and that you deal with them.

On the other hand, not only should we discover what is wrong with us, we can and must discover what is right with us. The former explores our depravity, which is beyond the scope of this book, while the latter explores our dignity, which is the purpose of this book.[1] And it is the latter that represents the positive side of knowing our identity—who we really are.[2] The following will put this into perspective.

Divine Design

Discovering who you are involves discerning your divine design. The process delves into your capabilities.

Your capabilities are your spiritual gifts, passion, temperament, natural talents and gifts, and other abilities that you have from God. They reside with each of us who knows Christ as personal Savior and in a sense are waiting to be discovered so they can be used in service for Christ. In fact it would seem strange that believers would not be excited and vitally interested in discovering the abilities with which God has blessed them. Everybody is a 10 somewhere,[3] and the discovery of your design helps to determine precisely where.

While you can grow and develop in many areas, your capabilities are sovereignly assigned by God and will not change over time. They do not change in essence before or after conversion. Consultants Mattson and Miller write:

> Our evidence demonstrates that motivational patterns do not change when a person becomes a Christian. The ingredients seen prior to conversion are seen after conversion. This is disturbing to people who expect it to be otherwise, but perhaps we will better understand our position in Christ if we see that God's intention for us is not replacement of who we are, but redemption of who we are. God's creation of us, including our basic motivational pattern, is not bad. . . . Conversion has us rejoicing in the fact that we are enabled to become who we originally were made to be, rather than becoming someone entirely different. The renewal takes place when we are resurrected in conversion; and sanctification causes a radical change, not in the gift we have, but in its purpose and use.[4]

Therefore it would be a waste of time to ask God to give us different spiritual gifts or to change us to another temperament.

Personal Character

Discovering who you are involves discerning your character.

Your character is the foundation of your ministry whether you minister from the perspective of a layperson or someone involved in vocational Christian ministry. It is the essential element that qualifies you to minister to others. Unlike your divine design, God does not sovereignly predetermine your character. Rather, it is subject to change and must be developed. In fact the development of Christian character is a lifetime process.

Character involves *being* and is a matter of your heart, whereas your design involves *doing* and is a matter of your gifts, talents, and abilities. For you to be effective in ministry over the long haul, being must precede doing, because what you do (your ministry) flows out of who you are (your character). If doing should ever exceed being, then the development and exercise of your design will ultimately suck the life out of your heart, and you will crash and burn.

Our character strengths are those positive traits that conform to Christ's character—our Christlikeness. Scripture refers to numerous character qualities that enhance the life of the believer. Representative is Paul's list of specific character qualities in 1 Thessalonians 2:2–8 that enhanced his ministry. One quality described in verse 2 is *courage*. Ministry has its ups and downs. In the down times, it takes men and women of courage who are willing to take faith-risks to serve the Savior. Hebrews 11 spotlights several faith cameos of courageous people who trusted God during ministry down times.

Another quality in verse 2 is *endurance*. Those who serve Christ in any way must not be too quick to quit. Most often it is through endurance of difficult situations that we learn our greatest spiritual lessons. A quick study of those who have achieved significant ministries reveals that they have the ability to hang tough rather than quit and run.

In verse 3 Paul reveals the character qualities of *integrity, purity,* and *honesty*. If we have any problems in these areas, the entire ministry suffers the consequences. Christian ministry in the 1980s and 1990s suffered adversely at the hands of professionals who professed Christ publicly but lacked personal integrity, purity of motive, and individual honesty.

Finally in verse 7 Paul describes his *gentleness* and *affection*, comparing himself to a caring mother. In verse 8 he assures those under his ministry of his affection. It is amazing what others can accomplish when they know we love them.

Scripture also cites specific character qualities as essential for leaders and followers. In 1 Timothy 3:1–13 and Titus 1:5–9, we find essential qualities for elders and deacons, such as self-control, respect, discipline, hospitality, gentleness, honesty, and trustworthiness. We find additional character qualities for leaders in Acts 6:3–5, such as the filling of the Spirit, faith, and wisdom. Scripture encourages every Christian to work toward maturity and Christlikeness (1 Cor. 11:1; Gal. 4:19; Eph. 4:13), to live by the Spirit (Gal. 5:16), and to evidence the fruit of the Spirit: love, joy, peace, patience, kindness, goodness, faithfulness, gentleness, and self-control (vv. 22–23).

Life's Circumstances

Discovering who you are involves discerning your life's circumstances. This process examines such areas as your age, marital status, race, education, gender, and health.

AGE

We are never too young or old to have a ministry in the body of Christ. Ministering on a part-time basis is possible for any Christian regardless of age. Early in his or her life, the divine design of a child is discernable, and parents would be wise to observe their children's ministry makeup and begin to encourage them to pursue certain ministries in the church. I believe that we need to involve children and young people in ministry rather than just ministering to them. Perhaps this would help stem the tide of their dropping out of church after completing high school.

Full-time ministry, however, does have some age restrictions. Particularly in the church environment, the current trend is to recruit pastors between their twenties and fifties, with the exception of those who minister to senior citizens. In the 1990s the average age of those entering seminaries climbed to nearly thirty, and an increasing number of Christians are pursuing vocational ministry as a second career. In the past most pastors stayed in the pulpit until God took them home. Today churches are discouraging this practice and tend not to hire men as senior pastors who are in their fifties or older.

MARITAL STATUS

For most ministry positions, married people are preferred over singles and the nondivorced over divorced Christians, especially in vocational (full-time, compensated) ministry. In the past this was because there were more marrieds than singles and more nondivorced than divorced, but the figures are shifting.

Divorced Christians carry a certain stigma with them regardless of their situation. The Baby Boom and Bust generations, however, seem more accepting of pastors who have experienced a divorce. While theologians debate the impact of divorce on the qualifications of those who pursue vocational Christian ministry in general and pastoral ministry in particular, most agree that it does not negate one's divine design. Regardless, it is much easier for divorced Christians to minister nonvocationally than vocationally.

RACE

A Christian's race should not affect his or her service for Christ. While Scripture acknowledges the difference between races (for example, Jews and Gentiles), it does not place any one race above another (Gal. 3:28). In fact Scripture does not tolerate discrimination on racial grounds, and the early church took action in such situations (Acts 6:1–7).

The issue of race becomes important in vocational ministry when we consider the homogeneous principle developed by missiologist Donald A. McGavran. The principle states: "Men like to become Christians without crossing racial, linguistic, or class barriers."[5] In effect it teaches that ministry is most effective among those who are of the same race, language, or social class as the minister, especially in evangelizing lost people.

This has become one of the most controversial principles in the Church Growth movement, and its critics attack it as racist and classist.

To be fair to McGavran, however, I must say that he is not arguing that this is the way things ought to be or that ministries should discriminate on the basis of race, language, or class. He is arguing that in most situations people of the same race, language, or class tend to minister best to one another, whether to Christians or non-Christians.

There are various reasons for this. One is that people from the same group understand best the culture, needs, and aspirations of those most like them. Another is that lost people generally think and act with an awareness of race and culture. Most will be attracted to a church where the people are like them in some way. I refer to this as the affinity factor. A third reason is that no church can be culturally neutral, and most people are attracted to a church that is closest to their culture. Regardless, it is a biblical imperative that a church must never discriminate for any reason against anyone on the basis of race, language, or class.[6]

EDUCATION

Our educational level impacts our ministry. Whether right or wrong, someone of inferior education will have difficulty ministering to those with an exceptional education. An education or the lack thereof affects the individual's ministry credibility. In a day when professionalism is at a premium, those who are considered unprofessional are at a distinct disadvantage. In most situations, people prefer that ministers have an education that is equivalent to or beyond their own. This is true in terms of nonvocational ministry and especially true of those in vocational ministry. It is difficult to pursue vocational ministry or training for ministry without certain basic educational credentials—a high school or college diploma.

GENDER

In the past women have been in the majority of those actively serving the Savior in nonvocational ministry. Those who have grown up in the church can usually remember a woman who had an impact in their lives for the Savior—but not a man, besides a pastor. Professional ministry and higher leadership positions, however, have been dominated by men.

In the second half of the twentieth century this began to change. More women have found professional positions on ministry teams. Some churches have women on their leadership boards serving as elders and deacons. The evangelical wing of the church has debated what the Bible teaches regarding the role of women in ministry in general and the church in particular. Can women be pastors of churches or elders on church boards? Can they teach men? Each Christian and each ministry must study this issue and follow through in ministry accordingly.

HEALTH

For obvious reasons those in good physical health have an advantage over those in poor health. Regardless of a person's divine design or spiritual character, poor health or disabilities can limit ministry in several ways. For example, someone confined to a wheelchair might have difficulty functioning as a traveling evangelist, and allergies could limit some ministries to a state such as Arizona.

Not only can one's own health affect a ministry, the poor health of a spouse or child or an aging parent can have the same limiting effect. The important thing to remember in any of these situations is that God is sovereign in our affairs (Dan. 4:17, 25, 32). We should attempt to serve him as best we can in the context of any particular health limitations.

Liking Who You Are

A second personal benefit of *knowing* who you are is *liking* who you are. The offices of Christian counselors and pastors are inundated with people who are struggling with poor self-esteem. The growing number of emotional and spiritual self-help books and articles indicates that the problem is becoming epidemic in proportion. Far too many Christians look in the mirror and dislike what they see. In many cases they habitually evaluate themselves in terms of their depravity and not their dignity. They have little knowledge of themselves and dislike what knowledge they do have. The result is a profound sense of insignificance and low self-worth.

The Command

Scripture teaches in a positive way that we should love ourselves. Jesus commands, "Love your neighbor as yourself" (Matt. 19:19). Paul conveys the same principle when he tells husbands "to love their wives as their own bodies. He who loves his wife loves himself. After all, no one ever hated his own body, but he feeds and cares for it, just as Christ does the church" (Eph. 5:28–29). And again in verse 33 he writes: "However, each one of you also must love his wife as he loves himself, and the wife must respect her husband."

The Problem

When Paul and Jesus command Christians to love others as they love themselves, are they advocating some form of narcissism? This would clearly cut against the grain of biblical truth. So much of Scripture addresses our responsibility to put others before ourselves. In Philippians 2:3–4, Paul exhorts believers: "Do nothing out of selfish ambition or vain conceit, but in humility consider others better than yourselves. Each of you should look not only to your own interests, but also to the interests of others." And in verse 21, he speaks negatively of those who put their own interests first: "For everyone looks out for his own interests, not those of Jesus Christ." Again in 1 Corinthians 10:24, Paul writes: "Nobody should seek his own good, but the good of others." Finally, one of the qualities of love mentioned in the great love chapter of the Bible, 1 Corinthians 13, is that "it is not self-seeking" (v. 5).

The Solution

The solution to this apparent contradiction lies as usual in a careful handling of the texts in their context. The key passages to unraveling the mystery are Ephesians 5:29 and 33. Paul follows his exhortation to love oneself in verse 28 with verse 29, which clarifies the meaning of the abstract concept of love with a concrete example—caring for and feeding the physical body. Certainly the physical acts of caring for and feeding one's physical body are self-focused. Yet most agree that they are necessary and vital to other acts that are others-focused and therefore are not to be considered narcissistic.

Verse 33 sheds more light on the meaning of the "love oneself" concept and introduces the emotional element. After Paul tells the husband to "love his wife as he loves himself," he again follows with a concrete statement that helps define what he means by the abstract term *love*. He adds, "and the wife must respect her husband." The key term here is *respect*. It is Paul's clarification of what he means by self-love—it involves self-respect. Consequently, loving yourself involves taking care of yourself physically and emotionally. These are necessary, permissible requirements if you are to function well in ministry.

The Implication

A critical factor in loving ourselves biblically is liking ourselves. That is where discerning our divine design is so important. It reveals our gifts, talents, and abilities in a favorable light. We discover what is good about ourselves as well as what is not so good. We maintain a healthy balance in the awareness of both our depravity and our dignity. Then, once our design is deployed in the proper ministry environment, we have an added, powerful sense of significance and incentive for more ministry that delights our souls and honors the Savior.

Being Who You Are

A third personal benefit of knowing your divine design is the fact that *knowing* and *liking* who you are naturally leads to *being* who you are. The former creates a powerful thirst for the latter, and the result is authenticity.

The Problem

People who do not like who they are often attempt to avoid who they are or try to be someone else. They put on false masks and play roles so others will not discover their identity and unmask their perceived ugliness. They fear that if people find out who they are, they will not like them and will reject them. If they do not like themselves, then it is only logical that others will not like them either. The pain from this would prove unbearable and must be avoided at all costs. The thing farthest from their minds is living authentically or modeling vulnerability.

The Solution

The solution is discerning our divine design. When we discover who we are in Christ and how God has uniquely designed each of us after his image to contribute in a significant, meaningful way to his kingdom, we are free to be authentic. But what is authenticity? It is integrity from core to crust.[7] What you see is what you get—personal reality. We take off our masks and stop playing fictitious roles because we know and like who we really are and no longer are ashamed of what God has made. The result? An authentic life that produces authentic ministry.

Another by-product is vulnerability. Those who do not know or like who they are, whether Christian or non-Christian, are not vulnerable people. Vulnerability means sharing Christ's strength in the context of our weakness.[8] William Lawrence writes, "It is the appropriate disclosure of an older brother or sister's pilgrimage that focuses on Christ in His conviction, faithfulness, grace, and blessing in such a way that attention turns to Him and the developing leader is encouraged, released from sin, and motivated to grow in confidence and impact."[9] Only as we become convinced of the wonder and beauty of our design and accept ourselves as God accepts us can we truly be vulnerable.

Over time our self-image blooms and matures as we discover a new freedom in Christ that we may never have realized in the past. In John 8:31–32 Christ says, "If you hold to my teaching, you are really my disciples. Then you will know the truth, and the truth will set you free." Truth has a liberating effect. And the truth of knowing, liking, and being who Christ has designed us to be frees us to become his special kingdom people.

The Organizational Importance of Your Design

How might the divine design concept help ministry organizations in general and churches in particular? When the leaders and the people in a church or other Christian organization discover their divine designs, the ministry benefits as a whole. Before going through the discovery process, many organizations are like an eight-cylinder car hitting on three or four cylinders. However, after completing the discovery process, they drive away a well-tuned machine hitting without a miss on all eight cylinders.

The Principle

New Testament ministry is team ministry. The concept is sprinkled throughout its pages. First, Christ ministered in a team context. He is God; thus he could have accomplished his ministry with a simple command. He chose instead to minister and pursue the Father's will through a small band of faltering Palestinian disciples. He began by traveling and teaching from village to village, calling the Twelve to himself. This led to his sending them out in pairs (Mark 6:7). Later, according to Luke 10:1, he appointed seventy-two others who were also sent out in pairs.

Second, Paul ministered through a team. Rather than attempt to fulfill the Great Commission mandate alone, he opted for a team. The initial team consisted of Barnabas and Paul (Acts 11:22–30). On the first church-planting journey, Paul added Mark to the team (13:2–3, 5). On the second, Silas (15:40), Timothy (16:1–3), Luke (Acts 16), and others (Acts 18) joined the three. Finally, additional people were added or used to form new teams (Acts 19–20).

The Problem

Reality teaches that people, even completely committed Christians, may experience difficulties and heartache in attempting to work together. This was true for the Savior, who was constantly disappointed by the disciples—Peter denied him, and Judas betrayed him. Before commencing the second missionary journey, Paul and Barnabas had a significant disagreement over whether or not to bring John Mark back on the team, because he had deserted them earlier. According to Acts 15:37–40, they agreed to disagree and pursue separate ministries. Interestingly, while Paul and Barnabas chose not to work together, they did not abandon the team concept (vv. 39–40). If godly men like Paul and Barnabas struggled as a team, then serious laypeople and ministry professionals are sure to struggle as well.

In addition to personal problems between team members, there is the problem of placing the wrong person in the wrong position on the team. Every ministry team will experience differences of opinion; some churches further exacerbate the problem by misplacing team members. We have all experienced the ecstasy of working on a good team and the agony of working on a bad one. As in athletics, it is critical that the right player be put in the right position to make a good ministry team. As long as the quarterback plays his position, the team has a chance to win. If the coach decides to move his quarterback to offensive tackle, the results can be disastrous.

The fact that so many ministry teams are voluntary organizations does not help matters. Laypeople working on a team in a church context have the option to quit and move to another ministry at the slightest provocation. Staff people do not have the same freedom. They have more to lose, and therefore the chances are better that they will work out a resolution to their problems.

The Solution

A solution to the problem of working on teams is the discovery of our design. Scripture makes an analogy between the human body and the church (Romans 12 and 1 Corinthians 12). Just as the body has various parts, such as a hand, an eye, arms, and legs, which are necessary for the body to function well in life, so the church is made up of different body parts that are crucial to the functioning of the body in ministry (1 Cor. 12:27).

The purpose of a quality program of assessment is to help Christian hands discover that they are hands and to begin to function as hands and not as feet or toes.[10] The ministry organization or church determines what it wants to accomplish. Then it recruits the appropriate lay and vocational people who best fit by design the various positions on the ministry team. The result is fewer problems among team members and more efficiency in ministry. If a ministry wants to reach out to street people in an urban area, it must look for someone with a passion for "down and outers" and the gifts of leadership and mercy. If an organization decides to plant a church, it looks for a church planter. If a plateaued or dying church wants to change its course and cast a new vision for ministry, it must find a change agent with a passion for reviving established churches.

Worksheet

1. Have you taken psychological tests that can surface emotional problems (such as the Minnesota Multiphasic Personality Inventory)?
   Does taking these inventories frighten you? How is discovering
   your divine design different?

2. What are some of the capabilities that make up your divine design?
   Can you change your capabilities? Explain.

3. How important is the development of your character? Does God
   predetermine your character? What are some of your character
   strengths?

4. How would your age, marital status, race, education, sex, or health
   be factors in your ministry?

5. At this point in your life, do you like who you are? Why or why
   not? What effect do the exhortations to love yourself in Matthew
   19:19 and Ephesians 5:28–29, 33 have on your liking who you are?
   Explain.

6. Do you find yourself wearing masks and playing roles to hide what
   you believe is your real identity? Why? What impact does this have
   on your ability to be authentic and minister authentically? How
   has it affected your vulnerability?

7. Are you currently ministering in a team context? Why or why
   not? If you are ministering on a ministry team, how well is the
   team functioning together? How would you explain this situation?
   Would discovering each member's unique divine design help the
   team function better?

3

THE COMPONENTS
OF YOUR DIVINE DESIGN

What Are the Pieces of Your Puzzle?

Tom was sleeping like a baby. It felt so good to wake up in the morning feeling rested and refreshed. No barking dog or passing car could shake him out of his slumber. What had changed his nights so dramatically and chased away his insomnia? The simple but monumental answer is not only that he had graduated from college, but he had also made a decision regarding life after college. His decision was to pursue vocational Christian ministry, and he was profoundly excited about it. Another answer concerning his life's purpose had fallen in place for him.

What were the circumstances that affected Tom's decision for full-time ministry? The Bible study he attended in a campus dorm had begun a study of spiritual gifts. Before that, he had no idea that God had given him certain abilities for service to others.

But Tom has uncovered only a part of all that God has done for him in his divine design for ministry. This design is like a puzzle made up of a number of pieces. At this point only one piece of the puzzle—spiritual gifts—is in place. What are the other pieces? Some of the components that provide him and all Christians with the big picture of God's design are spiritual gifts, passion, temperament, leadership role and style, evangelism style, and natural gifts and talents. Read this chapter carefully and prayerfully because you will use its contents as a vehicle in the next chapter to discover your divine design.

Spiritual Gifts

Discerning your personal design for ministry involves discovering your spiritual gifts. They are an important component or piece of the puzzle of your life. But what are spiritual gifts? To whom are they given? What are the individual gifts?

The Definition of Spiritual Gifts

A spiritual gift is a unique, God-given ability for service.[1]

First, a spiritual gift is unique. Not every believer has the same spiritual gift. In 1 Corinthians 12, Paul draws an analogy between the human body and the body of Christ—the church. In verse 14 he focuses on the body: "Now the body is not made up of one part but of many." In verses 15–17 he points to the uniqueness of the various parts of the body by singling out the foot, hand, ear, and eye. In verse 27 he applies this "body truth" to the church: "Now you are the body of Christ, and each one of you is a part of it." In verses 29–31 he closes the chapter with a series of questions that point to the uniqueness of each person's gifts: "Are all apostles? Are all prophets? Are all teachers? Do all work miracles? Do all have gifts of healing? Do all speak in tongues? Do all interpret?" It is obvious in the English and definite in the original language that the expected answer to each question is no.[2]

The greatest value of spiritual gifts is that they are unique and complementary. The human body functions poorly as only an eye or an ear (v. 17). All the body parts are necessary to function fully with maximum effectiveness. In the same way, the church of Jesus Christ functions best when different gifts come together to complement one another in ministry for Christ.

In addition to being unique, a spiritual gift is God-given. According to Scripture, all three members of the Godhead are involved in the distribution of our spiritual gifts. First, God the Father has a part in assigning our gifts. In Romans 12:3 Paul warns Christians against false pride. He encourages us instead to think about ourselves soberly. Then he adds, "in accordance with the measure of faith God has given you." Second, Jesus Christ, the Son, has assigned gifts to us. Paul writes in Ephesians 4:7–11: "But to each one of us grace has been given as Christ apportioned it. . . . He . . . gave gifts to men. . . . It was he who gave some to be apostles, some to be prophets, some to be evangelists, and some to be pastors and teachers." Third, the Holy Spirit distributes gifts. In a reference to spiritual gifts, Paul writes in 1 Corinthians 12:11: "All these are the work of one and the same Spirit, and he gives them to each one, just as he determines."

The reason for the involvement of all three members of the Godhead in disbursing gifts to the body is not stated in Scripture. However, other situations with this kind of divine involvement have been profound, momentous occasions, as in the work of creation and the cross. This underlines the importance of the biblical concept of spiritual gifts and encourages their discovery.

Another part of the definition of spiritual gifts is that they are God-given abilities or capacities. Christians have spiritual gifts that grant them the ability to accomplish various ministry functions. In this sense they have much in common with natural gifts or talents. A believer may have the natural ability to sing well, to play a musical instrument, to write novels or poetry, or to paint portraits. In a similar manner God gives Christians unusual abilities in such areas as teaching, leading, helping, shepherding, and evangelizing. The difference is the former are in some way present at birth and associated with natural birth, whereas the latter are given at the time of conversion and are associated only with the new birth.

As a person grows toward adulthood in life, it can be exciting, whether Christian or non-Christian, to discover the natural talents and abilities God has given. One individual may discover unusual abilities in basketball or tennis. How much excitement and fulfillment there must be in shooting a basketball well and experiencing all the right moves on the court. The same excitement and fulfillment can be present when believers discover and experience their spiritual gifts. Why would any serious Christian not want to know and exercise these special divine enablements?

Finally, spiritual gifts are unique, God-given abilities to be used for service. Though Scripture recognizes that not all Christians will become involved in full-time service for Christ, it does not condone noninvolvement. Any person who professes Christ should be involved in the service of Christ. God has not given us special, spiritual abilities to enable us to sit on the sidelines—he wants us in the game (1 Peter 4:10).

Since these gifts are spiritual gifts, they are used for spiritual service. For example, the gift of teaching involves teaching Scripture and not just any topic. Only Christians have the God-given ability to teach the Bible with spiritual power and insight. The ability to teach other subject areas, such as mathematics, English, and history, are natural gifts not spiritual gifts. God has given these natural abilities to unbelievers as well as believers for the good of humankind (common grace).

The Direction of Spiritual Gifts

Spiritual gifts are directed to believers not unbelievers. In four passages of Scripture, three penned by Paul and one by Peter, it is clear that God has given his gifts to every believer. Note the use of "each one" in the following verses (the italics are mine).

> But to *each one* of us grace has been given as Christ apportioned it (Eph. 4:7).

> Now to *each one* the manifestation of the Spirit is given for the common good (1 Cor. 12:7).

> All these are the work of one and the same Spirit, and he gives them to *each one*, just as he determines (1 Cor. 12:11).

> *Each one* should use whatever gift he has received to serve others, faithfully administering God's grace in its various forms (1 Peter 4:10).

The fact that God gives every believer a gift implies that each has at least one gift. The biblical evidence indicates, however, that some, if not most, have multiple gifts. Paul identifies at least three gifts of his own in 1 Timothy 2:7 and 2 Timothy 1:11: a herald (preacher), an apostle, and a teacher. It is possible that he had the gifts of evangelism, leadership, and a cross-cultural gift, for his passion was to preach the gospel to the Gentiles (Eph. 3:7–8; Acts 22:21; 26:17), and he appears to have been the leader of various ministry teams (13:7; 15:40; 16:3).

A helpful concept in determining multigiftedness is the believer's gift-mix and gift-clusters.[3] *Gift-mix* is a term that describes all your spiritual gifts. *Gift-cluster* describes a clearly dominant gift that is supported by the other gifts in the cluster. For example, your gift-mix might consist of the gifts of leadership, administration, evangelism, teaching, and helps (figure 1). Your gift-cluster will contain a single, dominant gift—in this case evangelism—which is supported by the other four gifts (figure 2).

Although many believers are multigifted, no believer has all the gifts. Again the body metaphor in 1 Corinthians 12 makes this clear. The body of Christ is made up of a multiplicity of parts because no single part is sufficient of itself. The point is that we desperately need one another (vv. 21–22). Carol's small church in south Texas is biblically inaccurate when it expects the pastor to do all the work of the ministry ("After all,

Gift-Mix

leadership   administration

evangelism   teaching

helps

Figure 1

Gift-Cluster

Figure 2

that's what we pay him for"). The fact that every believer is gifted argues that every believer is needed. When people hold back from ministry, they affect the entire body of believers as well as themselves.

The Description of Spiritual Gifts

The fact that the Godhead has sovereignly bestowed on each Christian one or more spiritual gifts raises several questions: What are the gifts? How would you know one if you saw it, either in yourself or in another person? Before answering these questions, I need to briefly address two issues.

The first concerns the number of gifts. Are all the gifts mentioned in the Bible available to Christians? Do other spiritual gifts exist that are not found in Scripture? The Bible seems to indicate there might be other gifts. In both 1 Timothy 2:7 and 2 Timothy 1:11, Paul mentions preaching ("herald") along with the gifts of apostleship and teaching. Although preaching (herald) is not listed among the gifts in Romans 12, 1 Corinthians 12, or Ephesians 4, in practice, it is apparent that some have a special ability to communicate Scripture better than others.[4]

Most likely many other gifts exist. However, we must be careful when we attempt to speak where Scripture does not. We can speak with certainty and authority regarding the gifts present in the Bible but with less certainty and authority regarding those that are not there.

The other issue is, Are all the gifts mentioned in the Bible still operative and available to Christians today? The focus of this question is the sign gifts of healings, miracles, tongues, and the interpretation of tongues. Godly, evangelical scholars land on both sides of this issue, which would seem to indicate that Scripture is not entirely clear.[5] I have chosen not to discuss these and certain other gifts because of the divisive debate that surrounds them and because we are not sure what they were or how they were used in ministry. A more positive approach is to examine the gifts that most people agree are available today.

Unfortunately the Bible does not offer a precise definition of each spiritual gift. Perhaps Paul and others felt no need to attempt this because their use was so common in the first century. I base the following descriptions on what Scripture does say about the gifts and on my personal ministry experience with Christians.

Administration (1 Cor. 12:28)

The gift of administration is the God-given ability to manage or order the affairs of a church or parachurch organization. It could involve several areas. One is working with leaders to determine ministry goals and then design a plan and budget to accomplish them. Another is creating an organizational structure around the plan and staffing that ministry structure. Monitoring the plan and solving problems as they arise are other areas. Often the mark of an administrator is the ability to accomplish these in a "fitting and orderly way" (14:40). This gift is not to be confused with that of leadership (Rom. 12:8), as the two are distinguished in the Bible.

Scripture presents examples of people with administrative gifts. Those who stand out for their administrative abilities in the Old Testament are Joseph and Jethro. Paul's directions to Titus might indicate that he had the spiritual gift of administration: "The reason I left you in Crete was that you might straighten out what was left unfinished and appoint elders in every town, as I directed you" (Titus 1:5). The gift of administration would have proved helpful during certain church meetings at Corinth (1 Cor. 14:40).

Apostleship (1 Cor. 12:28; Eph. 4:11)

The gift of apostleship is included here but not as the primary gift exercised by the twelve apostles. They are the men whom God used, along with New Testament prophets, to lay the foundation of the church (Eph. 2:20) and whose authoritative ministries were authenticated by certain sign gifts (2 Cor. 12:12). They literally witnessed the resurrection of Christ (Acts 1:8).

The gift of apostleship is used here in a secondary sense of people such as Barnabas (Acts 14:4, 14), Silvanus and Timothy (1 Thess. 1:1; 2:6), and Andronicus and Junias (Rom. 16:7). These were gifted individuals who were apparently sent out by the churches for ministry that often involved church planting. This gift may have included the capacity to minister cross-culturally (Eph. 3:7–8).

EVANGELISM (EPH. 4:11)

The gift of evangelism is the ability to communicate clearly the gospel of Jesus Christ (1 Cor. 15:1–4) to unbelievers individually or in a group context with the result that people respond and accept Christ. Believers with this gift care passionately about lost people and have a strong desire to see them come to faith. They feel compassion for them and authentically address their questions and their doubts. Thus lost people respond positively to their presence. People with the gift of evangelism become frustrated when they go for a long period of time without sharing their faith and gain great satisfaction in equipping others to share their faith.

In the New Testament Philip had the gift of evangelism and was referred to as "Philip the evangelist" (Acts 21:8). He is seen in Acts 8 witnessing individually to the Ethiopian eunuch. Timothy may have had the gift. In 2 Timothy 4:5 Paul encouraged him to do "the work of an evangelist." According to Ephesians 4:11–12, a primary function of those with the gift of evangelism is to equip others in the body of Christ for evangelism.

ENCOURAGEMENT (ROM. 12:8)

The gift of encouragement (or exhortation) involves encouraging, consoling, and when necessary, confronting and admonishing others so they are benefited spiritually in their walk with Christ. Christians with this gift have unusual sensitivity for and are attracted to those who are discouraged or struggling. People tend to pursue them for counsel. As a result of their ministry, believers are drawn closer to Christ or are won back to Christ. An excellent example is Barnabas. His name means Son of Encouragement (Acts 4:36). He encouraged such men as Paul (9:27) and John Mark (15:39).

FAITH (1 COR. 12:9)

The gift of faith is the ability to envision what needs to be done and to trust God to accomplish it even though it seems impossible to most people. Those with the gift of faith have a strong sense that God is going to accomplish something important through them or their ministry whether others see it as significant or not. They take Romans 8:28 literally and view obstacles as opportunities for Christ to accomplish his purposes in this world. They trust God in difficult, even impossible situations when others are ready to give up. This gift may cluster with the gift of leadership and can be found in some visionary Christians who dream big dreams, pray big prayers, and attempt big things for the Savior (Eph. 3:20).

Scripture presents several examples of people with great faith. In the Old Testament, Caleb and Joshua were men of unusual faith who led Israel in conquering and possessing the Promised Land. Nehemiah demonstrated his faith when he approached a hostile, pagan king and dared to ask permission to rebuild Jerusalem. The poor widow in Luke 21:2–4 showed great faith when she put practically all she had (two small copper coins) in the temple treasury for God. In the New Testament God may have given Stephen the spiritual gift of faith, for Luke describes him as "a man full of faith" (Acts 6:5).

Giving (Rom. 12:8)

The gift of giving is the ability to give eagerly, wisely, generously, and sacrificially to others. Regardless of the amount, people with this gift genuinely view their treasures, talents, and time as on loan from God and not their own. They find that God moves them to give to those with genuine needs. They take special delight in giving of themselves and what they have to others. Tabitha may have exercised the gift of giving, for Luke describes her as "always doing good and helping the poor"(Acts 9:36). It is also possible that some in the church at Philippi ministered to Paul through the gift of giving (Phil. 4:14–18).

Helps (1 Cor. 12:28) and Service (Rom. 12:7)

These two gifts appear to be the same gift and involve the capacity to recognize and provide assistance in meeting practical needs, thus making life a little easier for others. Often this gift concerns sacrificial, behind-the-scenes assistance and benefits others by freeing them up for vital ministries. People with these gifts were needed in Acts 6:1, where there was a dispute in the early church over its failure to serve the Hebraic widows. Phoebe probably exercised the gift of helps/service, according to Romans 16:1. Onesiphorus may have exercised this gift in Paul's life (2 Tim. 1:16), as did the household of Stephanas (1 Cor. 16:15). The term *deacon* is a form of the word for *service* (1 Tim. 3:8), and so those who are attracted to the office of deacon may have the spiritual gift of helps/service.

LEADING (ROM. 12:8)

The gift of leadership is found in people who have a clear, significant vision and are able to communicate it publicly or privately in such a way that they influence others to pursue that vision. They tend to gravitate toward the "point position" in a particular ministry and lead in such a way that others have trust and confidence in them and their abilities. This gift is not to be confused with the gift of administration (1 Cor. 12:28).

Scripture is replete with examples of those with leadership abilities. In the Old Testament, God used people such as Abraham, Moses, Joshua, Caleb, David, Daniel, Nehemiah, and certain judges and kings to lead his people. The Gospels present the most outstanding example and model of leadership in the Savior. In the New Testament other outstanding people who most likely had the spiritual gift of leadership were Paul, Peter, and James.

MERCY (ROM. 12:8)

The gift of mercy is the capacity to feel and express unusual compassion and sympathy for those in difficult or crisis situations and to provide them with the necessary help and support to see them through these times. They have the ability to "walk in another's shoes" and to feel the pain and burdens they carry. They do not stop there, however, but desire to embrace and make a difference in hurting people's lives for the Savior. Barnabas may have had this gift, as demonstrated by the mercy he extended to Paul in Acts 9:26–27, when he took him in and defended him before the other disciples. Dorcas may have also exercised the gift of mercy because she "was always doing good and helping the poor" (v. 36).

PASTORING (EPH. 4:11)

The term *pastor* literally means shepherd. Therefore, based on the function of a Palestinian shepherd, the gift involves leading, nurturing, caring for, and protecting God's flock. This gift is commonly associated with those who minister professionally in the church in the position of pastor. However, God bestows the gift of pastor on laypeople as well, including women. In fact most of the pastoral care in the church can and should be the ministry of laypeople. The recent biblical emphasis on small groups encourages this ministry, as lay-led groups provide an excellent context in which pastoral care may take place.

Some argue that the gift of pastor is to be associated with the gift of teacher, according to Ephesians 4:11. They believe two aspects or dimensions are combined in one gift. Thus someone with the gift of pastoring will have the gift of teaching, while the opposite may not be true. Though it is possible these gifts could cluster together (as is possible for any of the spiritual gifts), the original language does not demand it in Ephesians 4:11.[6]

In light of their function, the gift of pastor would be important to those occupying the position of elder in the church. In Acts 20:28 Paul instructs the elders in the church at Ephesus to "be shepherds of the church of God." In 1 Peter 5:2 Peter exhorts elders to "be shepherds of God's flock that is under your care."

TEACHING (ROM. 12:7; 1 COR. 12:28; EPH. 4:11)

The gift of teaching is the God-given ability to understand and communicate biblical truth. As stated earlier, it is not simply the ability to teach any truth, because God gives non-Christians the ability to teach general truth in areas such as business, medicine, computers, or music. Good teaching, however, does not merely involve the communication of Bible content but focuses on the insight it brings and its relevance and application to the lives of the hearers.

The importance of teaching is obvious in the New Testament. In James 3:1 Jesus's half brother warns those who would be teachers of the grave responsibility of their teaching position. In Hebrews 5:12 the writer uses teaching as a litmus test of spiritual maturity. In 1 Timothy 5:17 certain elders are not only responsible to lead the church but also to preach to and teach the church.

Passion

Discerning your design for ministry also involves discerning your passion. It is the second piece to your life's puzzle and marks the difference between ministry mediocrity and ministry excellence. For references to passion, see Acts 18:25; Rom. 12:11; and 15:20. In Romans 15:20 Paul uses the term *ambition* to describe his passion to proclaim the gospel to the Gentiles. But what precisely is a person's passion or ambition? Why is it important? Are there any good examples in the Bible?

The Definition of Passion

Passion is a God-given capacity to attach ourselves emotionally to something or someone (people, a cause, an idea, or an area of ministry) over an extended period of time to meet a need. Several elements make up this definition.

Emotion

Passion involves the emotions. It is a feeling concept. It is what you feel strongly and care deeply about. It is "a burning desire—even to the point of being irrational."[7] Others have described it as a "burning feeling deep in your soul" or as a "burning gut-feeling that a certain ministry is the most important place that God would have you."

Focus

Passion has an object. We say that a person has a passion for or toward someone or something. Thus passion serves to focus our spiritual gifts. It may include people: the lost, unchurched, unborn, poor and oppressed, or unreached peoples. Paul had a passion for the Gentiles, and Peter for the Jews (Gal. 2:7). It could include a cause or an issue, such as abortion, civil rights, women's rights, the gospel, the clarity of the gospel, or the family. It could be a situation or condition, such as poverty, oppression, abuse, addiction, dysfunction, or legalism. It might be a particular pursuit, such as theology, preaching, or teaching. It might include a place, such as an urban, suburban, or rural area or possibly a specific city, state, or country.

Tenure

Passion has tenure; it stays with you for an extended period of time. We must be careful to distinguish between passion and passing interests. Passion "sticks to the bones"; passing interests come and go. Paul writes, "It has always been my ambition to preach the gospel . . ." (Rom. 15:20). Some who are involved in a particular ministry acknowledge that they have wanted to be in that ministry for as long as they can remember. This is the tenure of passion.

Need

Passion often develops out of a strong sense of felt need. This need has a way of capturing our attention and pressing in on our hearts. Thus it prompts the exercise of our gifts. It may involve our own needs, the needs of others, or both. God used Chuck Colson's prison experience to impress on him the needs of those behind bars. God used the oppressive racial milieu in Mississippi to prompt John Perkins to pursue the Voice of Calvary Ministry.

The Importance of Passion

While our spiritual gifts supply us with the tools or special abilities for our trade, our passion focuses and motivates those spiritual gifts.

FOCUS

Passion provides us with the necessary direction for ministry in general and for spiritual gifts in particular. Thus it serves to focus our ministry. Three people may have the gift of evangelism. One may have a passion for children, another for students on college campuses, and the third for Asian people. The first could exercise his or her evangelistic gift with Child Evangelism, Inc. The second could minister with Campus Crusade for Christ. The third could consider the mission field in the Far East or the ministry of International Students in America.

MOTIVATION

Passion also provides us with the necessary motivation to exercise our gifts. It has a way of catalyzing or energizing us. It pushes and pulls us outside our comfort zones. It compels us to take some definite action. It spurs us to activity. It builds a fire in our soul that is only quenched momentarily by ministry activity.

Some Examples of Passion

The apostle Paul provides an example of passion. His passion was to preach the gospel to the Gentiles (the unchurched of the first century). He discovered his passion rather quickly (Acts 9:6, 15) but refined and sharpened it over an extended period of time. Initially his passion was to preach the gospel (1 Cor. 9:16–23) to both the Jews and the Gentiles (Acts 9:15; Rom. 9:1–3; 10:1). However, due to the rejection of the Jews, he later focused exclusively on the Gentiles (Acts 22:21; 26:17; Rom. 1:5; 11:13). This was further refined to preaching the gospel to Gentiles in places where Christ was not known (Rom. 15:20–21).

In his book *Honest to God?* Bill Hybels gives several examples of men and their passions. Dr. James Dobson, founder of Focus on the Family Ministries, has a powerful passion for the family. International evangelist Luis Palau has a passion for the lost in general. John Perkins, founder of the Voice of Calvary Ministries, has a strong passion for the poor and needy minorities. And R. C. Sproul, a reformed theologian and author, has a passion "to study and teach the very deepest truths of the Christian faith."[8]

Temperament

Discerning your divine design includes understanding your temperament. God-given spiritual gifts provide the special abilities for our ministries, and a God-given passion supplies long-term direction and motivation for those abilities. However, God-given temperament provides the unique personal characteristics and tendencies for ministry. Temperament is another vital piece of the puzzle. But what is temperament? Why is it important?

The Definition of Temperament

A careful reading of the general literature on human development and psychology reveals that often the terms *temperament* and *personality* are used synonymously. Consequently any definition of temperament must also comment on its relationship to the concept of personality. An examination of the two terms indicates that a distinction exists. While there is difference of opinion among those in the field of human development, Fergus Hughes and Lloyd Noppe indicate that a person's temperament is the foundation and forerunner for his or her personality.[9] They view temperament as a predisposition and precursor that contributes to our future personality makeup and its development.

If a person's temperament contributes to personality, then what is a definition of temperament? I define temperament as your unique, God-given (inborn) behavioral style. Hughes and Noppe define temperament as a person's "inborn behavioral characteristics."[10] The term *inborn* implies that the temperament characteristics were present at birth. In *Parenting Isn't for Cowards*, James Dobson writes, "It is my supposition that these temperaments are pre-packaged before birth and do not have to be cultivated or encouraged."[11] From birth it is evident that people have certain God-given behavioral characteristics already in place that are basic and unique to their makeup. It is possible that this is what Jeremiah is referring to in Jeremiah 1:5 and Paul in Galatians 1:15.

Next, temperament concerns behavior. In general, temperament is based on a person's actions or behavioral style. Each person has a unique behavioral pattern or style that involves a distinct way of thinking, feeling, and acting. This behavior can be motivated by a person's needs or values. The former affects how a person acts, the latter why a person acts the way he does. Most temperament tools concern needs-motivated behavior.

Finally, temperament focuses on a person's inborn behavioral characteristics, such as intelligence, initiative, self-assurance, and scholarship. Various terms are used besides *characteristics*, such as *tendencies* or *traits*. Regardless of the exact term, these inborn traits determine similarities and differences in the behavior of people. Ultimately the various organizations of these common traits constitute a person's individual temperament. In general these temperament characteristics remain constant over a period of time and are not permanently altered by temporary pressures from one's environment.

The Importance of Temperament

A knowledge of temperament is important for a variety of reasons. First, we can learn a great deal about ourselves and others when we explore the various temperaments and their behavioral types. While the Bible does not directly define temperament or personality, this concept serves as a convenient and helpful way to understand and describe the personal characteristics and tendencies of Christians and non-Christians that influence their thoughts, emotions, and ultimately their behavior.

Second, ministry involves working with all kinds of different people and behavioral styles. By identifying our behavioral styles and the styles of others, we have the potential to increase ministry effectiveness. This directly affects our servanthood. When we understand another Christian's temperament, we are better able to serve him or her (Mark 9:35; 10:43; Phil. 2:3–8).

Third, we must understand that people are different in fundamental ways, and that is okay. They have different wants, needs, motives, desires, goals, and values. The problem is not these differences but that we account for them in destructive ways. Our tendency is to see the differences in others as flaws, especially where they differ from us. We want to change people and make them more like us. The results can be disastrous in marriage, family, or team ministry.

The Description of Temperament

A number of different temperament models have surfaced in the past few years. Most of them derive from one of two prototypes.

The first is based on the traditional four-temperament model developed by Hippocrates two thousand years ago. He believed a person's temperament was based on the mixture of various fluids, such as blood and bile, in the human body. He named the four temperaments choleric, sanguine, melancholic, and phlegmatic.

The Personal Profile is based on the four-temperament model and is growing in popularity in the marketplace and with many Christian organizations. It was developed by John G. Geier and Dorothy E. Downey and based on the earlier work of William Marston, who popularized the DiSC model. DiSC is an acronym for the four behavioral temperaments: Dominant, Influencing, Steady, and Compliant. These are further broken down into fifteen profile patterns.

Another useful tool is the Biblical Personal Profile developed by Ken Voges. It uses the same terminology and methodology as the Personal Profile but applies the profiles to biblical characters in the interpretative stage.

Both tools allow individuals to analyze their behavior in nine specific categories:

1. Emotional tendencies
2. Goals
3. The criteria used in judging others
4. The means used to influence others
5. The perceived value one has to an organization
6. The tendency one has to overuse certain traits
7. The typical reaction under pressure
8. Fears
9. What one needs to do to increase personal effectiveness[12]

The other prototype is the Myers-Briggs Type Indicator (MBTI). It has become the most widely used tool for the nonpsychiatric population in America. It takes a different approach than the two profiles above in that it helps us discern our inborn preferences in four key functional areas of life.

First, the MBTI seeks to determine our preference for extraversion or introversion. This helps in knowing where we focus our attention (the inner or outer world) and what energizes us (people or ideas).

Second, the MBTI helps us discover how we perceive or take in information. We prefer either sensing, which involves receiving information through the five senses, or intuition, which gathers information intuitively or beyond the senses (a kind of sixth sense). People characterized by the former see things with their eyes and tend to be less visionary; the latter see things in their heads and are the world's visionaries.

Third, the MBTI helps us discover how we process the information we take in or how we make decisions. This involves a preference for thinking or feeling. These terms can be misleading. Those who prefer thinking make decisions based on logic and objective analysis, whereas those who prefer feeling make decisions based more on personal values and judgments. This does not mean that the former do not have values or that the latter do not think, as might be implied from the terms.

Finally, the MBTI helps in determining the lifestyle we adopt for dealing with the outer world. This involves a preference for judging or perceiving. Again the terms can be confusing. Those who prefer judging are not judgmental people but prefer to take a planned, organized approach to life. They like closure and are quick decision makers. People who prefer perceiving are adaptable and take a spontaneous, flexible approach to life. They do not like closure, preferring to wait until all the information is in before making a final decision.[13]

A shortened version of the MBTI is the Keirsey Temperament Sorter (KTS). I have taken the training and am fully qualified to give the MBTI. However, I prefer to use the KTS. It is easier to purchase, less expensive, and gives you virtually the same information. I will say more about it in chapter 4.

Some Examples of Temperament

Bill Hybels gives several examples of the impact of temperament on certain men and their ministries. James Dobson is an extroverted, relational man who deeply cares about this country, its people, and their needs. He is people-oriented. This puts his radio guests at ease and draws the interest of listeners around the world, especially those in struggling families. Luis Palau is an excitable, fiery person whose vision, focus, and intensity attract an audience and their undivided attention. R. C. Sproul, while an excellent communicator in front of an audience, is task-oriented and prefers being by himself for hours in his study, thinking and doing research. Finally John Perkins is a quiet, gentle, feeling kind of man. Hybels writes, "He just slips in and fits in with the group. Certainly that's one of the keys to his success in working with the downtrodden. His temperament is gentle enough to be nonthreatening and encouraging."[14] Hybels himself is an extrovert who is energized by being around people. He is a visionary (an intuitive) who saw Willow Creek Community Church in his head long before he planted it. He is also an "off the charts thinker" who is relatively unstructured, which is important in church planting.[15]

The Theological Justification for Temperament

Christians should be hesitant to use or be assessed with tools that might be influenced by so-called modern psychological principles. These principles could be based on unbiblical presuppositions. The question is, Do temperament tools such as the Personal Profile, the Myers-Briggs Temperament Inventory, and the Keirsey Temperament Sorter fall into this category?

GENERAL AND SPECIAL REVELATION

Evangelical theologians recognize two domains of revelation. One is special revelation, which refers to God's knowledge as found in Christ

(John 1:18) and the Scriptures (1 John 5:9–12). The other is general revelation, which refers to God's knowledge as found in his creation: nature,
science, and history. The former is the domain of the theologian; the
latter is the domain of both the scientist and the theologian. Christians
have no problems with knowledge based on the former. Most accept
the Bible as God's trustworthy, authoritative word. The problem lies in
knowledge based on general revelation—it may or may not be compat-
ible with Scripture. Psychological and temperament tests fall under the
category of general revelation.

ALL TRUTH IS GOD'S TRUTH

While all the content of the Bible is true (2 Tim. 3:16), not all
truth is found in the Bible. For example, scientists have discovered
the truth that if people brush and floss their teeth on a regular basis,
they will have fewer cavities. They have also found that cigarette
smoking is harmful to your health. Both truths are not found in the
Bible, yet few would challenge their validity. I could cite numerous
other examples. The point is that all truth is ultimately God's truth.
The problem lies in discerning truth from error in the domain of
general revelation. When Scripture addresses a topic, we have God's
truth on the matter. But how do we discern God's truth in matters
that Scripture does not address, such as the brushing and flossing
of our teeth, smoking cigarettes, or matters of temperament? When
dealing with knowledge based on general revelation, the Christian
must proceed cautiously.

The key to the truthfulness of any temperament or psychological
profile is its degree of accuracy in correctly detecting behavioral styles.
Those that prove accurate over time are most likely based ultimately
on God's truth regardless of their source, but those that do not prove
accurate are not based on divine truth. Consequently the validation
of a temperament tool is important to the Christian who is seeking
God's truth in the domain of natural revelation.[16]

Both the Biblical and Personal Profiles and the Myers-Briggs Temperament Inventory have demonstrated high reliability, as based on
professional studies of their validity. The Personal Profile has been
through a rigid validation process, and the results are available in
The Kaplan Report.[17] Katharine Briggs and Isabel Myers as well as
others have submitted the MBTI to rigorous standards of validity.[18]
That is why it is used so widely today in the nonpsychiatric population. Those of us who have worked with these tools over the years
have found from personal experience that they accurately detect behavioral styles.

WISDOM TRADITION

The Old Testament contains several books classified as Hebrew wisdom literature—Proverbs, Job, Ecclesiastes, and certain psalms that deal specifically with the topic of wisdom.[19] The Hebrew concept of wisdom was essentially practical. There was no distinction between the intellectual and the practical or the religious and the secular. For the Hebrews the whole of life was to be viewed from the religious experience, and wisdom was relevant to every area of man's existence.[20]

According to scholars, biblical wisdom literature reflects more influence from the ancient Near East than the other literature in the Bible. Roland Harrison writes, "It would seem clear, therefore, that not merely was Hebrew wisdom far from being an isolated literary or didactic phenomenon, but that in fact it was part of a large cultural heritage common to the whole of the ancient world."[21] However, Harrison is careful to point out that the Hebrew writers did not depend entirely on other ancient Near Eastern wisdom sources for their contribution.[22] In his commentary on Proverbs, Derek Kidner adds that parallels with the Book of Proverbs show that Israel's wise men sifted through and assimilated some of the wisdom tradition of the Near East.[23]

David Ward explains this process and how it interacts with inspiration:

> Under divine inspiration, Solomon and others sometimes took wise lessons from life captured in proverbs composed by pagan wise men, and reoriented their advice under the proper frame of reference. Namely, the fear of the Lord. Wisdom living had more to do with successful living in this world than it did with any redemptive vision of a future heaven. Therefore when wise insight was seen to help live for the true God more effectively, it was adopted as God's truth anyway. So it was not as much a case of being unoriginal and borrowing as it was a case of recovering truth for the believer's use that was God's truth in the first place.[24]

The point is that God's inerrant, authoritative Word under divine inspiration drew on lessons of truth and wisdom from the surrounding cultures. Again the reason is that all truth is God's truth regardless of where it is found. Consequently the careful use of insights from validated, reliable temperament tools closely parallels the wisdom process of Israel's sages.

Temperament and Spiritual Gifts

Some excellent work is being done in discovering how the spiritual gifts combine with the various temperaments, especially the traditional, four-temperament model represented by the Personal Profile (DiSC) and the Biblical Personal Profile. For example, the gift of teaching will function differently with the various temperaments. Those who combine the high D temperament (strong, direct, confident) with the gift of teaching are highly dedicated teachers who will strongly challenge students. However, they will need to work hard at relating to their students on a personal level.

The high I temperament (influential, expressive, enthusiastic, persuasive) with the gift of teaching will inspire students and influence them. These people are very articulate and prove to be excellent communicators. However, they can oversell their ideas and be manipulative.

The high S temperament (steady, dependable, relational) with the teaching gift tends to be a specialist who is consistent and works well with students. However, such teachers do not respond well to conflict in the classroom and people who differ with them or challenge their ideas.

Finally, those with the high C temperament (logical, persistent, conscientious) and the gift of teaching are methodical, analytical, and thorough. They highly value scholarship and may be scholars themselves. It is important to them that they be correct, and they like to develop methods to help people approach a particular discipline. However, they can become too detailed and picky.[25] In chapter 4 you will discover what your temperament is.

Leadership

Discerning your divine design involves discovering your leadership abilities. Christian leaders are godly servants (character) who know where they are going (direction) and have followers (influence). Determining your ability to lead is vital to your future ministry and involves two primary areas: your leadership role (if you are a leader) and your leadership style (how you lead). Both are important pieces of the design puzzle.

Leadership Roles

Determining your leadership role involves discovering whether you are a leader or a manager or a combination of both. Leadership is fundamentally different from management or administration.[26] Scripture makes a distinction between the gift of leadership (Rom. 12:8) and the gift of administration (1 Cor. 12:28). Many students of leadership make the same distinction. In the *Harvard Business Review* John Kotter writes: "Leadership is different from management, but not for the reasons most people think." He explains that "leadership and management are two distinctive and complementary systems of action. Each has its own function and characteristic activities."[27] Writers such as Ted Engstrom, Abraham Zaleznik, Bruce Jones, Mary Tramel, Helen Reynolds, and others also recognize this distinction.[28]

LEADERS

Tremendous change (megachange) is sweeping across North America and will make an impact on everything in its path, including church and parachurch ministries. A characteristic of good leadership is the ability to cope with the change that comes from outside the organization and channel it to create needed change within the ministry organization.[29] The result is that Christian ministries relate relevantly, effectively, and biblically to their contemporary culture.

The way leaders cope with and accomplish change is through influence. Leadership involves influencing people to change in the direction of maximum Christlikeness and ministry effectiveness.

How do leaders influence people? The answer is found in the definition of a Christian leader. I have defined Christian leaders as godly people who know where they are going and have followers. Leaders who have followers exert influence. If no one is following your leadership, then you have little or no influence. The key to influence is the first two aspects of leadership: godliness (character) and direction (vision). People who are servants with godly, Christlike character attract followers. Visionary people who know and are excited about where they are going in life also attract followers. And when character and vision combine in one person, that leader exerts a powerful influence over others.

In addition, leaders are adept at developing vision and strategies for their ministries and motivating people to accomplish those visions through their strategies. They are visionaries who tend to think inductively more than deductively. They are also more proactive than reactive, and many have both the spiritual and natural gift of leadership.

MANAGERS

Managers complement and work best under leaders by coping with the complexity of change. In fact a major distinction between the role of leaders and managers is that while the former cope with change, the latter deal with the complexity that change brings.[30] Managers or administrators attempt to bring order and consistency to this complexity.

In *Leaders*, Warren Bennis and Burt Nanus see another distinction between leaders and managers. They write, "*Managers are people who do things right and leaders are people who do the right thing. The difference may be summarized as activities of vision and judgment—effectiveness versus activities of mastering routines—efficiency.*"[31] The distinction may

Figure 3
The Leader-Manager Roles

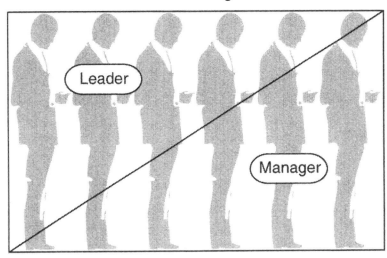

be that leaders exercise leadership functions intuitively. In the process of ministry, they naturally do things right. Similarly in *The Effective Executive*, Peter Drucker addresses the difference between effectiveness and efficiency in organizations. Effectiveness is the ability to get the right things done, whereas efficiency is the ability to do things right.[32] Leaders intuitively tend toward the former, managers the latter.

Managers bring order and consistency to the complexity of change through such activities as planning, budgeting, and organizing. Managers are godly people (character) who help us get where we are going (plan) and maximize our resources to get there (budgeting, organizing, staffing, controlling). Managers think more deductively than inductively. Often they are also more reactive than proactive and may have the spiritual and natural gifts of administration (1 Cor. 12:28).

LEADERS AND MANAGERS

Though a person can be a pure leader or manager, most tend to have qualities of both. A Christian could be primarily a leader with some administrative abilities or vice versa (see figure 3). Peter Wagner agrees:

Few pastors are pure leaders and administrators. Most are a mix of the two. But I have observed that pastors who tend toward being leaders, whether or not they are also administrators, will most likely be church growth pastors. Pastors who see themselves to be administrators and use that kind of management style tend to be maintenance-oriented. Making sure that the church functions smoothly and harmoniously is usually where a manager is. A leader, on the other hand, is willing to take risks and upset the status quo in order to move out toward new horizons.[33]

In *Leaders*, Bennis and Nanus studied ninety top leaders in an attempt to discover what it takes to be an effective leader as well as a manager. One interesting conclusion is that most organizations are overmanaged and underled. I would argue that this is true of most churches in North America as well.

Leadership Styles

Once you have discerned whether you are more a leader or a manager or, most likely, some combination of the two with one more dominant than the other, the next step is to identify your leadership style.

The style approach to leadership emphasizes leaders' behavior and how it consistently affects people when leading a church or parachurch organization or a ministry within one or the other. Leadership is composed essentially of two general kinds of behavior: task and relationship. *Task behavior* focuses on the accomplishment of one or several goals. An example would be Paul's life mission: "However, I consider my life worth nothing to me, if only I may finish the race and complete the task the Lord Jesus has given me—the task of testifying to the gospel of God's grace" (Acts 20:24).

Relational behavior focuses on how people relate to themselves and others. An example is Paul's comments on his ministry to the church at Thessalonica (1 Thess. 2:7–12). He says, "We were gentle among you, like a mother caring for her little children" (v. 7). The leadership metaphors and images of the New Testament fall into one of two categories—task or relationship.[34]

Leaders use either task or relational behaviors, or at times both, to influence followers to accomplish the ministry organization's God-given mission. These two behaviors, however, are separate and independent. Task behavior, which emphasizes ministry accomplishments, involves such activities as discovering and articulating core values, determining a mission, designing a strategy, preaching and teaching the Bible, organizing the ministry, providing structure, defining role responsibilities and expectations, scheduling ministry activities, defining policy, assigning ministry load, and evaluating ministry performance.

Relational behavior, which responds to the concerns and needs of people, involves such activities as building camaraderie, developing trust, developing teams, motivating followers, providing good ministry conditions, nurturing and supporting followers, building biblical community, promoting interpersonal relationships, counseling those needing direction, comforting the distressed, encouraging the discouraged, and many other biblical functions (see 1 Thess. 5:14–15).

Effective leadership depends on how the leader balances task and relational behaviors with the people in his or her unique ministry context or culture. Different ministry contexts or cultures require different leadership styles. All leaders will have an inherent, primary leadership style but will also need to adjust as much as their inherent style will allow to the context where they exercise leadership, whether over or within the church or parachurch organization. To grow and mature, some ministry situations require a task-related style, others require a relational style, while most require a combination of the two. Wise leaders and congregations will evaluate leaders and ministry contexts and attempt to align the best leaders for the particular ministry situation. I'll say more about this in chapter 4.

Evangelism

Discerning your divine makeup also includes discovering your evangelism style. It is an often ignored yet important piece of your life's puzzle. When most Christians, including many in vocational ministry, hear the term *evangelism*, they associate it with a confrontational style only. They picture the stereotypical evangelist with raised Bible in hand cornering some defenseless soul and shouting at the top of his lungs, "Repent!" They conclude that evangelism is not for them and avoid it all together.

Confrontational evangelism is a valid style and has resulted in a number of people coming to faith in the Savior. However, it is not for everyone. In *Honest to God?* Bill Hybels writes:

> Only a tiny fraction of unbelievers in this world will be reached by the stereotypical evangelist. The unbelieving world is made up of a variety of people: young and old, rich and poor, educated and uneducated, urban and rural, with different races, personalities, values, political systems, and religious backgrounds. Isn't it obvious it would take more than one style of evangelist to reach such a diverse population?
>
> That's where we come in. Somewhere in that multifarious group is a person who needs to hear the message of Christ from someone just like you or me. A person who needs an evangelist of your exact age, career, and level of spiritual understanding, or my exact personality, background, and interests.[35]

Then Hybels points to six evangelistic styles: confrontational, intellectual, testimonial, relational, invitational, and serving.

The Confrontational Style

The confrontational style is illustrated by Peter in Acts 2. Peter confronts more than three thousand Jews with this truth: "You, with the help of wicked men, put him to death" (v. 23). And later in verse 36 he says, "Therefore let all Israel be assured of this: God has made this Jesus, whom you crucified, both Lord and Christ." Peter witnesses unabashedly to this large group of the horror of what they have done, with little concern as to how his hearers might react. Peter's style may be described as confident, controversial, challenging, frontal, courageous, and straightforward.

After commenting on Peter's style and approach, Hybels, himself a confrontational style evangelist, writes, "Some people will only come to Christ if they are 'knocked over the head with truth' and confronted by someone like Peter. Fortunately, God has equipped certain believers with the combination of personality, gifts, and desires that make it natural for them to confront others."[36]

The Intellectual Style

The intellectual style is illustrated by Paul in Acts 17. The setting is a Jewish synagogue in Thessalonica. Paul entered the synagogue and "reasoned with them from the Scriptures, explaining and proving that the Christ had to suffer and rise from the dead" (vv. 2–3). Later in Athens (vv. 16–17), Paul again "reasoned in the synagogue with the Jews and the God-fearing Greeks." The same characterized his sermon to the Athenian philosophers on Mars Hill (vv. 18–31). Paul's style is best described as educated, intelligent, cogent, well-reasoned, logical, and accurate.

Regarding the intellectual style, Hybels asks, "What about you? Could you be an intellectual evangelist? Are you an effective debater? Do you enjoy examining evidence and reasoning through to a conclusion? Do you like to wrestle with difficult questions? Do you love it when cultists come to your door? Then take your calling as an intellectual evangelist seriously. Read, study, and train yourself."[37]

The Testimonial Style

The testimonial style is illustrated by the story of the healing of the beggar in John 9. Jesus healed a blind man on the Sabbath, which caused a split among the Pharisees—some thought he was a sinner; others thought he was from God. When the former asked the healed man what he thought about Jesus, he responded with a testimonial: "Whether he is a sinner or not, I don't know. One thing I do know. I was blind but now I see!" (v. 25). This style is excited, confident, firm, personal, biographical, straightforward, honest, concise, and powerful. People who use the testimonial style have a personal story to tell of how Christ has made a difference in their lives, and they tell practically everyone who will listen.

Hybels writes, "Testimonial style evangelists neither confront nor intellectualize. They simply tell the story of the miraculous work of Christ in their life. They say, 'I was spiritually blind, but now I see. Jesus Christ changed my life, and He can change yours.'"[38] This can take place between two men over lunch, across two neighbors' back fence, or between several housewives waiting for their children after school.

The Relational Style

The relational style is illustrated by the account of the demon-possessed man in Mark 5 who lived among the tombs. Jesus met him and cast the demons out. As a result of what Christ had done, the man begged the Savior to take him along on his ministry travels (v. 18). Mark states that, "Jesus did not let him, but said, 'Go home to your family and tell them how much the Lord has done for you, and how he has had mercy on you'" (v. 19). This style is highly personal, family-oriented, emotional, patient, passionate, and local.

Hybels adds, "Jesus, in effect, said, 'Don't go knocking on doors, doing "cold-turkey" evangelism with people you don't even know. You have family and friends who need to know what I have done in your life. Go home and live a transformed life in their presence. Diligently pray for them, then wait for divinely appointed opportunities to tell your story. Be available when someone says, "How can I get what you have?"'"[39]

The Invitational Style

The invitational style is illustrated by the story of the Samaritan woman in John 4. Jesus encountered a promiscuous woman of Samaria and after an extended conversation presented himself as Messiah (vv. 25–26). In her excitement she left her water pots, returned to her town, and invited all the people: "Come, see a man who told me everything I ever did. Could this be the Christ?" (v. 29). The result is found in verse 39: "Many of the Samaritans from that town believed in him because of the woman's testimony, 'He told me everything I ever did.'" This style is somewhat persuasive, persistent, opportunistic, and effective for those who are not good at articulating their faith.

Hybels describes the woman's evangelistic style: "The Samaritan woman was an invitational evangelist. She knew she wasn't prepared to articulate the message in a powerful way. So she invited her friends and acquaintances to come and hear someone who could explain it more effectively."[40] Then Hybels illustrates from his own ministry: "I estimate that fifty percent of the people who write and tell me about their conversion experience say something like this: 'I was lost. I was confused. I was lonely. Then someone invited me to a Sunday service—or to a concert, a holiday service, a special event. I kept coming back, and over time I came to know Christ in a personal way.'"[41]

The Serving Style

The serving style is illustrated by Dorcas in Acts 9. Scripture describes her as a disciple, "who was always doing good and helping the poor" (v. 36). Apparently she spent a great deal of her time serving other people in various ways not detailed in the text. She also had a great impact on the poor. This style is characterized by care, tenderness, compassion, love, patience, energy, hospitality, service, and quiet strength.

Hybels comments, "Dorcas was a service evangelist. She used her unique serving gifts as tangible expressions of the Gospel message. Like her, you may have a tender spirit and helpful heart. You may have gifts of mercy, helps, hospitality, giving, and counseling. You may be very effective evangelists as you connect sharing Christ with serving people."[42]

There are numbers of ways to evangelize through serving. We can mow a neighbor's grass while he is out of town or take food to one who is an invalid. We can help a coworker repair his automobile or provide a ride to work when his vehicle is in the shop.

The six styles of evangelism serve only to introduce us to the concept of discovering our natural, personal style. As many styles exist as there are different kinds of Christians. A more thorough study of the Scriptures, especially the biographical portions, reveals other styles as well. A Christian may have several styles of evangelism. Paul displayed not only an intellectual style but also a confrontational style (Acts 13:46; 14:3; 16:18). Both the invitational and testimonial styles are found in the Samaritan woman (compare John 4:29 with 4:39).

Natural Gifts and Talents

Discerning God's design involves discovering your natural gifts and talents. They are a more obvious component of your design from God and provide another missing piece of the puzzle. What are natural gifts and talents? They are abilities that God distributes to all people regardless of their spiritual condition for the benefit of all humankind. We will look at their source, essence, and recipients.

The Source of Natural Gifts

Natural gifts, like spiritual gifts, are from God. As the Master Creator and Designer, God delegates to each person certain talents and gifts. Unlike spiritual gifts, however, which are given at conversion, natural gifts are in place at birth. In some children they may manifest themselves at an early age, as seen in the child who teaches himself to play the piano or the one who paints extraordinarily well or the child who has the ability to multiply large numbers in her head.

The Essence of Natural Gifts

Natural gifts and talents are abilities or capabilities. Many spiritual gifts have corresponding natural gifts. Unbelievers have natural abilities to lead, administer, give, encourage, show mercy, help, trust, and teach, but they cannot have spiritual insight. When a natural gift and a spiritual gift are combined in a believer, he or she can exert a powerful impact in ministry.

Natural gifts may have little if anything in common with spiritual gifts. I am referring to such talents as the ability to write, draw, sing, play a musical instrument, participate in sports, analyze a problem, design objects, conceive ideas, persuade people, and many others.

The Recipients of Natural Gifts

God has given talents and gifts to all people, not just Christians. Natural observation and experience as well as history tell us that unbelievers are just as talented and gifted as believers. Natural gifts and talents are for the good of all, an aspect of God's common grace whereby he blesses everyone on the basis of his goodness and benevolence and not their personal worth or merit (Matt. 5:45). People without Christ are totally depraved, yet because of God's common grace they are not totally forgotten.

Other Components

I call the previous six components—spiritual gifts, passion, temperament, leadership role and style, evangelism style, and natural gifts and talents—the primary areas of design assessment. However, there are additional design components. I will briefly mention five.[43]

Style of spiritual growth. Numerous books have been written on how to attain spiritual maturity, and most prescribe a method or rules for all to follow regardless of how God has "wired" them. Mattson and Miller have a different perspective:

> The kinds of techniques that are embraced for the sake of spiritual discipline need to be individual. A set of rules made to discipline a person who has one motivational pattern may actually encourage unsanctified expression of another's pattern.
>
> Scripture does not outline one specific, step-by-step program aimed at maturing all Christians. Each individual requires a unique strategy. What one person needs will not work for another. What cripples one Christian may be a sign of health in another. This is troubling to those who want Christians in a more standardized package. God, however, has made each of us unique and never tires of ministering to every need.[44]

Learning style. We tend to assume that others learn as we do. This simply is not the case. Just as we have different leadership and evangelism styles, so we have different learning styles. Educators have found at least four.[45] I believe that many more exist, and the same is true of the other design components below. Regardless, knowing your learning style is crucial to your own learning and teaching.[46]

Conflict management style. Norman Shawchuck recognizes at least five styles people use to resolve conflict.[47] A knowledge of your style and the ability to recognize the style of another could make the difference between working harmoniously with another Christian and disaster.

Thinking style. Research indicates that people have a preferred style of thinking that falls into one of five areas.[48] At times we may use all of these styles or a combination of them.

Team-player style. Research has discovered that people who work together on a team display four styles.[49] Each team member's style contributes in different ways to the accomplishment of the team's goals and objectives. Also each style has a downside that can distract the team from realizing its vision. Since New Testament ministry is team ministry, Christians will benefit from discovering and implementing their team-player styles.[50]

Worksheet

1. Do you know how God has designed you for ministry? Why or why not?

2. How do you define a spiritual gift? Is your definition different from the one in this chapter? If yes, what is the difference? What is the difference between a natural and a spiritual gift?

3. What arguments would you give for the importance of spiritual gifts? Why might a person not want to identify his or her spiritual gifts? What is the difference between a gift-mix and a gift-cluster? Do you believe other gifts exist beyond those named in the Bible? Why or why not? What other gifts might there be?

4. What is the biblical justification for the concept of passion? Why is a person's passion important to his or her ministry design? Can you identify God-given passions other than those mentioned in this chapter?

5. Why is your temperament important to your divine design? Is temperament a biblical concept? Does it have to be? Why or why not? Name several people in ministry other than those mentioned in this chapter and identify their temperaments. How do their temperaments help or hinder their ministries?

6. What is your definition of a leader? Is it different from the definition in this chapter? If so, how? How important is influence to leadership? What is the key to influence?

7. What is the difference between role and style in leadership? Is there a difference between leadership and management or administration? If yes, what are some differences? Are some leadership styles in this chapter better or more right than others? Explain.

8. What is your natural reaction to confrontational evangelism? What might your reaction tell you about your style of evangelism? Is confrontational evangelism bad or good? Do other evangelistic styles exist besides the six covered in this chapter? Can you find others in the Bible?

4

THE DISCOVERY
OF YOUR DIVINE DESIGN

Do You Know Who You Are?

Like Tom, David has begun to get some sleep at night. He submitted his resignation to the church board, and his nightmare as a pastor is about to end. He had applied to a seminary as a doctoral student and has been accepted. When the good news arrived in the mail, his heart leaped inside him—a sense of joy he had not experienced back when he was first voted in as the new pastor of this church. Of course, he knows things won't be easy.

He will be committed to the doctoral program for the next three years, and after that his future is still uncertain. Teaching positions in North America are few and far between, so he will probably teach on the foreign mission field. But he isn't concerned because for once he feels a sense of self-esteem and significance—he is about to accomplish what he really wants to do with his life.

What prompted this change of direction? One morning an alumni letter from the seminary interrupted his sermon study, offering an assessment package that would help interested graduates discover their place in ministry. It was titled: "Discovering Your Personal Ministry Vision."

A few minutes later David contacted the alumni director by phone, and the assessment package was on its way. It took David several weeks to complete the divine design discovery process, but when he was done he knew better who he was and why he had to risk a change of ministry.

What was the process that David worked through? How did he discover his personal ministry direction, and how can you? It began with discerning his personal design for ministry—the components described in chapter 3—spiritual gifts, passion, temperament, leadership role and style, evangelism style, and natural gifts and talents.

Discovering Your Spiritual Gifts

At this point, you realize you have several different spiritual gifts (a gift-mix), and you have a working description of most of the gifts in the Bible. The next step is to discover your spiritual gifts.

The Importance of Discovering Your Gifts

Interest in spiritual gifts has ebbed and flowed for many years. Is the attempt to discover our spiritual gifts simply another Christian fad, or is it biblical? The Scriptures teach that it is indeed important—for two reasons.

In 1 Timothy 4:12–16 Paul instructs Timothy to maintain his integrity and continue his preaching and teaching of the Bible, and then Paul concludes: "Be diligent in these matters; give yourself wholly to them, so that everyone may see your progress." In 2 Timothy 1:6 Paul instructs Timothy to "fan into flame the gift of God." Paul is exhorting Timothy to involve himself heavily in the exercise of his gift. Both passages assume that Timothy has identified his gift(s).

In 1 Corinthians 12:31 Paul concludes a discussion on spiritual gifts with this imperative: "But eagerly desire the greater gifts." In chapter 13 he then describes our highest pursuit—love for one another. Then in 14:1 Paul brings the two ideas together: "Follow the way of love and eagerly desire spiritual gifts." This raises two questions: How could they "eagerly desire" spiritual gifts if they didn't know what they were, and why should they desire them if they are not important?

The Process of Discovering Your Gifts

In my ministry I have found the following eight-step, gifts-discovery process to be most helpful. It involves prayer, study, desire, analysis, experience, fulfillment, confirmation, and fruit.

PRAYER

John Bunyan said, "You can do more than pray once you've prayed, but you cannot do more than pray until you have prayed." The place to start in discovering your gift-mix is prayer. Indeed, the entire process must be bathed in prayer.

Pray for wisdom and insight for your personal ministry in general and your spiritual gifts in particular. Ask God to reveal to you your gifts in whatever way he deems fit. At the same time stay alert so that you do not miss any answers or opportunities he may send your way (Eph. 6:18).

This prayer must also be intentional. I suggest that you set aside a regular time each day for prayer and include specific requests for the identification of your gifts and abilities. The Savior set an example for us. According to Mark 1:35 he practiced the spiritual discipline of awaking early in the morning and traveling to a solitary place where he could pray without interruption. Whenever or however you do it is not as important as the fact that you do it.

Finally, your prayer time is a good time for an integrity check. Periodically ask yourself, Why do I want to discover my design and spiritual gifts? What are my true motives? Am I doing this for God or myself? The correct motive is to glorify God not ourselves. If there is a problem here, resolve it before you proceed.

STUDY

Another step in the process of discovering your gifts is to do a Bible study of the spiritual gifts. Turn in your Bible to the chapters on spiritual gifts (1 Corinthians 12; Romans 12; Ephesians 4; and 1 Peter 4) and read and pray over the gifts listed in these chapters. Though Scripture is not crystal clear as to the meaning of all the gifts, attempt to discern the nature of each gift and how it was used.

In chapter 3 of this book I provided a list of spiritual gifts. At this point, return to that list and read it carefully. Do you find yourself attracted to any of the gifts? If so, study those gifts in detail. Learn as much as possible about each one. Find someone with these gifts and learn what you can from them about their use.

This is a subjective approach to identifying your gifts and must be pursued carefully. The problem is you may select a gift based not on your actual abilities but your wishes. Some people wish for gifts and ministries that they and others admire but that are not true to who they are. For example, many Christians admire the ministry of Billy Graham and his gift of evangelism, and they want to be like him. However, they do not have his gifts and could waste much of their ministry by attempting the ministry of evangelism.

DESIRE

Next you must examine your personal desires. Ask yourself, What do I really want to do? While this is highly subjective and could mislead you, as in the Billy Graham example above, it may lead to the discovery of your gifts. David says, "Delight yourself in the Lord and he will give you the desires of your heart" (Ps. 37:4). In *The Dynamics of Spiritual Gifts*, William McRae writes that, according to this passage, God places certain desires in the believer's heart.[1] Whether or not this passage is specifically teaching that God gives us certain desires, it does teach that God may honor the desires of our heart. Consequently a specific desire to teach, evangelize, or show mercy could be from God or honored by God. Again we must examine the motives behind the desire.

ANALYSIS

Analysis is the next step in the discovery process. This is the objective side of the gifts discovery process that can serve to balance the subjective elements. It involves taking a spiritual gifts inventory. Many inventories are now available. I suggest that you take more than one, since each inventory has a slightly different format and approach.

Often the gifts inventories are divided into two groups. One consists of those that test for all the gifts, including the sign gifts, such as the Wagner-Modified Houts Questionnaire. The other group consists of inventories that exclude the sign gifts, such as the Houts Inventory of Spiritual Gifts or the Basden-Johnson Spiritual Gifts Analysis.

I have provided two spiritual gifts inventories for your use in appendixes A and B. It is important to realize that you are the final judge of your gifts, not some inventory. For a variety of reasons, the Spiritual Gifts Inventory or any of the other inventories mentioned in this chapter may not accurately reflect your design. If you doubt the inventory results, retake it now and several months later take it again. Now turn to the Spiritual Gifts Inventory in appendix A and complete it before you proceed.[2]

EXPERIENCE

It is difficult if not impossible to discover your gifts while sitting around your dining room table at home or in a pew at church. If you are a student, it will be difficult to discern your gifts if you spend all your time in the school library or in the classroom (unless you have had several years of prior ministry experience). The process happens much faster and more accurately if you are involved in ministry. In *The Making of a Leader*, Robert Clinton writes, "Gifts normally emerge in the context of small groups or when a leader has a ministry assignment. Most lay leaders will discover gifts by using them, without recognizing that they are spiritual gifts."[3] The same is true for those who desire full-time vocational ministry. If, after taking the preceding steps, you believe God has given you the gift of evangelism or teaching, then you need to share your faith or involve yourself in a teaching ministry. While the experience could prove awkward initially, given a little time, you will know if you are gifted.

Clinton adds two other helpful insights. First, he writes, "Potential leaders are intuitively attracted to leaders who have the same spiritual gifts."[4] For example, you might feel a strong attraction to the preaching or teaching aspects of your pastor's ministry. Or you might feel attracted to a layperson who ministers with the gift of helps in a nearby hospital.

Second, Clinton writes, "Potential leaders respond intuitively to ministry challenges and assignments that call for their spiritual gift, even if not explicitly known."[5] For example, you might find yourself jumping at the opportunity to preach, lead a ministry, administer a project, or encourage a group of Christians.

FULFILLMENT

The next step after experience is fulfillment. As you focus on specific gifts and minister and experiment with your gift-mix, there will be a sense of personal satisfaction and a feeling of significance. You believe that what you are doing counts for something special, that the body of Christ is better because of you and your gifts, and that you would be missed should you cease to minister with your gifts.

Although the motivation for using our gifts is unselfish—their ultimate purpose is to glorify God (1 Cor. 6:20), and they are for the common good (12:7) not for ourselves (13:5)—this sense of fulfillment is an important by-product that encourages us in the exercise of our gifts.

CONFIRMATION

Confirmation of your gifts comes from two sources: your abilities and other people. First, as you become involved in various ministries, over time your gifts and abilities will begin to surface. When you focus on them and use them, you should see improvement and a corresponding desire to develop them further. You will begin to realize that these are, indeed, God's special gifts for you and you will look forward to their use.

Second, other people will confirm your giftedness. The advice and counsel of others is a characteristic of wisdom: "Plans fail for lack of counsel, but with many advisers they succeed" (Prov. 15:22). Wise counselors include people such as a pastor, spouse, family, friends, and those to whom you minister. Give full attention to those who speak the truth in love. You do not need someone who tells you what they think you want to hear or someone who is caustic and always negative. You need the input and confirmation of those who care about you and have your best interests at heart.

Fruit

When you discover your gifts and exercise them, you will see ministry fruit or results. You need to ask, When I exercise my gifts, is there any fruit? If the Holy Spirit is operating through your gift-mix, there will be fruit. If you have the gift of evangelism, people will come to faith, or you will equip people who bring others to faith (Eph. 4:11–12). If you have the gift of teaching, your hearers will grow in knowledge of Scripture and biblical insight, and they will apply it to their lives. Also your class or small group will, under most circumstances, grow numerically. If you have the gift of leadership, people will follow you.

Discovering Your Passion

According to chapter 3, your passion is your God-given capacity to attach yourself emotionally to someone or something over an extended period of time to meet a need. You will need to follow both an objective and a subjective approach to discover your passion.

The Objective Approach

Read the following questions carefully. Give yourself plenty of time to think about them and feel free to return to them periodically. Remember, the discovery process will take place over an extended period of time. You need not answer all the questions below, nor is there a right or wrong answer to each, but several of them should catalyze your thinking and the ultimate discovery of your passion.

1. Make a list of everything about which you feel strongly and care deeply.
2. Do you have a "burning conviction" that a certain ministry is the most important place that God would have you? If so, what is it?
3. Does your gift-mix or gift-cluster point in a particular vocational or nonvocational direction? For example, Billy Graham has obvious

gifts in evangelism, preaching, and leadership. His primary gift is evangelism, which is supported by his other gifts. These have pointed him vocationally toward the leadership of an evangelistic ministry that involves preaching.

4. Do you have a "burning, gut-level desire" to reach a particular group of people, such as the lost, unchurched, undiscipled, unborn, poor, oppressed, youth, children, college age, adults, business people, street people, alcoholics, homosexuals, AIDS sufferers, internationals, refugees, a particular ethnic group, cults, unwed mothers, single parents, young couples, singles, divorced, street gangs, military people, apartment dwellers?

5. Do you have a strong desire to pursue a particular issue as your ministry? Do any of the following causes stir you emotionally: the family, abortion, physical and emotional abuse, emotional problems, divorce, drug abuse, alcoholism, civil rights, politics, women's rights, poverty, AIDS, starving children, legalism, the clarity of the gospel, demonism? This could include a particular issue or cause in your church or community.

6. Does the pursuit of a particular subject area excite you? Examples include apologetics, cults, theology, the law, business, leadership, politics, government, finances, the arts.

7. Do you find yourself strongly attracted to a particular geographical area for ministry, such as an urban, suburban, or rural area located in a specific city, county, state, or foreign country?

8. Do you have a significant attraction to a particular area of ministry in your church, such as leading a small group, teaching a class, ministering to a particular age group, maintaining the building and grounds?

9. If money, family, and time were not factors, what would you want to do for the rest of your life in your work, in your ministry, in your church?

10. Do you have a secret ambition, something you have always wanted to pursue but were afraid to tell anyone?

The Subjective Approach

Turn back to the section on passion in chapter 3. When you first read this section, did you get a sense of what your passion might be? Carefully reread the section focusing on the elements of passion: emotion, focus, tenure, and need. In light of these elements, write down any initial thoughts regarding your passion.

Discovering Your Temperament

The identification of your temperament will help you deepen your understanding of yourself and others, allowing you to see more clearly the strengths and the liabilities you and others bring to ministry. The approach to discovering temperament will be both objective and subjective.

The Objective Approach

The objective approach involves taking a temperament inventory and should prove more valid than the subjective approach. The problem with the subjective approach is that intentionally or unintentionally you can influence the results. You may choose a temperament type that appeals or seems best to you but does not reflect who you are. The objective approach attempts to eliminate the subjective element by asking a series of random questions that surface your real temperament identity. I have provided two objective temperament inventories in the appendixes at the back of this book.[6] Temperament Indicator 1 uses the four descriptors that are in Model 1 below. Temperament Indicator 2 uses the descriptors that are in Model 2 below. Turn to Indicator 1 in appendix C and complete it before reading any further.

I recommend that in addition to these inventories you take either the Biblical Personal Profile or the Personal Profile. They have been carefully refined and are sophisticated instruments that will result in a far more accurate assessment of your temperament.[7] If you take one of the two profiles and your results differ from Indicator 1, then use the results of the profile in light of its validity.

Also helpful are several books that are based on the four-temperament model. In addition to taking one of the profiles, read Voges and Braund's *Understanding How Others Misunderstand You* and Phillips's *The Delicate Art of Dancing with Porcupines*.[8]

Now turn to Temperament Indicator 2 in appendix D and complete it before proceeding. In addition to Indicator 2, you should take the Myers-Briggs Temperament Inventory (MBTI).[9] Like the two inventories above, it is a reliable instrument and will go into much greater depth than Indicator 2. A shorter form of the MBTI and one that is easier to obtain is the Keirsey Temperament Sorter (KTS).[10] If you desire more information on both forms, purchase a copy of the book *Please Understand Me* by David Keirsey and Marilyn Bates from your local bookstore.[11] This book contains the Keirsey Temperament Sorter. If the results of either of these inventories differ from that of Indicator 2, use the results of the MBTI or the KTS.

Once you have taken the MBTI or the Keirsey Temperament Sorter, several books may prove helpful. *Please Understand Me* gives further knowledge and insight into your temperament, based on the MBTI. Another work that applies the MBTI material to professional ministry is *Personality Type and Religious Leadership* by Roy Oswald and Otto Kroeger.[12]

The Subjective Approach

The subjective approach to discovering your temperament is an affinity approach that involves reading a general description of the temperaments and determining which best describes you.

MODEL 1

Model 1 (so named for the sake of discussion) uses the traditional four temperament descriptors that go back to Hippocrates and is a variation of the Personal or Biblical Personal Profile. Read through the following descriptions and determine as best you can whether you are primarily a doer, influencer, relator, or thinker.

DOERS

Doers attempt to control or overcome their environment to accomplish their ministry vision or mission. They are more task-oriented than people-oriented. They are catalytic people who love a challenge and are not afraid to take risks. Doers make quick decisions and like immediate results. They prefer change and love to challenge the status quo. In their ministry environment they need freedom from control and supervision and desire opportunities for individual accomplishments. They are "upfront" and "out-front" people. They are Ds on the Biblical Personal Profile. A biblical example is Paul.[13]

INFLUENCERS

Influencers attempt to persuade people to accomplish the ministry's vision. They are more people-oriented than task-oriented. They are persuaders and promote their ideas to bring others into alliance with them. Influencers enjoy contact with people and desire to make a favorable impression. They are articulate, motivational, and enthusiastic. They, too, prefer change and will challenge the status quo. In their ministry environment they need freedom from control and detail to function at their maximum ministry effectiveness. Influencers, like doers, are upfront and out-front people. They are usually an I on the Biblical Personal Profile. A biblical example is Peter.[14]

RELATORS

Relators cooperate with others to accomplish their vision. They are more people-oriented than task-oriented and prefer the status quo unless given good reasons to change. They are patient, loyal, and good listeners. They are well-liked and pleasant to be around. They minister best in a secure and somewhat safe environment where they receive credit and appreciation for their accomplishments. While they can serve out-front, they prefer remaining behind the scenes. They are Ss on the Biblical Personal Profile. A biblical example is Abraham.[15]

THINKERS

Thinkers tend to be diplomatic with people and comply with authority. They shape their ministry environment by promoting high quality and accuracy in accomplishing the ministry's vision and mission. Thinkers are more task-oriented than people-oriented. They are analytical and critical thinkers who focus on key details and accuracy. In their ministry environment, they desire to work under known circumstances and prefer the status quo. Like relators, they can minister out-front, particularly as teachers and preachers, but often they prefer to minister behind the scenes, especially in terms of leadership. They are often Cs on the Biblical Personal Profile. An example is Moses.

MODEL 2

The second model is that of the Myers-Briggs Temperament Inventory. This model assumes that people approach four key areas of life in ways that are different but equally correct. These areas are called preferences because each person prefers one over the other, much as we prefer to throw a ball with either our right or left hand. Carefully read through the following descriptions and determine which most accurately describes your preferences.

EXTRAVERTS/INTROVERTS

The first area looks at where people like to focus their attention and interests and what is their source of emotional energy.

Extraverts like to work with the outer world of people and things. They prefer variety and action. They are energized by contact with large numbers of people and are good at greeting people. When they are by themselves for long periods of time, they become fatigued and seek out people who stimulate and revitalize them. Consequently they have many friends and acquaintances. Usually they communicate freely and act quickly, sometimes without thinking.

Introverts like the inner world of concepts and ideas. They prefer to spend time alone reading, studying, or meditating and are emotionally drained if around many people for a long time. When fatigued, they are revitalized by "getting away from it all." Often they have trouble remembering names and faces. Consequently they have a limited number of acquaintances and only a few close friends. They are careful with details and like to work on projects for long periods of time without interruption.

SENSING/INTUITION

The second area looks at how people take in and process information. *Sensing people* prefer to take in information through their senses. They focus on facts and details that can be observed through the five senses—what they can see, hear, touch, taste, or smell. They are practical people who prefer to do ministry rather than study ministry, and they like to follow established, traditional ways. They are steady workers who love to follow systems and procedures and to reach conclusions one step at a time. They dwell on present reality (the here-and-now), so for them "seeing is believing." An example in the Bible is Thomas, who needed to see and touch the Savior to believe (John 20:24–25).

Intuitive people take in information holistically, preferring the world of ideas, possibilities, and relationships. They are big-picture types who shy away from meticulous facts and figures. They like to solve problems and work in bursts of energy powered by enthusiasm. They do not care for systems and procedures but would rather pursue change and new ideas. Intuitive types prefer to follow their inspirations, whether good or bad. They are visionary people who focus on the possible future (what could be). For them "believing is seeing." A biblical example is Nehemiah, who could see the rebuilt walls of Jerusalem before they had been rebuilt.

THINKING/FEELING

The third area concerns what you do with the information you take in, or how you make decisions.

Thinking people make their decisions on the basis of logic and objective analysis and are relatively unemotional. They prefer to win people over by their logic. They take a more impersonal approach to decision making in ministry and can come across at times as insensitive and not interested in people's feelings. The truth is important to them, and they are task-oriented. They are not people-pleasers and can minister in a team environment where there is some disharmony among the ministry team.

Feeling people make their decisions on the basis of personal values and motives. They are aware of other people and their feelings. They prefer to win people over through persuasion. Feeling types take a personal approach to decision making and communicate warmth and harmony.

Human values are important; consequently they are more people-oriented. They can be people-pleasers and prefer a ministry environment where there is harmony among the ministry team.

JUDGING/PERCEIVING

The last area deals with how you orient to the outer world and to structure and the time it takes to make decisions.

Judging people prefer a more structured approach to life because they desire to control and regulate life. Thus they are organized and deal with the world in a planned and orderly way. They minister at their best when they can plan their work and follow that plan without change and interruption. They may not see new things that need to be done, however. Preferring to have things settled and behind them, they pursue closure and tend to make decisions quickly.

Perceiving people seek to understand life and adapt to it, and so they take a less structured approach to life. They are adaptable, flexible, and spontaneous. They tend to start too many projects and have difficulty finishing what they start. Perceiving people are curious about and enjoy exploring new ideas and ministries. They have little need for closure and prefer to make decisions only after all the facts are in.

Discovering Your Leadership Role and Style

Leadership is critical to the success of any work for Christ. As the leadership of a ministry goes, so goes the ministry itself. Two important leadership areas are your leadership role and style.

Your Leadership Role

There are two primary leadership roles, leadership and management or administration. Most likely you are some combination of both, but one role will dominate. Discovering your leadership role involves first an objective and then a subjective approach.

THE OBJECTIVE APPROACH

To help you discover your leadership role, I have designed a tool called the Leadership Role Indicator.[16] Turn to the Leadership Role Indicator in appendix E. Complete and score it.

THE SUBJECTIVE APPROACH

Turn back to the section on leadership roles in chapter 3. As you read through this section, did you identify with or feel an attraction to leadership or to management? Carefully reread this section paying particular attention to the descriptions given for both leaders and managers. Note the definitions, differences, and the possibility that you may be a combination of both leader and manager. If the latter, which is stronger—leadership or management?

Your Leadership Style

While everyone does not have the gift of leadership, people often find themselves in situations where they need to lead. An example would be the father in the home. Your style of leadership reflects how you lead people when you do lead, regardless of the circumstances.

Before reading further, you should turn to appendix F and take the Leadership Style Inventory (LSI). Once you've completed and scored it, the following explanation of the leadership styles will help you understand the results.

What Does All This Mean?

There are four dominant, primary leadership styles that characterize all leaders. I've organized each style around three areas: the ministry context or situation where the particular style is most effective, the style's strengths, and the style's weaknesses.

One of the following styles will be your primary leadership style and should accurately describe you and how you typically influence or affect people in certain contexts. You might find it helpful to underline the characteristics that describe you, since some will not. Most likely, some of the characteristics of a second and possibly a third leadership style will help to make up your leadership style. Read carefully the information describing the other styles and try to determine what is true and not true of your style.

DIRECTORS—THE STRONG LEADERSHIP STYLE

Context. Directors are task-oriented leaders and they bring this strength to ministries that need more task orientation. In ministry contexts Directors often gravitate to the lead positions. They make good primary leaders or leaders of ministries in churches and parachurch settings. If you want something accomplished, assign it to a Director. He or she loves a challenge and will get the job done.

Directors are proactive, risk taking, hard charging, challenging leaders who set a fast pace for their ministries. Studies indicate that as lead pastors, they often make good church planters and church revitalizers, especially if they have some characteristics of Inspirationals, who are strong in relating to people. Directors are often change-oriented and attempt to bring change to most ministry contexts. They also lead well in a crisis situation.

Strengths. Directors excel at the task-oriented aspects of leadership. Some are visionaries and may set lofty goals for their ministries and then regularly challenge people to accomplish those goals. They're change agents who question the status quo and may struggle with maintaining traditions, especially if traditions prevent the organization from accomplishing its mission.

Directors are hard workers who seek opportunities for individual accomplishment and pursue high personal performance in their ministries. They are quick to recognize and take advantage of opportunities that God brings their way. They excel at managing problems and tackling complex situations and are fast decision makers with the ability to size up a situation quickly and act on it. Often those who evangelize take a direct approach, and those who preach like to impact people and challenge them to live for God.

Weaknesses. While Directors are strong, task-oriented leaders, they often struggle with the relational side of leadership. They have to resist the temptation to take control of a ministry and to work around rather than with a ministry team. They can intimidate people who, in response, either give them control or leave and look for another ministry. Directors can be bossy, make hasty decisions, and appear cold and unfeeling. Some need to learn how to relax and enjoy people.

Directors must consider the needs of others as well as their own. They have a tendency to judge people based solely on their ministry performance. Consequently ministries they lead can be too task-oriented with little regard for relational issues. Directors can balance this somewhat by working hard at developing people skills. They would benefit by teaming with those who have complementary ministry skills and by listening to wise counsel.

INSPIRATIONALS—THE PERSONABLE LEADERSHIP STYLE

Context. Inspirationals are people-oriented leaders who bring this strength to ministries that need a more relational orientation. Like Directors, Inspirationals often gravitate to lead positions, especially in church contexts. They lead best in ministry situations that call for an inspiring, motivational, compelling, exciting, sincere person. They prefer to work in teams where they can use their leadership skills. They insist on having fun and desire that people enjoy ministry. Inspirationals don't do well in strong, controlling environments where there is little freedom to lead and express themselves. They will work hard at changing such circumstances. Indeed, they are change agents who are open to new ways of ministry, setting a fast pace for the ministries they head.

Inspirationals make good pastors in a variety of situations, such as church planting and healthy church and parachurch contexts. They'll struggle somewhat in difficult situations where people are fighting with one another and will work hard at bringing them together. They perform best in situations where they have moderate control (things are neither completely under nor out of their control) as opposed to very high or minimal control. Studies indicate that Inspirationals with strong Director qualities are very good at revitalization.

Strengths. Some temperament tools call Inspirational leaders influencers because they tend to be natural leaders, relating especially well to people. People who work with them appreciate their visionary capabilities and the warm, personable way they relate to them. Inspirationals have a nose for new opportunities while being sensitive to the ministry's past. They're good troubleshooters in a crisis and have the ability to inspire people to work together in good spirits.

Often Inspirationals are articulate, and if they preach or teach, they speak with emotion, and their style of evangelism is very relational. In fact they relate to people on more of an emotional than intellectual level. In their messages, they seek to inspire and motivate with insight from the Scriptures. Some gravitate toward and enjoy counseling and supporting others.

Weaknesses. Some Inspirationals can be loud and obnoxious. They enjoy being the center of things, and that often bothers their followers. While Inspirationals are strong relationally, they may struggle at accomplishing necessary leadership tasks. They start projects that they may never finish because, when the newness wanes, they become bored and restless.

Inspirationals struggle with details, rules, and unpleasant tasks. Often they miss deadlines, ignore paperwork, misjudge others' abilities, and may not manage their time well. They want to be liked by all; consequently they seek to please people. This means that they'll shy away from speaking directly and confronting those who are problematic. Most Inspirationals need to be more objective when making decisions and make fewer promises.

DIPLOMATS—THE SUPPORTIVE LEADERSHIP STYLE

Context. Diplomats are people-oriented leaders who, like the Inspirationals, bring a relational orientation to the ministry context. They lead best in situations that call for a person who is caring, supportive, friendly, and patient.

Diplomats are strong team players who lead well in specialty areas, such as small groups, counseling situations, and other similar people-supportive settings. However, they often minister best in supportive roles rather than in organizational lead positions. Diplomats struggle in situations where there is bickering, disharmony, and uncertainty about their future. They prefer a somewhat slow ministry pace with standard operating procedures. They resist change environments because they're concerned about the risks change brings and how it will affect people.

Strengths. Other leaders praise Diplomats for their loyalty and support, especially in difficult times. These same leaders appreciate their taking direction and accepting and following instructions without hesitation. Diplomats are most skilled in ministering to and calming the troubled and disgruntled. They have learned to listen well so that people feel heard and understood. They are great team players who cooperate well with their teammates in accomplishing ministry tasks. People also admire them for their commonsense approach to ministry.

Diplomats are very patient, supportive leaders who get along well with most people in the ministry organization. (If you can't get along with a Diplomat, the problem is with you not them.) They take responsibility willingly and follow through on their promises. As evangelists, they prefer a relational style. Those who speak or preach like to console, comfort, and encourage others with the Scriptures.

Weaknesses. Some people complain that Diplomats are so nice that it's hard to be angry with them when you need to be—you don't want to hurt their feelings. They can be so loyal to their leaders and ministries that they miss God-given opportunities. They can be so softhearted that they fail to confront and deal with difficult people.

Diplomats need to work hard at developing task-oriented skills, such as being more assertive and learning how to say no when they are stretched to the limit. They must also learn not to blame themselves when others fail. In difficult situations they tend to seek compromise rather than consensus. Diplomats would benefit from being more proactive and taking the initiative in ministry opportunities.

Analyticals—The Conscientious Leadership Style

Context. Analyticals are task-oriented leaders. Thus they can bring certain complementary, task-oriented abilities to their ministry contexts. They lead well in ministry situations calling for people who are analytical, factual, probing, and detail-oriented. They are assets in ministries that demand high quality, such as an academic or teaching setting in a Bible college or seminary. They also function well as lead pastors of churches that emphasize a strong pulpit, characterized by in-depth Bible teaching—the teacher-pastor model. Often you will find Analyticals teaching Sunday school and similar classes in churches where people want strong Bible teaching.

Analyticals tend to lead best in support positions where they know what's expected of them, having responsibility for individual accomplishments, such as preparing for and teaching a class. However, they prefer not to work with strong leaders, such as Directors, who often focus more on reaching people and doing ministry than on the quality of ministry.

Strengths. Analyticals are conscientious, self-disciplined leaders who are self-starters. They are good at evaluating their church and ministry programs and holding churches to their theological moorings. People who work with Analyticals appreciate their ability to be consistent and dependable; they keep their word. They prefer assignments that require analytical and critical skills in problem solving.

Analyticals relate to people more intellectually than emotionally, and often ask "why" questions that help others think deeply. They prefer to do evangelism as apologists more than as confronters or relators. Some people are attracted to Analyticals for their careful, accurate Bible teaching. Analyticals who preach prefer to cover the Bible in depth, using lots of facts and details to support their conclusions.

Weaknesses. In their leadership roles, Analyticals attempt to maintain the status quo or even look to the past and tradition for direction. In situations where there is dissatisfaction and much conflict, such as in a revitalization context, they do not lead well. They struggle with fast-paced, change-oriented ministries because they're concerned that change may adversely affect the accuracy and quality of the ministry. Consequently they may not see the need to move into the future and consider new ministry approaches.

Analyticals may struggle with other vital organizational leadership functions such as vision casting, team development, change management, strong direction, and risk taking, all of which are key to ministry in the twenty-first century.

People often complain that Analyticals are too picky and become so involved in getting accurate facts and details that they fail to complete their ministry assignments. Analyticals have a tendency to be critical of innovative leaders who do ministry differently, and they may even stir up negative feelings toward them.

Often Analyticals need to work hard at the relational aspects of ministry. They tend to overwhelm and intimidate people with their logic and depth of information. At times they are cool, distant, and reserved. At other times they may want to please people. This makes it difficult for others who want to know Analyticals better and those who work with them on teams. Most would benefit from developing strong relational ministry skills.

These leadership styles combine to form at least sixteen different styles, and most people will have a combination of two or more of the four primary leadership styles. For example, the Director style could have any of the following combinations: Director-Inspirational, Director-Diplomat, and Director-Analytical.

What Difference Does All This Make?

Once you know your leadership style, its ideal context, and its strengths and weaknesses, you may wonder what difference it makes in your leadership and ministry. What should you do with this information?

Your Ideal Context

The Leadership Style Inventory will help you understand where you lead best—your ideal context. The next step is to analyze your current context. Is your current situation a good fit? A good fit provides you with the opportunity to do what you do best practically every day.

If your current situation is not a good fit or if it is questionable, can you adjust your style enough to make the context a better fit? If not, you would be wise to seek a context closer to your ideal context that aligns with your leadership style. If you are not currently involved in a ministry but want to be, you would be wise to evaluate the various opportunities in light of your ideal context.

Your Weaknesses

The results of the Leadership Style Inventory will surface some of your weaknesses. Your weaknesses are those skills and abilities that you do not have but need if you are going to do your job well. There is a popular myth and common assumption that says to become strong you must improve or at least minimize your weaknesses. However, you cannot excel in leadership by merely fixing or minimizing your weaknesses. To excel, you must maximize your strengths. This does not mean, however, that you simply ignore your weaknesses. The solution is to work around them where possible.

There are several ways to do this. First, you must realize that you cannot be proficient at everything. God did not design you to excel in every area of ministry. Those areas outside your design are limitations not weaknesses. If it is necessary for effective ministry, a limitation becomes a weakness. The solution is to staff to your limitations and weaknesses. Find people who are strong in the areas of your limitations and let them help you.

Knowing your limitations can work to your ministry advantage in two ways. One advantage is that you avoid ministry burnout. Involving yourself in a ministry that calls for a divine design that is different from your own will, over a short period of time, lead to ministry burnout and in time ministry dropout.

The other advantage is that knowing your limitations aids you in working toward maximum ministry effectiveness. By knowing what you do not do well, you can focus significant time on what you do well. An important by-product of the process is you learn when to say no.

To lead your ministry well, there are certain skills you must have. If you are weak in these required skills, you have no choice but to try to improve in them. However, you must keep in mind that you will always struggle in these areas to some degree, so don't be too hard on yourself when they don't become strengths.

You can also attempt to work around your weaknesses. If you have trouble remembering good ideas, keep a scrap of paper and a pen with you so that you can write them down when they come to you. If you want to remember to pray for someone, write his or her name on a Post-It note and stick it on the dash of your car.

Your Strengths

The results of the Leadership Style Inventory lets you know your strengths as a leader. This is the most helpful feature of this tool. To excel at leadership and make the greatest contribution to your organization and God's kingdom, you need to know and cultivate and thus maximize your strengths. Good leaders are learners who continue to pursue growth in their expertise as leaders. The greatest room for your personal growth and increasing competence is in these areas of strength. You should focus your training and development on building your strengths, not working on your weaknesses.

When you know your strengths as a leader, consider the following questions: How can I best develop each strength? Is there a course I can take, a book I should read, or a practice I should pursue? Perhaps the answer is a mentor who shares your strengths. Regardless of your answer, it is imperative that you develop and pursue a personal leadership development plan and begin it as soon as possible.

Another question is how do those whom you lead perceive your leadership style? How do you come across to others? Your people will respond to your leadership on the basis of how they, not you, perceive your style. (This is a good reason for others to rate you on the inventory as well.)

Most likely you will be a combination of two of the four temperaments in the Biblical Personal Profile or the Personal Profile. One will be primary and the other secondary, and your resulting leadership style will reflect characteristics of both. For instance your style may be primarily democratic (if you are high I) and also autocratic (if you are a secondary D). For further insight on leadership in general, I encourage you to consult my books *Being Leaders* and *Building Leaders*, both published by Baker Books.

Discovering Your Evangelism Style

Little has been written regarding the Christian's style of evangelism. Therefore this approach to discovering your style or combination of styles is more subjective than objective.

The Objective Approach

A clue to your evangelism style is how you relate to people in general. Therefore one of the more objective temperament inventories, such as Temperament Indicator 1, the Biblical Personal Profile, or the Personal Profile, can give you insight into how you prefer to evangelize.

I have observed a correlation between a high D temperament and a confrontational evangelistic style. Those who use a confrontational style experience a lot of rejection—doors slammed in their faces, people rudely saying they are not interested. While all the temperaments struggle with rejection, Ds tend to handle it best. Also I see some correlation with the testimonial style. Those who use it deal primarily with the facts. For example, the blind man healed in John 9 kept responding to his questioners, "One thing I do know. I was blind but now I see!" (v. 25). High Ds also place great value on facts.

I have noted a correlation between high I and R or S temperaments and the relational and invitational styles. Both high Is and Rs or Ss are people-oriented temperaments, and the relational and invitational styles involve time and interaction with people. They focus on winning family and friends to Christ. In Mark 5 Jesus told the man delivered from demon possession: "Go home to your family and tell them how much the Lord has done for you, and how he has had mercy on you" (v. 19). In John 4 the Samaritan woman went back to her people and said, "Come, see a man who told me everything I ever did. Could this be the Christ?" (v. 29).

I have observed a correlation between the high T or C temperaments and the intellectual style. Those who use the intellectual style tend to be extremely intelligent, analytical, and able to put together good arguments for their belief systems. They enjoy grappling with the tough questions of Christianity. People with the high T or C temperaments are also analytical and intelligent.

Each temperament will have strengths and weaknesses in evangelism. A high D temperament with the gift of evangelism will be a self-starter who will see many come to faith in Christ. This person may be seen as overbearing and pushy, however. A high I temperament gifted in evangelism will be an enthusiastic, articulate witness who relates well to unbelievers and wins many to Christ. However, Is tend to worry too much about what others think about them. The high S temperament with the evangelistic gift will be a steady, faithful witness for Christ and will get along extremely well with non-Christians. However, he or she tends to be easily intimidated and will not take risks like the high D or the high I. Finally, the high C temperament with the gift of evangelism is careful in witnessing to the lost. They are analytical and concerned with details. It is important to them to have the correct answers for any questions an unbeliever might ask. However, they can be too cautious and inflexible.[17]

The Subjective Approach

To determine your style subjectively, reread the section on evangelism styles in chapter 3 and think about your past activity in evangelism, which should give you some idea of what works for you and what does not.

If you have had any evangelism experience, for example, most likely you have been exposed to the confrontational style. You may have knocked on people's doors, gone witnessing in a college dorm, or handed out tracts on a street corner. You are either attracted to this style or repelled by it.

You need to expose yourself to other styles as well. Your church may be a good place to start. If your church doesn't offer opportunities for evangelism, I have two suggestions. First, look for people in your church who are individually sharing their faith. Most likely, they would be delighted to help involve you in some form of evangelism. Second, contact a parachurch ministry in your area that specializes in evangelism. Most are looking for workers and would be willing to help you. However, be aware that some churches and parachurch ministries specialize in only one style of evangelism: confrontational.

Discovering Your Natural Gifts and Talents

No doubt you have always been more aware of your natural God-given gifts and talents than your other design components. Since they were inborn, you have lived with them longer than your spiritual gifts. Also the world around you focuses more on these abilities and their discovery than some of the other areas of your design, so they are more familiar and recognizable.

The Objective Approach

Turn to the Natural Gifts and Talents Inventory in appendix G and complete the inventory before you proceed.

If you plan to pursue full-time vocational ministry, you may need to consider additional part-time opportunities outside of the church and parachurch. This applies to pastoral ministry in particular. Presently the supply of pastors is larger than the demand. Also the majority of churches in North America are small. Often pastors need additional employment ("tent-making") to supplement their salaries. I have provided a Natural Gifts and Abilities Indicator in appendix H. If you do not anticipate vocational ministry, this indicator can help you further identify your natural abilities for your present or future vocation.

Various individuals and organizations have developed a number of tools or have set up organizations to help people discover their unique, motivated abilities. One helpful vocational tool is the Campbell Interest and Skills Survey.[18] In addition, you may want to contact a vocational counselor or vocational testing service in your community, located at some public high schools, community colleges, and universities.

The Subjective Approach

Depending on your age, you have already determined many of your natural abilities. For example, you may have taken piano or voice lessons beginning at an early age and have determined your abilities to play an instrument or sing. However, you have other abilities that you are only vaguely aware of or have not discovered. To continue the process of bringing them to the surface, reread the section on natural gifts and talents in chapter 3, especially the part on the essence of natural gifts.

A helpful tool in discovering and confirming your natural abilities and the other components of your design is the "life map" or "lifeline," which is a pictorial representation of your life from birth to present. A careful examination of the past serves to bring to light patterns of consistent behavior that, in turn, reveal your giftedness and various styles through which you operate. To develop your life map, trace your life from as far back as you can remember up to today, searching for clues and hints that help you discover your spiritual gifts, passion, and temperament. Look

Figure 4
Life Map

Time Line

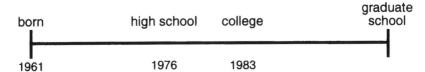

born　　　　　high school　college　　graduate school

1961　　　　　　　1976　　　1983

Cycle

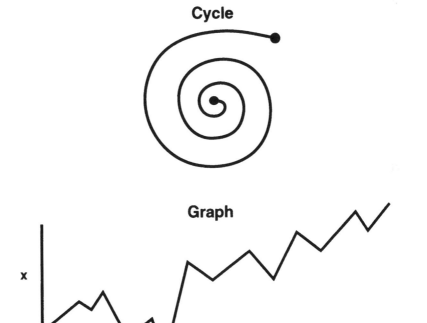

Graph

x

y

for important accomplishments, hobbies, jobs, interests, and trends that reveal natural abilities and other divine design elements.

The life map often surfaces design features that you may not have realized. You might discover that you have always been motivated to start new things. For example, in grade school you may have organized a lawn-mowing business in the summer to earn a few extra dollars. Then in high school you started a documents-delivery service. Later in life you started another business, not to mention a neighborhood Bible study. This pattern demonstrates that a significant part of your design is starting new ministries, whether as a lay or professional person in a church or parachurch ministry.

In *The Leadership Challenge*, Kouzes and Posner present a helpful, abbreviated version of a lifeline exercise developed by Shepard and Hawley.[19]

> On a blank piece of paper, draw your "lifeline." Start as far back as you can remember and stop at the present time.
>
> Draw your lifeline as a graph, with the peaks representing the highs in your life and the valleys representing the lows.
>
> Next to each peak, write a word or two identifying the peak experience. Do the same for the valleys.
>
> Now go back over each peak. For each peak, make a few notes on why this was a peak experience for you.
>
> Analyze your notes. What themes and patterns are revealed by the peaks in your life? What important personal strengths are revealed? What do these themes and patterns tell you about what you are likely to find personally compelling in the future?[20]

The life map can take several forms. Kouzes and Posner suggest a graph. However, you may find another figure is more to your style. Some people have used a straight timeline, a corkscrew spiraling from the inside out, or a picture (see figure 4). Whatever form you use, the composition of your life map is critical ultimately to discovering and understanding your divine design. It will open your eyes to how God has wondrously designed you (Ps. 139:14) and will motivate you to use your design in his service. Before you proceed with the following exercise, be sure to develop your life map according to the guidelines above.

Worksheet

To see a complete picture of how God has designed you, place all the information you have gleaned from this chapter under the appropriate topic.

    1. What are your spiritual gifts? Is one a primary gift around which the others cluster in support? If so, list it first and circle it.

        a.

        b.

        c.

d.

e.

2. What is your passion(s)?

3. What is your temperament? (Circle the appropriate letters.)
   a. Temperament Indicator 1: DIRT
   b. The Biblical or Personal Profile: DiSC
   c. Temperament Indicator 2

E	I
S	N
T	F
J	P

   d. The Myers-Briggs Temperament Inventory

E	I
S	N
T	F
J	P

4. What is your leadership role?
   a. Leader
   b. Manager
   c. Leader-manager
   d. Manager-leader

5. What is your leadership style? If you express two styles, circle both and underline the one that is dominant.
   a. Director
   b. Inspirational
   c. Diplomat
   d. Analytical

6. What is your evangelistic style(s)?

7. What are your natural gifts and talents?

8. Optional: What is your style of spiritual growth, learning, conflict resolution, thinking, and teamwork?

9. List any other relevant observations about your divine design.

PART 2

DETERMINING YOUR DIRECTION FOR MINISTRY

The second part of this book will help you understand that God has a limited range of ministries for you in the body of Christ. Once you have discovered your ministry identity (part 1), the next step is to use this information to determine what ministry God has for you (part 2)—which is the ultimate goal of this book.

5

THE CONCEPT
OF MINISTRY DIRECTION

Is Every Member a Minister?

Carol sat down with a cup of steaming black coffee and the day's mail, feeling puzzled and a little troubled. The church's lay-ministries consultant, Bruce Smith, had mailed the results of her spiritual gifts inventory. No explanation accompanied the results, just a note saying, "Drop by and see me at your convenience so we can talk about your results and your ministry direction."

The inventory said God had given her the spiritual gifts of leadership, mercy, and pastor. The first two she understood. However, she had some concern over the gift of pastor—what did that mean? She did not believe women should pastor churches, and she thought you had to be "called" to be a pastor. She had never had a deep, emotional experience like her pastor back home in south Texas, where God speaks in a vision and calls a person to go into the ministry and pastor a church. Isn't that what a "ministry vision" is?

Lately Carol's new pastor had said that a major goal for the people in this new paradigm church is "Every member a minister." But what does that mean? She was perfectly happy as an attorney—was God telling her to change professions? *First thing tomorrow,* she thought, *I'll call and make an appointment with Bruce Smith.*

Once you have discerned how God has wired you for ministry (your divine design or ministry identity), the next step is to discover your ministry direction (your design-based direction). Now that you have some knowledge of who you are, you need to discover what you can do. But before you attempt this, we must answer several questions. First, who is to be involved in ministry? Can every member be a minister? Should everyone in church pursue vocational ministry? Second, what is a ministry vision? Is it an emotional experience in which God speaks to you in a dream and tells you what to do? Finally, we will look at several issues that swirl around the concept of ministry direction, such as, Does a person have to experience a divine call to be involved in ministry?

Who Is Involved in Ministry?

So far this book has assumed that every Christian is to be involved in some form of ministry whether full- or part-time. But does the Bible teach this, and are most believers involved to some degree in ministry?

The Plan for Ministry Mobilization

Is every member a minister? Yes! God desires that all who know the Savior be involved in ministry to some degree. Our loving Father's plan is to bless us and others through our involvement in serving him and the church. God does not recognize the lay-clergy division that has characterized the church for so many thousands of years. Clergy are not paid to do the work of the ministry in our place. This is evident from God's many divine accomplishments in our lives.

1. God created each of us with a unique design (Gen. 1:26–28; 2:15; Exod. 31:1–5; Ps. 119:73; 139:13–16; Jer. 1:5; Luke 1:15; Gal. 1:15). This includes our temperament and natural talents and gifts.
2. God has given the Holy Spirit to each of us. At the moment of our conversion to Christ, God, the Holy Spirit, indwells each of us (1 Cor. 3:16; 6:19), supplying us with the power we need to accomplish our ministry direction in this world (Eph. 3:16, 20).
3. Christ has placed each of us in a unique relationship in a community of believers, called the body of Christ (1 Corinthians 12). In this context he has also given each of us one or more spiritual

gifts, which are an addition to our design when we come to faith in him (Eph. 4:7–11).

4. We are all believer-priests due to our position in Christ (1 Peter 2:5–9; Rev. 1:6) and are here for the purpose of serving God.

5. The Father has placed all of us in various difficult situations in life for more effective service (2 Cor. 1:3–7). No one will experience all of life's difficulties. Instead, God allows different Christians to go through trials and tragedies and then uses them to minister to others in similar situations. For example, a mother who has experienced the death of a child can have a significant ministry in the lives of other mothers who have lost children.

6. Christ has given us some gifted individuals (prophets, evangelists, pastors, and teachers) "to prepare God's people for works of service" (Eph. 4:11–12).

We are never more like Christ than when we serve him, and these divine accomplishments enable us to minister his grace in the lives of believers and unbelievers alike. God desires more from us than merely showing up on Sunday and filling a pew.

The Problem of Congregational Mobilization

Far too many Christians are not involved in any ministry, while others are not properly involved, having been placed in positions contrary to their designs.

You'll recall from chapter 1 that Larry Richards and his colleagues quizzed five thousand pastors about the greatest needs in their churches. From a list of twenty-five items, nearly 100 percent of the pastors selected as the top or second priority "Getting my lay people involved as ministering men and women."[1] This is why Carol's pastor developed the slogan "Every member a minister." He is not suggesting that the entire congregation give up their current professions and pursue vocational ministry as pastors. His desire is to mobilize them for ministry in the body of Christ (Eph. 4:11–12).

There are several reasons for inactivity and wrong activity. One is the typical North American church service that takes place on Sunday morning, particularly in churches that place an emphasis on teaching over worship. Teaching is a necessary but passive function that can encourage passivity on the part of Christians. The pastor or teacher does all the work while the congregation sits and listens. In most churches this is the main event for the entire week; everything else pales in significance.

A second reason is the way some churches recruit people for ministry. The process is based on emotion or coercion. The pastor or a well-meaning Sunday school superintendent plays on the emotions of members until they agree to serve. They may pester members or preach "serve or burn" sermons until members finally give in and agree to take that class of dysfunctional fifth graders.

A third reason for the "unemployment" rolls is the lack of knowledge and expertise of pastors doing the recruiting. They simply do not know what they are doing. Their seminary or Bible college never offered a course on lay mobilization.

A fourth reason why lay people often do not respond is they are waiting for a personal invitation. Many churches make an announcement regarding the church's needs and then sit back and wait for people to respond. Some people do, but many do not. I have discovered in ministry that people respond more to a personal, private invitation. They are not opposed to involvement; they simply want someone to come and ask for it.

A fifth reason is some pastors do not recognize or value the ministry of lay people. Their attitude may be "If you want it done well, then you have to do it yourself." Some feel that since they have been to seminary, they are responsible to do the work of the ministry; after all, that is their job. Others attempt to minister out of codependency. They do all the ministry because they feel good when others need them.

A sixth reason behind lay inactivity is many lay people are convinced that ministry is the pastor's responsibility. This is a reversal of reason five. This is the attitude of the people in Carol's church in south Texas. Since the pastor has been to school or in ministry for a long time, he is responsible to do the work of the ministry. Their job is to be faithful and committed, which means showing up on Sunday morning and putting their tithe in the offering plate.

The discovery of your divine design and personal ministry direction is one major solution to these problems. God wants all believers involved in ministry because that is what is best for them and the body of Christ. The proper discovery of your design and direction will motivate you not only toward involvement but the right kind of ministry involvement.

What Is a Personal Ministry Direction?

It is one thing to realize and accept that God desires the involvement of all Christians in ministry. It is another to understand what this involvement entails. Developing your ministry direction can give you that understanding.

A personal ministry direction resembles an organizational ministry direction. Both concern people. One difference between them, however, is that organizational direction affects all the people who make up that organization; whereas personal direction primarily affects the individual alone. In my book *Advanced Strategic Planning*, I discuss organizational direction.[2] It is not to be confused with the ministry organization's purpose. The same is true for personal ministry direction.

Purpose

Just as a ministry organization has a purpose for its existence, so does each individual Christian. The purpose of both is to glorify God, just as the purpose of the nation of Israel was to glorify God (Ps. 22:23; 50:15; Isa. 24:15). The Hebrew term for this idea means to honor or value someone who is worthy of respect and obedience. To honor or value them is to enhance their reputation privately or publicly. In the New Testament as well, the church's purpose is to glorify God (Rom. 15:9; 2 Cor. 9:13). The New Testament term also means to honor or value someone and is literally translated "honor" in 1 Corinthians 6:20. Consequently the people of God are here on earth to value and honor God in their lives, enhancing his excellent reputation before a watching world.

That is our proper purpose in life—it is why we exist. It is the key to the meaning of our entire existence. It is the thread that runs through the history of each of us, connecting all its events and relationships, giving true meaning to our lives. Without it life becomes superficial, empty, and meaningless (read Ecclesiastes!). While each event and each person in our lives has a unique purpose, they all are subsumed under a greater purpose: God's glory. To miss that greater purpose is to miss life altogether, because all of life is centered in God not us (Col. 1:15–20; Heb. 1:1–4). Unfortunately, this is difficult to see and realize from our limited view of life.

In Acts 13:36 Paul summarizes David's entire life with the words: "For when David had served God's purpose in his own generation, he fell asleep; he was buried with his fathers and his body decayed." David's life served God's purpose. Most of what he did (certainly not all) brought honor to God and enhanced God's great reputation before others. That is why David existed.

Understanding your life's purpose is critical to discovering your life's direction. It assumes you understand why you exist. However, your ministry direction is not to be confused with your purpose. Instead, it serves to accomplish your purpose—God's glory. Ministry direction is not the same as purpose but is subsumed under that purpose.

Ministry Direction

Your ministry direction is the same as your design-based direction or, in more contemporary terms, your ministry niche or ministry portfolio. It is where you fit in the body of Christ. It is your specific ministry or range of ministries—what you can do in serving the Savior.

Believers, like ministry organizations, have a mission in life. The mission of the church is the Great Commission (Matt. 28:19–20; Mark 16:15), which in turn serves our greater purpose—to glorify God. The mission of each Christian is his or her particular place in the accomplishment of the Great Commission.

Therefore for a Christian's purpose, I could use the terms *ministry vision* or *ministry mission*. There are some similarities and distinctions between the two. Both answer the "what" question: What is my ministry in obedience to the Great Commission? However, your personal ministry mission is more goal-oriented. It is a short, straightforward statement of what you do, as might be found in a job description: I am a Sunday school teacher, a small-group leader, a teacher of adults, a greeter, a senior pastor, a worship director.

Your personal ministry vision articulates what that ministry looks like as you see it in your head or attempt to communicate it to others. It is what you see when you think about your mission. It is usually longer and contains more imagery than the mission statement. Rather than the kind of thing you would read in a job description, it is what you might see in a promotional brochure. For example, a person who goes into vocational ministry as a church planter might have the following ministry mission: "My mission is to plant Great Commission churches that plant other churches throughout Dallas, Texas." Whereas a ministry vision might be "My ministry vision is to birth significant Great Commission churches throughout the city of Dallas that will see unchurched, lost people embrace the Savior and hurting families healed and brought back together in Christ. These in turn will plant other reproducing churches with the result that in fifteen years Christian influence will be increasingly felt all over the metroplex, the state of Texas, and abroad."

A ministry mission for a layperson might be "I teach a class of junior high boys at our church." It could be expanded into the following vision statement: "I spend several hours each week providing spiritual insight and wisdom from Scripture for a group of young men who are at a critical time of development in their personal lives." The vision is the mission statement fleshed out in imaginative, descriptive terms of the community and the people who live in it.

The distinction between a personal mission and vision may be only slight, but there is a difference. In some cases, the difference is how the statement affects the listener. What might be a mission statement for one could be a vision statement for another if it elicits a strong mental picture of what the ministry will look like. Consequently the terms *vision* and *mission* may be used synonymously in this book along with other terms, such as *ministry direction, ministry niche, ministry job, ministry portfolio*. For the sake of clarity I will try to make a distinction between *ministry mission* and *vision* as well as *direction*.

Regardless, you should take time out of your busy schedule to begin writing your personal ministry vision, beginning the process as you finish this chapter and having it fully developed by the end of chapter 6. This is a very important part of the formation of your vision or mission statement. I suggest that you set aside a morning or two each week for this process or, better still, spend a day or two in a quiet spot, perhaps in the mountains or at the beach, to think about and write your personal ministry vision. The format is not important. Perhaps one of the samples above will prove helpful.

Ministry Direction Issues

Much of Carol's confusion in the introduction to this chapter stems from various issues that have collected like barnacles to the concept of Christian ministry. Some of the issues that affect the concept of ministry direction are calling versus design, old versus new paradigms, church versus parachurch, and gifts versus office.

Ministry Calling versus Ministry Design

The concept of the calling of God is widely used by many as an indispensable factor in determining God's will for the believer's life in general and the believer's pursuit of a vocation in particular. Pastor Kent Hughes writes, "My call to ministry was *real*! And I am convinced that God calls certain of his children to this special service. To be sure, my experience of the call is not normative for anyone else, for the experience of God's call is as varied as there are people; only the reality is the same."[3]

In this view, professional ministry is a higher calling for Christians than professions such as law or banking. In fact it is the "highest of calls." Hughes quotes Dr. Will Houghton, a former pastor: "The highest calling man can know is the call to the Christian ministry. While it is true that every Christian is commissioned to labor together with Christ, it is also true that he has chosen some to undertake special service for him in their day and generation."[4]

In this view, God issues a special, higher mystical call for a lifetime of vocational ministry to certain individuals whom he has chosen. Again God is active in choosing, while man passively receives. Most often the call is to the vocational ministry of a pastor or missionary. God accomplishes this call in a variety of ways, most of which are described as a subjective "inner call." For example, the Holy Spirit may call men through a special inner conviction, an unusual urge to preach the gospel, or by impressing a particular passage of Scripture on one's mind.

Regardless of what constitutes a special call to vocational ministry or how that is accomplished, the real issue is whether or not the concept is scriptural. Hughes believes it is. He writes, "Those who would deny or minimize the fact that God calls individual Christians to special service must not only discount the facts of human experience but the evidence of Scripture, which records the calls of Moses, Isaiah, Jeremiah, Paul, and the commissioning of the apostles."[5] The classic text in support of this idea is Isaiah 6:1–13, where God calls Isaiah the prophet. Hughes believes this particular call has all the classic elements common to the experience of those who have obeyed God's call to minister: a vision of God's holiness, a vision of our unholiness, the forgiveness of sin, and obedience.[6]

However, further examination of the Bible indicates the concept of a special, divine call is questionable biblically and is not normative for all believers for several reasons. First, to argue for this concept on subjective grounds alone raises problems and questions that most who hold this view will acknowledge. Its validity must rest on scriptural evidence. To argue for a special inner call, those who embrace the concept must demonstrate that the experiences of Moses, Isaiah, Jeremiah, and Paul are normative experiences for all who pursue vocational ministry in all ages. That these Old Testament prophets and some apostles had a special call from God does not necessarily mean others must as well. This argument is a non sequitur.

Also these were prophets who spoke God's word and prophesied future events (Isa. 1:1; 7:14; 9:6; Jer. 1:7–9). Paul was an apostle with apostolic authority to record divine revelation. Neither Old Testament prophets nor New Testament apostles are the equivalent of the contemporary pastoral office.

Second, the offices or positions of elders and deacons in the New Testament are the closest equivalent to today's office of pastor. In light of the significant size of the early, first-century churches, the elders spent a lot of time with their ministries and were compensated for them (1 Tim. 5:17–18; 1 Peter 5:2). Much of that ministry involved shepherding God's flock (Acts 20:28; 1 Peter 5:1–2) as well as preaching to and teaching God's people (1 Tim. 5:17). Of the fifteen or more qualifications for elders and deacons listed in 1 Timothy 3:1–13 and Titus 1:5–9, a special inner call is not mentioned. Also, 1 Timothy 3:1 indicates that people can "desire" or set their heart on being an elder. This clearly teaches personal proactivity on the part of the believer and contradicts the idea that God is active in the divine call while man remains passive.

Third, the New Testament uses the term for *call* or a form thereof more than 150 times. However, the term is primarily used of the divine call to salvation and, in turn, to ministry involvement whether vocational or nonvocational. If there is a call to ministry, then the call to salvation is the call to ministry. Thus all are called to ministry.

Fourth, in the analogy that the New Testament makes between the church and the human body (1 Corinthians 12), no body part is separated out for special or separate ministry. While mention is made of the head, there is no indication that it was a special or divinely "called" body part.

Fifth, the New Testament teaches the priesthood of all believers (1 Peter 2:9–10; Rev. 1:6). There is no mention of a special priestly caste or a hierarchy of the few who are set aside for pastoral or missionary service.

Another concept that is important here is the confirmation of others in the body of Christ. I covered this under Confirmation in chapter 4 and I deal with it under The Consultation Phase in chapter 6. In determining your ministry direction, it is important that you have the blessing of those in the body, especially those who are spiritually mature. It is imperative that you consult with them, asking them to confirm your ministry design and direction. If they question your conclusions, you would be wise to revisit the process.

The most important point of this brief study is the same one made earlier in this chapter—all believers are to be involved in ministry. The key to the exact nature of that ministry is not some special inner call from God but a person's divine design. Therefore men who desire the pastoral office in particular do not need to wait for a call to that office but need to determine if their design best suits them for such a position. Often this pastoral design consists of such gifts as leadership, administration, teaching, and pastor.

Having said all this, do I mean that God cannot issue a special call to ministry? My answer is no. As we have seen, God has done this with some, such as certain Old Testament prophets. However, a call is neither necessary nor normative for all who go into ministry. Of course, it is possible for God to call someone today through a subjective moving of his or her spirit. I would not deny this. My point is that you should not let the lack of such an experience hinder you from stepping out and serving God through the gifts and abilities he has given you.

Old Paradigms versus New Paradigms

A frequently used term in literature on leadership, change, and ministry is *paradigm*. A paradigm is a shared set of assumptions and beliefs, a mindset or viewpoint about reality or how things are.[7]

Each ministry represents a paradigm. A church's paradigm is the particular assumptions, beliefs, or viewpoints about reality adopted and shared in common by the congregation. It includes not only the church's doctrinal beliefs, but what the congregation thinks about other areas of its life, such as the style of its music, where people sit in the service, what they wear to that service, if an invitation follows the service, and how the offering is taken. In short, "It's how we see and do things around here." Consequently the church's paradigm serves as a pair of glasses through which its people view the world and reality. It affects all they see and do.

No two churches have precisely the same paradigm. However, a number of churches share similar paradigms. A large number are referred to as traditional churches because they prefer church music that favors the grand old hymns of the faith played on an organ; the sermons may last forty-five minutes to an hour and may be preached from a particular translation of the Bible; the men wear coats and ties, and the women dresses; and there is a Sunday morning and evening service with a Wednesday evening prayer meeting. They are old paradigm churches because they see and do church the way it was done in North America back in the fifties and earlier.

Other churches view life through a different set of glasses. They prefer a style of music that is more upbeat and use instruments such as the guitar and drums. The worship consists of contemporary praise hymns that are printed on the bulletin or projected on screens placed at the front of the sanctuary, and the people dress casually as well as formally. The sermons are much shorter and attempt to be practical and relevant to the times. These are commonly referred to as contemporary or new paradigm churches. While new paradigm churches can be ministry restrictive (they have limited opportunities for lay ministries), most seem to offer a broader ministry menu than old paradigm churches. For example, few old paradigm churches include the fine arts as a part of worship or ministry (ballet, drama, painting, sculpture); as a result lost people naturally gifted in these areas are not attracted, nor do they find a place to exercise these gifts when they come to faith.[8]

In the past, paradigms have proved virile. Once in place they prevail over a ministry for years, decades, even centuries. However, today, with change occurring at lightning pace, paradigms are turning over more frequently. Consequently contemporary churches will soon become tomorrow's traditional paradigms, and new congregations with new paradigms will appear on the scene and be called contemporary or emerging churches.

Christians who serve in any capacity in a ministry must be aware of their paradigm preference. While some people in the older paradigms attempt to argue that their paradigm is the correct biblical paradigm corresponding to the first century church, no correct biblical paradigms exist. The real issue in most evangelical churches is not what is biblical and what is not—but which paradigm you prefer. An old paradigm church may not have a place of ministry for someone whose ministry direction is drama or leading a small group. A new paradigm church may not have a place of ministry for another whose ministry mission involves playing the organ or leading or singing in a choir. The issue in both examples is not which is biblical, since neither is forbidden in Scripture, but which you prefer. The same applies to people interested in vocational Christian ministry. Those who desire to pastor a church must be aware of their paradigm preference as well as that of the church. The ministry world is full of horror stories of what happened to the young new pastor with a new paradigm mentality who tried to minister to a church with an old paradigm mentality.

Church versus Parachurch

Should you attempt to minister in a church or a parachurch setting? Before going any further, I need to define these terms. The key to the term *parachurch* is the prefix "para," which means "along side of." *Parachurch* literally means "along side of the church." Here the term *church* refers to the local church and not the universal body of Christ (the fellowship of all believers).

In the last decade some have begun to use the term *para-local church* instead of *parachurch*. In this book I use the terms *parachurch* or *para-local church* for any ministry other than that of a local church. This would include such ministries as some missions organizations; Christian colleges, universities, and seminaries; youth ministries; ministries to children; ministries to international students; ministries to college students; ministries to cults; ministries to military personnel; ministries to athletes; ministries to ethnic groups; evangelistic ministries; counseling ministries; and publishing ministries.

Some trace the beginnings of the parachurch movement back to the Pietists in 1669, though the causes that promoted these movements were evident before then.[9] In the twentieth century the movement experienced its greatest expansion since 1860.[10] Leith Anderson writes that a large number of parachurch organizations were born and blossomed with the post-World War II "Baby Boom."[11] However, he believes that at the end of the 1980s many of these parachurch groups reached their zenith: "But like the baby boomers, these organizations are starting to show signs of aging. Many of the founders are gone; many will go within the next decade or two. And the current generation of leaders, who often seem to lack the vision of the founders, are accused of merely managing others' dreams."[12] Still, I suspect and hope that the parachurch movement will continue to minister effectively in this world until the Savior returns. Indeed, early in the twenty-first century, parachurch ministries appear to be "holding on."

In deciding where to pursue your ministry vision, the local church or parachurch, you might find it helpful to consider the advantages and disadvantages of both.

There are numerous advantages to ministry in the local church. Most churches, especially the large ones, offer a number of diverse ministry opportunities, which provide you with more settings in which to minister and receive ministry. Another advantage is ministry accountability. Even if a believer joins a parachurch ministry, he or she should also be part of a local church, which has the greatest potential for ministering to and holding a broad number of Christians accountable for their lives and service.

A third advantage of ministry in the local church is that churches often minister to a broad range of people. While people are attracted to a particular church on the basis of some affinity, most churches, especially larger churches, reflect some variety of people along racial, educational, social, and economic lines. A fourth advantage is consistent theology. Most churches have a doctrinal statement of their beliefs that is embraced by its members. A fifth advantage is most churches observe some form of the ordinances. Jesus Christ commanded believers to be baptized and partake of the elements of the Lord's Supper. The local church offers these to its people.

There are some disadvantages to ministry in the church. First, some churches focus on their buildings and not their people. Much time, money, and energy can go into bricks and mortar rather than people. Second, a tendency exists in some churches to place all their ministries in the hands of a few professionals. This creates an overworked clergy and a passive, lethargic laity. Third, most churches are slow to change. They are locked into old paradigm ministries that tend to be ministry restrictive. Fourth, far too many North American churches are having little if any evangelistic impact, especially in the unchurched community.

In *The Church and the Parachurch*, Jerry White lists several advantages to parachurch ministry. First, independent mission agencies have primarily been responsible for developing and initiating missions ministries over the last two centuries. Second, since lay people are at the core of most parachurch ministries, these ministries have done a good job of equipping and involving them in ministry. Third, parachurch organizations have done a good job of equipping and involving women, both single and married. Fourth, parachurch ministries have become experts in how to penetrate and evangelize the unique groups that make up our culture. Fifth, many of the finest educational institutions from elementary through graduate school are parachurch ministries. Sixth, parachurch ministries appear open to change and innovation, realizing that it takes all kinds of ministries to reach all kinds of people.[13]

White also lists several disadvantages. First, with some organizations no accountability exists except to the organization itself. Second, parachurch organizations often do not relate well to or support the local church. Third, because parachurch organizations are independent, there is needless duplication of some ministries and a lack of coordination with others. Fourth, most organizations begin with and often focus on one person whose vision and drive carries the ministry. This can result in obsessive control and the potential for a personality cult. Fifth, parachurch ministries are specialized, focusing only on part of believers' needs, not their total needs. Thus a special focus may be blown out of proportion, whereas other areas are missed entirely.[14]

Gifts versus Office

A final issue that affects the implementation of your ministry vision—in a church in particular—is the difference between ministry gifts and church offices.

Every church consists of a body of Christians who have a cluster of spiritual gifts (1 Corinthians 12; Romans 12). Therefore the ministry of the church is the responsibility of all the people in the church. The corporate ministry of any church will only be as effective as the individual ministries of the believers in that church.

Every church will also have officers. Most argue that according to the Bible only two offices exist: elder (1 Tim. 3:1–13) and deacon (vv. 8–13). Some would include women in the office of deaconess (v. 11) and point to Phoebe as an example (Rom. 16:1). One unique view identifies four offices in the church: Christ as the head (Col. 1:18; Eph. 1:22), elders (1 Timothy 3), deacons (1 Timothy 3), and priests (1 Peter 5:9). The latter includes all believers.[15]

With the exception of the last position, most agree that not all Christians in the church will hold an office though they are encouraged to seek the office of elder (1 Tim. 3:1). The offices, however, come with certain qualifications. Not only does one have to be a Christian, as is true with spiritual gifts, but a mature Christian (vv. 2–13; Titus 1:5–9).

The differences between spiritual gifts and the offices of the church are evident. Every believer will have one or more spiritual gifts but may never occupy a church office. Believers do not need to seek spiritual gifts but do need to seek an office, at least the office of elder. And the only qualification for spiritual gifts is faith in Christ, whereas specific qualifications need to be met to hold an office.

Many confuse offices with gifts. For example, confusion exists between the gift of pastor and the office of pastor. The reason for this is the common practice in most churches of being led by an individual called a pastor. Actually this is more a cultural phenomenon than a biblical imperative. A thorough search of the Scriptures reveals that this practice is not biblical. That does not mean that it is wrong or should be abandoned, only that its practice cannot be defended from the Bible. This would be true of much of what takes place in the typical evangelical church on Sunday morning. Much of what churches do is dictated by the culture not by Scripture.

Confusing gifts with offices affects your ministry vision. For example, many believe that the office of pastor in a church should be filled by a man and not a woman. From this they conclude that a woman could never be a pastor in a church. While it is true that a woman should not hold the office of pastor (or better, elder), she may have the gift of pastor and exercise that gift in the local church, especially with the other women of the church.[16] Most churches in North America desperately need women with pastoral gifts and a ministry vision to shepherd other women. A person with the gift of pastor, whether a man or woman, does not necessarily have to function as *the* pastor of a church but can shepherd people in a small group or any other context.

Whether the office of pastor must be filled by someone with the gift of pastor depends on the role the pastoral position plays in a particular church. In most small churches the pastor is expected to have shepherding skills because the people want to be nurtured. Small churches should seek someone with the gift of pastor and a pastoral ministry vision. In larger churches, however, the pastor is expected to be a leader, preacher, and teacher. He is not expected to literally shepherd all the people because the church is too large. Large churches should seek a man with the appropriate gifts and ministry vision.

Finally, a person's ministry design could include an office and spiritual gifts. This would be true of the office of elder. In Acts 20:28 and 1 Peter 5:1–2, the elders are told to pastor or shepherd God's people. While the gift of pastor is not necessarily a requirement, its presence in the individual enhances his performance dramatically.

Vocational versus Nonvocational Ministry

In general, the terms *vocational* and *nonvocational*, when used of ministry, do not distinguish between those who have received a divine call and those who have not (according to the discussion above). Instead I use the terms in this book to distinguish between those who work regularly in that ministry and those who do not.

This involves several components. One is time. Often the terms *full-time* and *part-time* are used of a person's involvement in ministry. If the majority of your time is spent in the ministry rather than another vocation, then you are considered full-time. But if the majority of your time is not spent in that ministry, then it is part-time.

Another component is income. Those in vocational ministry derive their chief income from that ministry. Those in nonvocational ministry look to other sources for their primary income, such as the legal profession or the construction industry. Nevertheless, a lawyer or a carpenter should consider their professions as ministries for the Lord. Here the traditional line drawn between the sacred and the secular blurs. Certainly the construction skills of Bezalel and Oholiab were used for the Lord (Exod. 36:1–3). Consequently the distinction is not found necessarily in the Bible but in the attitudes and expectations of both Christians and non-Christians toward the ministry and their professions in general.

In terms of your ministry direction, you must make two decisions. First, do you desire to spend the majority of your time pursuing your ministry direction or only part of your time? Second, will you receive your income primarily from the pursuit of your ministry direction or some other source? For you who believe in a divine call to ministry, the answer depends on whether or not you have received that call. If you do not believe in a divine, inner call, the answer to both questions can be more difficult. For some ministry directions, few if any paid positions exist, and the answer is simple. An example would be a woman with the gift of pastor in a small church.

Answering these questions is more difficult when you consider positions involving remuneration. If every Christian left the work world to pursue a full-time ministry in the local church, the results would be disastrous. The same would hold true if the example is reversed. I suggest you determine the area in which you believe you can have the greatest impact for the Savior—your job or your ministry.

Worksheet

1. Would you categorize yourself as an active or nominal Christian? Why? Are you one of the "employed" who is involved in ministry, or among the "unemployed"? If you are among the "unemployed," what is the reason?

2. What does the Bible say about why you exist? Do you agree with that? Why or why not?

3. What is the biblical mission of the church? Is this your church's mission? What is your ministry mission? Have you begun the process of writing it down? How does it relate to your purpose? What is the difference between your ministry mission and your ministry vision?

4. Do you believe that God issues a distinct, inner call to those who are to go into vocational ministry? Why or why not? Have you received such a call? If so, describe it.

5. What is a paradigm? Is your church an old or new paradigm ministry according to this chapter? What is your paradigm preference? Why?

6. What is the difference between a church and a parachurch (or para-local church) ministry? Do you plan to minister in a church or parachurch ministry? Why? Name some of the advantages and disadvantages you will face in this ministry.

7. What is the difference between a vocational and a nonvocational ministry? Do you plan to pursue vocational or nonvocational ministry? Why?

6

THE DISCOVERY
OF YOUR MINISTRY DIRECTION

What Is Your Ministry?

Although Tom did not realize it at the time, the discovery of his spiritual gifts was just the starting point. The purpose of the Bible study in the dorm was to uncover more than spiritual gifts; it was to help college students discover their divine design and then determine their personal ministry direction. The Christian organization that sponsored the campus Bible study valued this concept highly, and so it brought in a specialist who lived in the community to teach and work with the students in this area.

As a result, Tom saw the rest of the pieces of his "puzzle" begin to fall into place. Not only did he identify his spiritual gifts, he also discovered his passion, temperament, leadership abilities, and some natural gifts. The next step in the process, according to the specialist, was to determine his personal ministry vision—what he would do with his God-given design. There are two chronological steps to discovering your personal ministry direction: the direction identification step and the direction confirmation step.

The Identification of Your Ministry Direction

The identification step helps you determine as precisely as possible your personal ministry direction. Most likely it will not pin down your exact vision, but it will provide you with a process for someday zeroing in on that vision. It consists of two phases that I will handle separately but that, in fact, work together. One focuses on ministry positions and the other on ministry people.

Ministry Positions

The focus on ministry positions involves two vital concepts: ministry matching that starts with the position for ministry and then moves to the person who is most wired to fill that position and ministry projecting that starts with the person and then moves to the ministry position.

MINISTRY MATCHING

Ministry matching starts with the various positions in the ministry organization and matches them to the personal ministry design of the individual. For example, a local church may be adding a small-group program to its ministry menu and needs people to lead and shepherd those groups. First, it focuses on the ministry position of a small-group leader, drawing up a reasonably detailed ministry description (similar to a job description) that consists of the necessary spiritual gifts, passion, temperament, and so on needed for this ministry. Then it will seek someone with a design that most closely matches the small-group leader's ministry description.

Matching presumes that two important events have already taken place. First, the ministry organization needs to have identified its ministry positions and drawn up precise ministry descriptions for each position. The church will do much more than announce in the bulletin: "We have an immediate opening for a Sunday school teacher with the junior high girls." Willow Creek Community Church in northwest Chicago has developed a ministry description for each of the ministries in the church. This ministry description contains a concise statement of what the person is to do, the necessary spiritual gifts, the passion, the minimum spiritual maturity requirements, any needed talents and abilities, the preferred Myers-Briggs temperament (such as ENTP or ISTJ), the ministry target (adults, children), the necessary time commitment, and where the ministry will take place. To this could be added the score on the Biblical or Personal Profile.

This is a critical process that will make it more likely that Christ's people will be mobilized and have an effective ministry (Eph. 4:11–12).

All too often the rule of thumb is to fill a slot with a warm body. For example, a church that has an opening on its leadership board will often fill that position with an individual who has been faithful in attending the church services and has shown an interest in the church's affairs. Instead, the church should look for a Christian with the spiritual/natural gifts of leadership, since the position calls for a leader. Those who are responsible for finding people for ministry must carefully and thoughtfully articulate the kind of design necessary to accomplish that ministry with maximum effectiveness and Christlikeness. If there is no one who comes close, then the organization is not ready for that particular ministry. When it is, Christ will raise up the right person with the right design.

Second, the ministry organization needs to have implemented an effective program for discovering the believer's divine design. It is the key to the mobilization and assimilation of its people. The program might consist of three stages.[1] The first is education that will provide believers in the ministry with instruction on the various divine design elements (as found in chapter 3) and then help them determine their personal ministry direction (as in this chapter). The second stage is consultation, in which people meet with a lay or professional person who provides personal ministry consultation one-on-one or in a small group. The third stage is mobilization, as the consultant helps believers determine where they can minister within the ministry organization and then connects them with that ministry.

MINISTRY PROJECTING

Ministry projecting also helps in determining your ministry direction. You should practice both ministry projecting and ministry matching because the two work together in determining your best ministry fit. Ministry projecting involves projecting from your divine design to your ministry position. Contrary to ministry matching, it begins with the person and then looks to the position. For example, if you have the gift of evangelism, you would look for a ministry that involves evangelism. You examine each piece of your completed ministry puzzle (spiritual gifts, passion, and so on) and attempt to project or determine what God might do with it in a ministry context. In essence, you build the position around the person. Your design from God dictates your direction for God.

Your ministry design translates into your ministry style, and every style is unique. Adopting another's exact ministry model is a grave mistake. For example, to mimic Billy Graham's evangelistic ministry would most likely result in failure even if you have practically the same design. Because of your uniqueness, you must allow your ministry model to take shape based on your design. Pastors who are planting or revitalizing churches in one part of the country often attempt to replicate a popular, successful church in another, hoping for the same success. There are numerous problems with that. One is that it is not authentic and does not flow from the leader's own style but from that of another. While we can learn certain principles from others' ministries, we face dire consequences if we copy them.

When projecting your personal ministry direction, you may discover a single, precise direction, such as leading and preaching in an evangelistic organization. However, you may also discover your direction includes several related ministry positions. The concept of ministry range can be helpful in this process (see figure 5). A ministry range consists of the various ministries (represented by the crosses) in a particular ministry organization on a continuum with the ministries that make up your best fit on the extreme left, a questionable fit in the center, and no fit on the extreme right.

Ministry Range

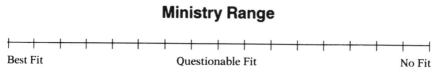

Best Fit   Questionable Fit   No Fit

Figure 5

It is possible, as the best-fit area shows in figure 5, that several related ministry positions fall within your ministry direction. One layperson might discover that she could best serve the Savior in a church as a greeter on Sunday mornings and as a volunteer counselor two evenings each month. Another might discover he could serve Christ full-time by functioning as the senior pastor in a church or by teaching homiletics (preaching), church leadership, and other ministry topics in a seminary setting. He would need to decide which he prefers to pursue.

After projecting your preferred ministry position, you may discover your church or ministry organization does not have a position that accommodates your specific design but would benefit greatly from it. Pray about asking the ministry's leaders to create a new ministry position.

Ministry People

The concept of ministry people moves from the ministry position to the ministry person. It focuses not on the various ministry positions but on the person who is ministering well in a particular ministry position. It is person-centered not ministry-centered. Employing the ministry people concept in addition to or along with the ministry positions concept aids you even further in detecting your personal ministry vision.

The Concept

The ministry people concept looks to particular individuals whom God has chosen to bless in a particular ministry over the years. It is obvious by what God is accomplishing through them that they have found their ministry visions.

On the one hand, they may be as well-known as Billy Graham, Chuck Swindoll, Mother Teresa, Charles Colson, E. V. Hill, Elisabeth Elliot, Bill Bright, James Dobson, Anthony Evans, or Joni Eareckson Tada. On the other hand, they may be known only in a particular area, or they may not be well-known at all. Most likely, a ministry person is someone in a church: the pastor, a godly lay leader, or the church custodian. It would be a mistake to assume that those who are well-known are more spiritual or faithful than those who are not. God has seen fit in his sovereignty to allow the public spotlight to shine on some and not on others. We must take care when considering well-known ministry figures. Be aware of your motives. Does your design and direction truly come close to that person's, or are you trying to be someone you are not? Many seminarians would love to have a ministry like that of Chuck Swindoll for a variety of reasons—some good and some not so good. But there is only one Chuck Swindoll.

The ministry people concept looks at the designs of the person in focus, in particular the ones that are most like yours. Based on the similarity of designs, it considers whether the ministry directions are similar as well. You might have the gifts of evangelism, leadership, and preaching. Sound familiar? That is the point! Since you and Billy Graham have the same gifts, the possibility exists that you might have similar ministry directions. Or you might discover that you have the same gifts as your pastor, the director of the church's drama team, or the lady who serves as the part-time counselor. Consequently you could carefully probe their ministries to discover if your ministry direction is the same or similar to theirs.

Another example is a dynamic, church-planting pastor. You are aware of his ministry because of the impact it is having on the unchurched, lost people in your community. Many have come to Christ and been discipled, including the mayor. As you investigate this pastor's divine design, you discover you have much in common—the same approximate gifts, passion, temperament, and so on. The concept of ministry people teaches that in light of this affinity you should prayerfully consider leading a church planting team in a ministry similar to the one just described. It is also quite possible that God may use you similarly—but differently—because of some divine design differences. Regardless, you have benefited in the personal vision process and saved time.

Where the ministry people concept is most effective and beneficial for determining your ministry direction is in the ministries that do a good job overall in helping all their people discover their designs and ministry directions. Most likely these will be organizations that employ a program such as the instruction, consultation, and implementation stages mentioned above, requiring it of all their people or at least making it available to them. The advantage is that those responsible for this ministry will have an awareness of or information on all the people with the same or similar designs and will use them as potential indicators of personal ministry direction.

THE RESEARCH

Recently those thinking and working in the field of assessment have made some significant contributions to the concept of ministry people. Most research has focused on those in two full-time, vocational ministries: church revitalization and church planting. Much of the church ministry taking place in the twenty-first century will be in these two areas.

Church revitalization. Robert Thomas has written a doctoral dissertation attempting to answer the question "What types of personality traits are characteristic of an effective revitalization pastor?"[2] Among other things, the study sought to develop a working profile for use in identifying and placing pastors designed for the ministry of revitalizing churches.[3]

In his survey of twenty Baptist General Conference pastors (ministry people) who had a proven record of renewing churches, Thomas used the Biblical Personal Profile to isolate their specific personality or temperament characteristics. He discovered that of fifteen possible patterns, all the effective revitalization pastors he studied fell within one: the persuader pattern.[4] The profile supplies the following temperament description:

> Persuaders work with and through people. That is, they strive to do business in a friendly way while pushing forward to win their own objectives. Possessing an outgoing interest in people, Persuaders have the ability to gain the respect and confidence of various types of individuals. This ability is particularly helpful to Persuaders in winning positions of authority. In addition, they seek work assignments which provide opportunities to make them look good. Work with people, challenging assignments, variety of work and activities which require mobility provide the most favorable environment for Persuaders. However, they may be too optimistic about the results of projects and the potential of people. Persuaders also tend

to overestimate their ability to change the behavior of others. While Persuaders seek freedom from routine and regimentation, they do need to be supplied with analytical data on a systematic basis. When they are alerted to the importance of "little things," adequate information helps them to control impulsiveness.[5]

The value of Thomas's work is that the Biblical Personal Profile or the Personal Profile can be used to help pastors determine if their ministry designs are conducive to a ministry vision of renewing established churches.[6] Voges writes, "The Biblical Personal Profile (BPP) measures behavioral tendencies. It is not meant to be a prescriptive tool. You and others do not 'have to behave' like your profile. *However, it is a fairly accurate predictive tool. You will 'tend' to behave as described.*"[7]

Church planting. In *Planting Growing Churches for the 21st Century*, one chapter title asks, "Are You a Church Planter?"[8] While a number of designs are suitable for those who would be part of a church planting team, there is a unique design for those who would plant solo or serve as the point person on a team. This design includes such spiritual gifts as leadership, faith, evangelism, and preaching.[9] Their passion is often for lost people in general and unchurched, lost people in particular. On the Biblical or Personal Profile and Indicator 1 in appendix C, they tend to be high Is or Ds or a combination of the two.

The Christian Churches/Disciples of Christ performed a survey using the Personal Profile to correlate the personality types of 66 church planters (ministry people) with the growth of their churches. The survey revealed that the high D planters had an average attendance of 72 after the first year and 181 after an average of 5.2 years. The high Is had an average of 98 after the first year and an average of 174 after 3.6 years. The high Ss had an average of 38 after the first year and 77 after 6.3 years, while the high Cs had an average of 39 after one year and 71 after 4.3 years.[10] This reveals that if church planting success is to be measured in terms of reaching and ministering to people, then the Is and Ds have the edge when planting either by themselves or leading a team of church planters.

There are some additional design elements. In terms of leadership, solo church planters are primarily leaders with some ability to manage in their roles and either directive or inspirational or a combination of the two in their styles.[11]

Robert Thomas makes the following insightful comment on the use of the Biblical Personal Profile for those anticipating full-time ministry:

This profile has been said to meet a major need for many denominational executives. The development of other operational profiles could further assist them in the difficult task of screening candidates for ministry. Suggested areas for further study are a church planter profile, an interim pastor profile, a small, medium, and large church pastor's profile, and an associate minister's profile. It is interesting that the few large church pastor profiles this writer observed were all "task oriented," "High 'D'" profiles. It is quite likely there are different personalities for each of the suggested areas of need.[12]

The need, however, is for similar work to be done in the area of ministry direction inhabited largely by laypeople. The limited amount of research thus far has focused on professional ministry. Research in lay ministry areas as well will prove vital to mobilizing the full body of Christ for powerful, significant ministry in the twenty-first century.

The Confirmation of Your Ministry Direction

While the identification step serves to help you discover your ministry direction, the confirmation step seeks to validate the accuracy of your discovery. It consists of three phases that are distinct but work together to confirm your ministry direction.

The Observation Phase

The observation phase involves self-observation based on the knowledge of your past consistent behavior or ministry experience. You carefully examine the results of the identification process and ask yourself, Is this true of me? Is this what I think I can do? The reason why this phase is so important is we are the ones who ultimately determine the accuracy of any phase of any assessment program. We can use highly sophisticated tools, such as the Biblical Personal Profile or Myers-Briggs Type Indicator, to determine our design, but they reflect only the information we give. If the information for our direction is based on what we want to do or what someone else thinks we should do, then at best it tells us nothing and at worst it leads us astray. Next to our omniscient God, we are the ones who know ourselves best. As we weigh the results of all assessment, it is our responsibility to determine its accuracy based on our self-observation.

However, there exists the ever present problem of subjectivity. We are working on the basis of how we feel or what we think. For various reasons we have the potential to distort the information. Two other phases help us detect this: the consultation and experimentation phases.

The Consultation Phase

The consultation phase involves intentionally seeking and accepting wise counsel and advice from others regarding the accuracy of your ministry direction. Its purpose is to confirm or correct your ministry direction through the help and input of other significant people. This phase is not temporary but will last a lifetime because of the constant need to evaluate and refine the direction of our ministries in light of additional personal insight and ministry experience. Initially it should consume much time and energy and then gradually decrease in intensity over the years.

THE IMPORTANCE OF CONSULTATION

Scripture advises us to seek the counsel and advice of wise people. Proverbs 15:22 says, "Plans fail for lack of counsel, but with many advisers they succeed." Most often the counsel of others brings wisdom. Proverbs 19:20 advises, "Listen to advice and accept instruction, and in the end you will be wise." Other passages encourage the same (12:15; 13:14, 20; 20:18; 24:5–6; 27:9).

Getting counsel adds an objective element to what otherwise can be a subjective experience. We may carry a hidden agenda and not be aware of it. We may rationalize and distort the feedback we receive from the various indicators and tools because we want to be or do something other than what we have been designed to be and do. Wise counsel serves to offset and correct this problem.

A third reason for consultation is some people are confused as to who they really are. They may have grown up in a situation where they were pressured to be who they were not. Paul and Barbara Tieger explain, "Children are particularly vulnerable to others' expectations and often suppress their own natural preferences in order to fit in and be accepted."[13] Again they write, "Children who are discouraged from using their innate strengths can grow up to be confused and ambivalent about their perceptions and inclinations—and this confusion can affect every aspect of adult life, including career issues."[14] Other people can see through all this and help them discover their true identity.

THE SOURCES OF CONSULTATION

We must seek advice from the right people, however. Good counselors display several characteristics. First, they are people who know you reasonably well. High on the list is your spouse. Your husband or wife may know you better than any other person in your life, and so I suggest you have your spouse also take the indicators (located in the appendixes) on you. If the results are similar to or the same as yours, then you probably have an accurate feel for who you are. If they differ, then you would be wise to discuss these differences and possibly repeat the process. The same holds true for the confirmation of your ministry direction. Other people who could prove helpful as advisors are your parents, close friends, children, and pastor.

A second source of good counsel is those involved in a ministry similar to that for which you have a vision. Since these people are serving in the ministry firsthand, they can give you an idea of all that is involved. Often we see only the surface of a work, or what we want to see. We have no idea what goes on behind the scenes. Thus our picture of a ministry may be distorted or entirely inaccurate. Spending some time interacting with those in the ministry should help us catch reality and gives them an opportunity to get to know us and determine if we are a good fit for that ministry.

A third source is Christians who have demonstrated unusual wisdom in life and who display keen insight into people. They have the unusual ability to see things in you that others, including you, may not see. They can not only confirm obvious gifts and talents but spot dormant abilities and bring them to our attention so we can cultivate them in ministry for Christ.

A fourth source for confirming your ministry direction is people who are truth-tellers. Truth-tellers don't tell you what they think you want to hear or what you actually do want to hear. They tell you the truth. Some will speak the truth with love; others will tell you the truth with little regard for your feelings. While they come across as harsh, they are doing you a favor. Do not make the mistake of rejecting their counsel because of how they communicate their thoughts.

A fifth source is people who are on your side. In general, you want to pursue those who have your best interests at heart, who are "on your team." They desire God's very best for you not only in life in general but your ministry in particular.

A sixth source of confirmation is the consultant. Some churches have begun to use consultants—either from within or outside the congregation—in mobilizing their people for ministry. If this is your situation, consider yourself blessed and use the services provided. If this is not your situation, look for a consultant in a nearby church or find one online.

The Questions for Consultants

When you seek the counsel and advice of another person, you should ask certain specific questions. One is, What do you see me doing or not doing with my life? The words *doing* and *not doing* will help them approach the issue from two sides. The same question asked differently is,

If you were in my shoes with my design, how would you serve Christ? Once you have asked a question, sit back and let the person talk. Resist interrupting, except to clarify any points you do not understand. You may have to prod the consultant at first, letting him or her know you want to hear the truth, whatever that may be. By doing this you give the person permission to relax and be a truth-teller.

After the consultant is finished, say something like, "I'm thinking about pursuing a certain ministry. I value your opinion and want to know what you think. In your opinion, would I make a good Sunday school teacher of adults (leader for a small group, campus evangelist, a pastor of a church)?" Watch for visual cues while listening to their words. They may say one thing and signal another. When this is the case, seek further counsel from others.

Another question is, Why do you feel the way you do about my ministry vision? The reason behind the positive or negative response may be as important as the response itself. For example, a trusted friend may counsel you not to pursue vocational ministry as a campus evangelist at the present. The reason: "You are task-oriented, and evangelism requires someone with developed people skills. Wait a year or two until you have had more time to further develop your people skills."

The Experimentation Phase

Pursuing the counsel and wisdom of others to confirm your ministry direction should prove most valuable. A third complementary phase involves experimenting with your vision by getting ministry experience.

THE VALUE OF EXPERIMENTATION

Ministry experience supplies "seasoning." It is one thing to think and talk with others about your direction; it is another to experience it. You need to spend some time experiencing your ministry niche before claiming ownership. You don't know for sure if you can drive a car just by listening to a lecture in a driver's education class. The true test comes when you slip behind the wheel and get out on the road.

As you involve yourself in a ministry, you should feel a sense of significance and fulfillment in at least 60 percent of what you do. If you drop below 50 percent, chances are good you will experience burnout and will eventually drop out. This does not mean your ministry direction will be problem-free. Every ministry has its "bedpans." However, when you are in the right ministry, even the bedpans seem easier to clean, and the problems are less threatening.

OPTIONS

Those considering professional ministries in a church or parachurch should pursue an internship. The general rule is the longer the internship the higher the learning curve. The shortest internship should be equivalent to a semester of school—about four to six months or a summer. However, this is minimal and works best in quality organizations that place a premium on training men and women for ministry. The best internships last from one to two years because this period of time allows the ministry seasoning process to take place.

Laypeople need experience as well. Bruce Bugbee suggests giving people three opportunities. If the first is not the right ministry fit, then the person can try the second and third. Each ministry is responsible to train a new person "on the job." If no position is suitable to someone's design, then a new ministry could be designed around that person.

SUGGESTIONS

For ministry experience to prove valuable in confirming your direction, it must take place with the right people in the right context. As with seeking wise counsel and advice, not just any ministry will do. Seek a quality ministry organization. You want to be trained in the best situation possible. Seek a ministry that fits your ministry direction. If you plan to minister in a new paradigm church, then do your training in a similar setting. Look for a ministry staff that is committed to training its people. Agree on the expectations of the trainer and trainee in advance. This will prevent major problems later on. Develop a ministry training plan. Without a clear, personalized plan you will waste your time and that of others.

Worksheet

1. Does the ministry you are a part of have a detailed ministry description for its key ministry positions? If not, why not?

2. Does your ministry have a program for helping people discover their divine designs? If yes, how effective is it? If not, why not?

3. Are you aware of most of the ministry positions in your church or parachurch? As you practice ministry matching, what ministry position(s) best matches your ministry design?

4. Based on your divine design, project the kind of ministry you should pursue. Does your ministry organization have such a position? If not, is it willing to start one?

5. Do you know of a person or persons whom God is blessing in ministry who has a divine design similar to yours? What is his or her ministry? Do you feel an affinity for that kind of ministry?

6. If you are considering vocational pastoral ministry, is your design similar to that of a pastor involved in church renewal or church planting? Is your ministry vision church renewal or church planting?

7. At this point in your discovery process, what is your ministry direction (ministry mission and vision)? Have you written it down on paper? No matter how accurate your statement, it is most important that you begin the process of writing it out as soon as you finish this chapter. It may go through a number of revisions, but that is part of the process of articulating a significant personal ministry direction. Use the format provided by the examples in chapter 5 as your initial guide.

8. Have you consulted with anyone regarding the confirmation of your ministry direction? If not, why not? If yes, who? Do they meet the qualifications for a good source of counsel? What was their response?

9. What ministry experiences are available to help you confirm your direction? What is the attitude of those in these ministries toward working with you? In light of your design, which is the best possible ministry environment to test your direction? Has any experience thus far either confirmed or contradicted your ministry mission and vision?

PART 3

DIRECTING YOUR DEVELOPMENT FOR MINISTRY

The last part of this book will help you accomplish or realize your personal ministry direction. Now that you know who you are (your ministry identity) and what God wants you to do (your ministry direction), the third and final step in the process focuses on your ministry development. It answers the question, How do I best prepare for my ministry or range of ministries? The answer is to design a unique, personal ministry training plan.

7

INITIATING THE MINISTRY PLAN

What Can You Learn from a Professor or a Pastor?

David is now back at the seminary. He spends much of his time in the library quietly doing research in preparation for his doctoral courses. Sometimes he thinks he has died and gone to heaven. He loves what he is doing, and God is providing for his family's material needs. The company where his wife worked during his prior studies rehired her and increased her salary substantially. Since they have no children, they should be able to get by financially until he completes his program.

The last two years in the pastorate have proved profitable. Not only has God used this time to direct him to the teaching ministry, but David has gained practical ministry knowledge, experience, and some ministry skills, enough that he has been invited to preach regularly at a small church located thirty miles from downtown.

Through the knowledge of his ministry design and the discovery of his ministry direction (mission and vision), David knows that much of his ministry preparation will involve classroom-based education. He is preparing for a professional ministry that requires a graduate degree from an accredited theological institution.

But what ministry preparation is necessary for Tom and laypeople like Carol to realize their personal ministry dreams? Actually David, Tom, and Carol are far ahead of many in the process. Most Christians work through the process in reverse order. They know they want to serve the Lord but are not sure how. So they begin the process with the preparation stage hoping that somewhere along the way they will find their personal ministry directions. They may enroll in a Christian college or seminary even though they have no future ministry vision or an ill-defined, inaccurate one. Because so little information is available on the divine design concept, they may never have considered the design stage and have not discovered their gifts, temperaments, and natural abilities.

David, Tom, and Carol are ahead in the process because they have taken each step in the proper order. First, they discovered their divine designs for ministry (chapters 1–4). Next, based on those designs, they determined their personal ministry directions (chapters 5–6). Now it is time for them to take the third step—ministry development (chapters 7–9)—which involves preparing a ministry plan.

In light of who you are (your design), how can you best prepare to accomplish your personal ministry vision (your direction)? You can answer that question by designing a lifetime personal training plan tailor-made for your individual ministry situation. This is the concept behind the development stage. This plan is designed to take you from wherever you are and move you to where you want to be in ministry. It consists of three steps: initiating the plan (chapter 7), designing the plan, (chapter 8), and working the plan (chapter 9). The rest of this chapter will cover initiating the plan. It will address the concept of and guidelines for the plan.

The Concept of the Plan

Your Divine Design

A personal training plan assumes you have a reasonable knowledge of your ministry design. This depends on where you are in the design discovery process. Some people know themselves well. They have always been sensitive and alert to who they are. Thus they are ahead in the process. Others, however, do not know themselves as well. For a number of reasons they may not have been as observant, so they are behind in the process. These people are often late bloomers. They discover their design and become productive in ministry later in life. Others look at them and are amazed at the change. This often contributes to the mistaken view that people can change their temperaments, when, in reality, they are just discovering and realizing their true identity. Regardless of whether you are advanced in the divine design process or a little behind, you are so unique and wonderfully made that you will continue to discover and refine your design for the rest of your life.

Your Ministry Direction

The development of your ministry plan assumes a reasonable knowledge of your ministry direction (your personal mission and vision). Since the discovery and development of your design is an ongoing process, you will need to regularly refine and adjust your direction. It is like focusing a movie projector on a screen. Time is on your side. The longer you think about and work with the concepts in this book, the clearer they become. Keep in mind that this is a process that does not take place overnight.

Your Ministry Development

With a reasonable knowledge of your ministry design and direction, you are ready to pursue your ministry development. Everyone needs preparation. Even if you are an unusually gifted person, you are aware of your present need for ministry development. And this, too, does not take place overnight. Like the discovery of your design and direction, it takes time and hard work. A man with the natural talent to play the piano needs to take lessons and practice regularly. A woman with the gift of evangelism will need some instruction and experience in sharing her faith.

Most likely you have already given your ministry development some thought. In fact you may have unknowingly begun the process at this point rather than with the design and direction phases. For example, you may be in school with little idea of your design or direction. If this is the case, you may need to make some minor adjustments or major changes. You may have thought that God wanted you to be an accountant but now realize he has designed you to pastor a church. You are enrolled in business school, preparing to be a CPA. You may need to leave school and pursue seminary training. Others may need to leave seminary and begin training to become a CPA, farmer, or plumber.

Not only does everyone need preparation, they need to think in terms of a lifetime of preparation. Those who are serious about serving the Savior, whether lay or professional, need to tailor a lifetime training program. All too often churches and schools look at training as "front end" preparation, as introductory, as if those in ministry had somehow arrived and have no further need for development.

Church and parachurch ministries may take pride in the fact that they provide training for their people—although many in their ranks have not even progressed this far. How often is a recently recruited third grade Sunday school teacher still simply handed a lesson book and pointed in the direction of the class? Still, many who have progressed beyond this point fail to see the need for lifetime continuing education. David Ludeker writes of the professional minister: "The passivity of clergy in planning learning goals is widely known. There is a heresy in the American culture which has permeated the Church: 'that professional training ends with entry training.' The result is that many clergy fail to see the need of planning a life-time program of learning."[1] The result is that they grow stale and fall behind the times.

Lay and professional people who are serious about ministry must take charge of the process of tailoring a lifelong training program that will equip them for their various ministry positions. In light of the speed of change at the beginning of the twenty-first century, this planning is more short- than long-range. This calls for periodic planning and replanning throughout our lifetime as circumstances change. Life is too short to wait on churches or schools to offer the necessary programs; instead, we must plan proactively and seek the necessary training. This will not be easy. Like anything else worthwhile, it will require your time and attention. It is imperative that you discipline yourself to stay on the leading edge.

The Guidelines for the Plan

Build on Your Strengths

In chapter 4 I discussed the concept of strengths and weaknesses. Actually I prefer to use the term *limitations* about which I will say more below. You have certain strengths based on how God has wired you. And you know what they are now that you know your divine design. These will help you excel in your ministry direction and make the greatest contribution to God's kingdom. Your goal is to have the greatest possible impact for Christ over your entire life, and this can happen only when you focus on your God-given strengths and what you do best.

In addition, you will feel most energized and challenged when you focus on your strengths. Before you read this book, it is most likely that you already knew some of your strengths. Think of how you felt when you were actively using one or several of those strengths. You felt optimistic and positive about your service and gained a sense of self-confidence that God was using you in a wonderful way. For these reasons, you would be most wise to discover your strengths and build on them.

Our God is a God of grace who has blessed us immeasurably. It is my view that the discovery of our divine design in general and our strengths in particular is an ongoing process. As we involve ourselves in his service in ministry, we will constantly discover new aspects of how he has designed us, with strengths we didn't know we had. As we employ these strengths for him, we will experience what David experienced—a sense that God is using us to serve his purpose in this our generation (see Acts 13:36).

Good servants are learners who continue to pursue growth in their expertise as servers in the body of Christ. The greatest room for your personal growth and increasing competence that will glorify God is in your areas of strength. You should focus your training and development on building them, not on improving your weaknesses.

Develop Only Necessary Limitations

We all have limitations. They are our areas where we are not strong, areas that are outside our design. God did not design us to do everything well. As Paul describes it in 1 Corinthians 12, an ear is not an eye. Our limitations consist of areas in which we are not talented. The problem is that every ministry will require that we function in some of our areas of limitation to do our job well. A limitation becomes a weakness if it is necessary for effective ministry.

There is one view that argues that to become strong and serve well, you must improve or at least minimize your weaknesses or limitations. Therefore, you should focus on improving your limitations not your strengths. However, as I said earlier, you cannot excel in your ministry direction by merely fixing or minimizing your weaknesses. To excel you must maximize your strengths.

This does not mean, however, that you simply ignore your limitations—some are necessary for effectiveness in your ministry context. Thus you have no choice but to try to improve in them. However, you must keep in mind that you will always struggle to some degree in these areas, so don't be too hard on yourself when they don't become strengths. And above all, do not spend as much time trying to develop them as you spend on developing your strengths.

Establish Priorities

Once you have developed your training plan, you will need to establish certain priorities. It is impossible to work on and implement all of your plan at the same time. If you do not understand this, you will frustrate yourself and others and will likely walk away from the process altogether.

Here are the questions to answer: What do you need to develop now that will help you most in serving Christ and accomplishing your ministry direction? What should get your attention? Do you need to address an area of character development, or focus on a specific skill? Which is most important to you and necessary to implement to make the biggest difference now?

I suggest that after you complete much of your plan, you review it and assign priorities. Focus on no more than five or six, depending on your wiring and what you can reasonably expect to accomplish in the time you have.

Remain Flexible

People respond differently to making plans. Much of it has to do with how God has designed us and our temperament. For example, thinkers are likely to be better planners than doers in terms of discipline and sitting down and actually designing a development plan. Thus the idea that one size fits all is not valid when formulating a plan for the future. It is a very personal process based on your divine wiring.

In the next two chapters I introduce some ideas to help you determine your development plan. As you know, working the plan and accomplishing the development goals must be squeezed into your already busy schedule. Do the best you can under your individual circumstances. To fail to plan is to plan to fail, so make an effort to develop and follow your plan, but do not beat up on yourself if you do not accomplish it as well as someone else might.

8

DESIGNING THE MINISTRY PLAN

David, Tom, and Carol are excited about how God has "wired" them for ministry, and they are delighted in the direction of their personal ministry visions. Perhaps for the first time, they feel a strong sense of meaning and spiritual purpose. Many of the missing pieces of the puzzle have fallen into place. Like King David (Acts 13:36), they have a growing desire to serve God's purpose in their generation. As long as they are alive, there will be no sitting on the sidelines for them. They plan to pursue their God-directed ministries with a passion.

They are convinced they need to develop a ministry plan, a road map to move from where they are to where they hope to be in the near future. This chapter will focus on three areas that make up the training plan. The first is design considerations. It addresses three areas that you must consider or keep in mind as you design your plan. The second is the major design ingredients that are competencies that make up the plan. There are four: character, knowledge, skills, and emotions. The last is the format that the plan will take or what it will look like. There are two options: the short-answer format and the long-answer or prose format.

The Design Considerations

As you work through the development process, there are three design considerations that you should keep in mind: your learning style, your training methods, and your life circumstances. All three will have a major impact on the final product.

Your Learning Style

How do you learn? Do you know? Some people are most aware of their style or styles of learning and some are not. Regardless, you have a preferred way of learning that feels most natural to you. You are wise to know what that style is and to leverage it in the planning process. Research shows that people learn best when they use their particular style of learning.[1]

There are several tools available to help you discover your learning style (see http://www.learningfromexperience.com and http://www.hay group.com). I have developed one that consists of four learning styles: the dynamic style, the imaginative style, the commonsense style, and the analytical style. There are two ways to discover which is your style. The first is the more subjective approach. Read through the following descriptions of the styles and try to determine which fits you or feels right based on your life experience. The second is to review your score on Temperament Indicator 1, as the learning styles here compare favorably with those four temperaments as well as those that comprise the Personal Profile or DiSC tool. Keep in mind that you will likely have a combination of two, possibly three, styles.

Commonsense Learners

1. *Temperament*: Doers (the D temperament on the Personal Profile)
2. *Life-orientation*: Goal/purpose
3. *Characteristics*: Realistic, practical, logical, competitive, impersonal, decisive, persistent, direct, efficient, doers, risk-takers, problem-solvers; they view Christianity in terms of action, read the Bible for hands-on information, are interested in "real life."
4. *Key learning concept*: These learners don't want to talk about something, they want to do it. They're pragmatic. They enjoy practical, hands-on approaches to learning.
5. *Their learning question*: How does this work?

6. *Learning environment*: They don't like lectures, prefer to work alone, are competitive, innovative, visionary, and want freedom from control.
7. *Teaching methods*: Problem-solving, challenge, independent study, projects, logical problems, activities of physical skill, demonstration.

Dynamic Learners

1. *Temperament*: Influencers (the I temperament on the Personal Profile)
2. *Life-orientation*: People/relationships
3. *Characteristics*: Natural leaders, flexible, curious, insightful, inspiring, expressive, future-directed, enthusiastic, unpredictable, risk-takers, intuitive, optimistic, outgoing, good communicators, fun-loving, talkative, popular, loud; they enjoy people and have a sense of humor.
4. *Key learning concept*: These learners enjoy coming up with creative, unique applications for what they learn.
5. *Their learning question*: What can this become?
6. *Learning environment*: Experimental, creative, motivating, patient, student-directed; they prefer options.
7. *Teaching methods*: Drama, brainstorming (more than hands-on), case studies, open-ended discussion, problem solving, moral dilemmas, projects.

Imaginative Learners

1. *Temperament*: Relators (the S temperament on the Personal Profile)
2. *Life-orientation*: People/relationships
3. *Characteristics*: They are idea people, enjoy listening and talking, like people, see facts in relation to people; they are easygoing, sociable, sincere, dependable, friendly, quiet, empathetic, kind-hearted, compassionate, in touch with feelings, patient, understanding, experience-oriented, loyal, supportive, steady, agreeable, likable, nonconfrontational, submissive, quiet.
4. *Key learning concept*: These people learn best as they listen and share ideas. They like to be personally involved in the process.
5. *Their learning question*: Why? and Why not?
6. *Learning environment*: In small groups with other people, consistent, stable, with little conflict.

7. *Teaching methods*: They dislike lecture and memorization; like skits, mime, role-playing, discussion, creative listening, storytelling.

Analytical Learners

1. *Temperament*: Thinkers (the C temperament on the Personal Profile)
2. *Life-orientation*: Goal/purpose
3. *Characteristics*: They are interested in ideas and concepts, are data collectors, read the Bible for concepts and ideas; they are factual, analytical, thorough, sincere, perfectionistic, intellectual, accurate, logical, theoretical, detailed, disciplined, emotionally reserved, responsible, serious, scheduled, skeptical, compliant.
4. *Key learning concept*: These learners just want the facts. For them learning occurs as they think through ideas to form reality.
5. *Their learning question*: What do I need to know?
6. *Learning environment*: Quiet, planned, predictable, private, low risk, with clear policies and procedures and expertise.
7. *Teaching methods*: Straight lecture, self-study, demonstrations, memorization, lists, technical information.

Summary of Learning Styles

Commonsense Learners	Doers
Dynamic Learners	Influencers
Imaginative Learners	Relators
Analytical Learners	Thinkers

Your Training Methods

I have developed four methods or means for training ministry personnel: learner-driven training, content-driven training, mentor-driven training, and experience-driven training. Work through the following descriptions of each and determine which method would be most effective for you in your ministry development. Some of the methods will be available to you, whereas some may not, such as those involving school.

Learner-Driven Training

Learner-driven training is where believers take responsibility for their own growth. The training question is, Who is ultimately responsible for the individual's training? The obvious answer is the individual. This is self-training for the purpose of self-development in character, knowledge, skills, emotions, and so on. It may be planned or unplanned and may occur at any point throughout the week, depending on the individual's schedule. This training is for all who want to initiate their own training. Rare is the church or ministry that is intentional in its ministry training, so most people need to take charge and assume responsibility for it.

What can leaders and servers do on their own to function well or competently in their nonvocational or vocational ministries? Here are some suggestions:

- Read books and periodicals on their ministry areas.
- Listen to tapes and view videos by prominent leaders that teach ministry knowledge and skills.
- Make appointments with and interview experienced, competent servers.
- Attend classes, seminars, and conferences that focus on leadership and ministry development.
- Visit churches in your geographical area that God is blessing, observe what they do and ask lots of questions.

The emphasis of self-directed training is that people pursue these opportunities on their own initiative or at the suggestion of a leader-trainer.

CONTENT-DRIVEN TRAINING

Content-driven training focuses on the transfer of knowledge. "Content-driven" means that someone other than the learner has structured a body of information that determines the basis for the training experience. Thus a predetermined outline, lesson plan, or curriculum guides the training process. This training involves a lecture approach or a one-way communication from a knowledgeable person to one seeking that knowledge. Most seminars, classroom settings, and conferences are venues for content-driven training. Practically speaking, most leadership and servant training fall into this category. After all, gaining a basic knowledge of the ministry task at hand is an important beginning point for any ministry and leadership.

Content-driven training comes in all shapes and sizes. For example, the content may be relatively focused and presented in a three-hour seminar. Or the content may be comprehensive enough to require a three-year curriculum. Also, the nature of the training varies widely from formal to informal. Informal training, on one end of the continuum, includes a myriad of church-based and volunteer-led training. Formal training, on the other end, includes accredited degree programs and even seminary training. Let's take a quick look at informal and formal environments for training.

Informal content-driven training takes place any time a church, parachurch, or individual develops training content and teaches others in the local ministry context. Usually this training takes place in short time periods, is planned and supervised, and does not result in some kind of degree or academic credential. The goal of the church or parachurch ministry is to train its people intentionally for leadership and ministry.

An example of informal training is the pastor or a staff person who uses a classroom within the church to teach members and attenders about the church. The emphasis is on ministry content or information more than actual experience. A leader might use the classroom context to cover the church's history, any denominational affiliation, polity, theology and philosophy of ministry, core values, mission, vision, strategy, doctrinal position, and so on. In addition, the pastor, staff, or a professor from a nearby college or seminary could teach a class of interns or volunteer leaders Bible study skills, various books of the Bible, systematic theology, church history, how to preach and teach the Bible, Christian education, spiritual formation, missions, as well as other subjects.

Formal content-driven training is used in training staff and potential staff to best prepare them for leadership and ministry. Colleges, universities, and seminaries provide formal training that prepares leaders for various kinds of ministry. It's longer in duration than the others and involves academic training, which culminates in a diploma or degree, such as a bachelor's degree (B.S. or B.A.), master of ministry (M.Min.), a master of divinity (M.Div.), a doctor of theology (Th.D.), a doctor of ministry (D.Min.), or a doctor of philosophy (Ph.D.).

Leaders in particular must ask if formal training is vital to their ministry preparation. Classical programs that attempt to prepare future pastors for ministry provide in-depth training primarily in such areas as Bible, languages, theology, and church history. Some organizations—especially the mainline denominations—may require that a pastor of one of their churches have a theological degree from an accredited school. Thus formal education serves to credential prospective leaders in these ministries.

Serious disadvantages of formal content-driven training are that it tends to be too academic, ignores leadership training and people skills, tends to be out of touch with the culture, and doesn't involve the student in enough hands-on ministry experience. In addition, most training programs still require that the emerging leader move to where the institution is located to pursue training. In their research, Kouzes and Posner rated formal education and training a "distant third" in comparison to the value of hands-on "trial and error" experience and the help of other people, such as coaches and mentors.[2]

The exceptions are the master of ministry and the doctor of ministry programs that schools have designed and adopted for those in professional ministry. These programs focus on the practical aspects of ministry. Also, some schools are adopting distance-learning programs that allow emerging leaders to stay where they live and minister in their home churches while pursing an academic degree on the Internet.

It has become the practice of some megachurches to select and hire for leadership roles people from within the church who have proven their ability, rather than take a chance with a seminary graduate with little experience. Future leaders who pursue formal training would be wise to invest themselves heavily in ministry while attending school.

MENTOR-DRIVEN TRAINING

The third type of training takes place when a leader or member works intentionally and closely with a mentor or coach. The involvement of a trainer distinguishes this from the other training types. For example, someone, such as the pastor of leadership training, brings together aspiring leaders with proven leaders, and the latter train the former directly or indirectly. The coach or mentor could involve the leader in actual hands-on experience or a classroom context or both. The coach is there for the emerging leader and advises and directs him or her.

The oversight of an experienced, godly mentor is invaluable. In my own experience, I've learned much from poor leaders about how not to lead. And that's instructive. However, we must also learn from godly, competent leaders. Good leaders who model servant leadership, challenge us, trust us, and are willing to spend quality time with us are the most instructive. Prospective leaders would be wise to identify servant leaders in their communities and form a mentoring relationship. If initially the leader refuses to take on a mentoring role, the emerging leader should persist, asking what it would take to establish such a relationship and showing a sincere commitment to growing as a leader.

What precisely do mentors do with leaders and other participants in training? Is there a process they follow? Good mentors take their trainees through the following four steps:

1. *Instruction.* Mentors must provide their people with the knowledge necessary to lead and minister at their particular level in the ministry. This encompasses the second core competency—knowledge or headwork—but by no means excludes the other three (character, skills, and emotions). I will say more about these competencies shortly. The emerging leader needs instruction in all four core

competencies. Again, the key question is, What must he or she know to lead at the ministry level? The mentor will have some of this knowledge but will also use other resources, such as books, seminars, and other staff.

2. *Modeling.* Conveying knowledge alone isn't sufficient. Good mentors model when possible what they have taught their students. Modeling moves the student from theoretical understanding to observation of actual or simulated ministry experiences. The emphasis is on the third core competency—skills—but doesn't exclude the others.

3. *Observation.* Not only do good mentors instruct and model competent leadership and ministry, they observe emerging servers as they attempt what the leader has modeled. They let the developing servers lead and minister. They involve them in the process.

4. *Evaluation.* Here is where the trainer and trainee evaluate how the latter is progressing. I have included it here because this is the natural place where it falls in the process. However, good evaluation is sprinkled throughout the process. After trainees have ministered, they need to know how well they accomplished a particular skill. Periodically they also need times when the mentor assesses their overall performance, looking in particular for the trainee's strengths more than his or her weaknesses. This is to be a most encouraging experience for the mentee.

EXPERIENCE-DRIVEN TRAINING

In experience-driven training the emphasis is on the doing of ministry, actual hands-on experience. The ministry seeks to offer the kinds of experiences that will help leaders lead and people serve more effectively. The focus is on actual practice of and experimentation with skills in a context where the person is doing ministry, such as leading a small group, counseling a troubled person, visiting the sick, teaching a class, conducting a baptism, consoling the bereaved, welcoming visitors to the church, presenting the gospel to a lost person, and many other experiences.

You can't learn ministry in a classroom or a seminar exclusively. It's best learned while actually involved in the ministry. Then you can apply and evaluate any classroom or seminar instruction in real situations. In their book *The Leadership Challenge*, Kouzes and Posner refer to their studies as well as those done by Honeywell Corporation and the Center for Creative Leadership. They conclude: "What is quite evident from all three studies is that, whether you are talking about managing or leading, experience is by far the most important opportunity for learning." They continue, "There is just no suitable surrogate for learning by doing."[3]

They add, "The first prescription, then, for becoming a better leader is to broaden your base of experience."[4]

However, you cannot limit experience-driven training to the hands-on experience alone. Learning takes place in a context or environment. Actually, ministry always takes place in a broader context that also contributes toward experience-based learning. People's values, personalities, attitudes, perceptions, and so on have a way of "rubbing off" on the aspiring minister. The environment includes spontaneous interactions and unplanned relationships that contribute toward the overall atmosphere of the church or ministry. Much of this environment is intangible, like the collective enthusiasm of the people or a clearly demonstrated value for excellence.

The uniqueness of the environment is that it is always influencing people and most don't realize it. The church or parachurch ministry must ask how their environment is subconsciously training its people for leadership and ministry. Keep in mind that this training consists of everything that trainees are exposed to and learn from the total experience during the training time. Much of it takes place in the ministry context. For example, learning takes place—even though we may not be conscious of it—when we're attending a worship meeting, a board meeting, or simply standing around and talking with people after a ministry event. Things that are said or the way that they're said teach learners how people feel about the church's pastor, other leaders, programs, and key areas of ministry. All of this results from mere exposure to the environment.

Your Life Circumstances

Another consideration for training is your life circumstances, a concept that I discussed in chapter 2. A vital aspect of discovering your divine design is discerning your life situation. With your divine design and direction in mind, consider carefully each of the following areas, collecting pertinent information that will impact the development of your training plan.

AGE

In light of your present age, how should you prepare for your ministry? If you are in your twenties or younger, you have your life ahead of you. If you decide that a formal, content-driven ministry is to play a significant part in your plan, then you need to pursue it at this time in your life. Your goal is to have the greatest impact for Christ during the brief time you have on this earth (1 Cor. 9:24–27; Acts 13:36), and there is a decided advantage to pursuing any formal training early as it may be difficult to go to school later on in life. However, avoid the temptation to pursue this training in exclusion to experience-driven, ministry-based training. While it may take a little longer to finish school, you need not be in a hurry.

If you are a layperson, your church will be delighted to use your skills and abilities regardless of how long it takes you to complete the process. If you are preparing for professional ministry, such as the pastorate, you will discover that most churches will be more interested in your ministry when you are seasoned and in your thirties. Use your twenties to complete the majority of your formal, classroom-based training and to get as much experience-driven, ministry-based training as possible. If you plan to pastor, consider a one- or two-year internship at a well-established church before diving into the ministry.

If you are in your thirties, you still have a significant portion of your ministry life ahead of you. It is wise to pursue formal-driven, classroom-based education, but do so as soon as possible. It is imperative that you gain experience-driven, ministry-based training because you will enter ministry sooner than if you were in your twenties.

If you are in your forties, fifties, or older, and a layperson, you are approaching a prime time for ministry. You have experienced enough of life to have matured and gained much wisdom. Parachurch ministries and churches will welcome your services with open arms. However, if you are considering beginning a professional ministry, you may not have time for lengthy formal, classroom-based education. Unfortunately many ministries overlook those in their late forties and especially their fifties unless they have already put in a lifetime of significant ministry.

MARITAL AND FAMILY STATUS

If you are single and disciplined, you may have more time to invest in preparation for your ministry than do those with family responsibilities. If formal, classroom-based training is to be a part of your preparation, try to complete as much of it as possible before you marry. Mixing a heavy work schedule with school is hard on marriages.

However, if you are married, you need to consider several critical factors. First, it is important that your spouse support your ministry plans. Sometimes you can minister as a nonprofessional without spousal support. However, such support is essential to professional ministry. If your spouse is not in favor of it, then ask God to change your spouse's heart. If this does not happen, stay and minister in your present circumstances.

Second, if you have children, you must consider them and their circumstances in your plan. It is easier to pursue school while they are young, as long as you spend time with them. However, if they are in their teens and in high school, you may want to delay any plans to move or attend a school until they have graduated. Moving kids from place to place during adolescence can prove harmful to their emotional and spiritual health.

Third, divorced people will face problems in ministry. This has become less a problem in nonvocational church ministries because a significant number of Christians have experienced divorce. It may not be a problem for those pursuing a parachurch ministry. However, few churches will consider divorced people for the pastorate and in some cases for staff positions.

PRIOR EDUCATION

The education you have acquired at this time in your life will affect your ministry plan. If you are young and have not completed high school, then you need to do so as soon as possible. A high school diploma or its equivalent is basic to effective ministry in most situations in North America. The question you must consider is, Do you have the basic educational foundation on which you can build a ministry? The answer to this question relates directly to your plans for any further content-driven, classroom-based education.

If you have a high school diploma or its equivalent, college may or may not be necessary. Certainly a college education will enhance to some degree any ministry, but there are many situations where you can minister without one. In our day of professionalism, however, a college degree has become almost a necessity if you plan to lead an organization or work on staff with a local church. It grants you a certain degree of credibility.

GENDER

Although women have been at the foundation of Christian ministry for centuries, men have dominated the ranks of professional ministry in North America. This has begun to change in the second half of the twentieth century. Most Christian colleges and seminaries make their degree programs available to women on both a master's and doctoral level. Also some evangelical seminaries now have some women on their faculties. There are a few evangelical schools that will not allow women to pursue pastoral studies. Regardless, a growing number of women in evangelical churches are filling such positions as elder, deacon, worship director, counselor, and director of Christian education.

If you are a woman, you will have professional ministry opportunities in the twenty-first century experienced by few women in the past. Therefore it is imperative that you determine the biblical role of women in ministry. You need to arrive at answers to such questions as, Can I serve as a senior pastor in a church? Does the Bible allow for women elders or deacons? Should women teach men? Whatever your answers to these and other questions like them, you should be ready to defend your position from the Scriptures.

HEALTH AND DISABILITIES

A major factor in your ministry plan will always be your health and that of your family and elderly loved ones. Health involves both the physical and emotional dimensions. Those in good physical health have priority over those in poor health. Vocational and nonvocational ministry often require long hours. This will place a constant strain on you and your family both physically and emotionally. If you are struggling with any serious emotional difficulty, you should not pursue ministry. The top priority on your ministry plan is to get help. But do not give up hope for future ministry. A number of people who have had emotional difficulties have experienced healing and served the Lord professionally, some as excellent lay and professional counselors.

If you have a disability, you will discover that a number of ministries are available to you. The problem is finding a ministry willing to hire a Christian with a disability. In spite of much progress, many Christians still do not understand or are afraid of those with disabilities. The reality is that most will choose a person who is not disabled. Therefore, be prepared for disappointment and rejection until you are able to find the setting that recognizes and values your unique gifts for ministry. Unfortunately, people with various disabilities are often ignored by the average Christian ministry but provide a mission field of activity for those who understand them and have a passion for reaching them.

FINANCES

Preparation for ministry may or may not prove costly. Most laypeople involved in part-time ministry incur few expenses. Most churches are willing to provide training at no cost to the trainee. However, the reverse is true if you desire full-time ministry. Any formal, classroom-based education is expensive, and it is best to get your education without taking a part-time job. This frees you to pursue both classroom- and ministry-based education. One way to accomplish this is to raise funds to cover your expenses. When you make application to a school, inquire about any available scholarships or grants. Talk to your pastor and friends about possible support.

The Major Design Components

Competency and authenticity in ministry walk hand in hand. Christians who are incompetent at what they do are inauthentic, and as a result people will not trust them. You would not trust an incompetent heart surgeon with your life, no matter how good his or her character. Therefore all who serve Christ must strive for competency in that sphere of service. There are four major design components that make up the competencies necessary for effective ministry: your character (being), knowledge (knowing), skills (doing), and emotions (feeling). You will need to determine how all of these fit into your lifetime ministry plan because all are necessary for a competent, high-impact ministry.

Developing Your Character

An authentic ministry development plan starts with the ongoing development of your character. You must begin with the character question, Who do I need to be? As briefly stated in chapter 2, for you to be effective in any ministry, being (or character) precedes doing (or ministry). We cannot drive far on an empty tank. God accomplishes through us what he has accomplished in us. To do otherwise is to be guilty of what Howard Hendricks describes as "trafficking in unlived truth." While it is not necessary that you have personally experienced everything you address in ministry, it is crucial that you have experienced an authentic walk with God.

It is possible to discover your divine design and direction for ministry and fail to cultivate your heart and soul for them. It is exciting to discover your God-given spiritual gifts and talents, begin to minister with them, and have a significant impact in people's lives. However, it is easy to be distracted by all this and allow your soul to shrivel in the process. Initially the result of such a ministry approach is ministry burnout, which is God's early warning system. Failure to take note and respond appropriately will in time result in ministry dropout.

God does not use and abuse his people. He desires to accomplish a work in your life that will supply all you need to minister in the lives of others. As you have an enduring impact on others, he desires to have an enduring impact on you. Therefore time must be set aside in your life to develop your character as well as employ your gifts, talents, and abilities.

This can take place in two contexts. The first is private and individual. It involves a hearty, robust quiet time alone with God. The Savior has set the example (see Mark 1:35; Luke 6:12; 9:18). This time usually includes prayer, worship, and Bible study.

The second is public and corporate. It is a mistake to emphasize the devotional approach to the exclusion of the community approach. By itself the devotional, private approach can feed the independent and competitive appetite that already predominates ministry preparation and practice. But Christ accomplishes far more in community than in private. This includes spiritual formation in such contexts as mentoring, small groups, and public worship that incorporates the proclamation of Scripture.

Broadening Your Knowledge Base

A realistic ministry development plan also includes the expansion of your knowledge base for ministry. You must ask, What do I need to know? While being (character) must precede doing (ministry), knowing (content) must walk hand in hand with doing. On the one hand, there is the problem of training people in the classroom for ministry (content-driven, classroom-based learning) without the balance of experience in the field (experience-driven training). This circumstance plagues those preparing for professional ministry exclusively in Christian colleges and seminaries. On the other hand, there exists the problem of involving people in ministry without an adequate knowledge base. This problem affects both lay and professional people who pursue ministry without sufficient knowledge to be competent at what they do. These people learn how to minister by trial and error, which is roughly analogous to learning how to drive by having a series of accidents. Neither is satisfactory and both can prove painful.

What kind of knowledge complements experience? Christ's servants must have a working knowledge in a variety of areas. One is a knowledge of the Scriptures. The Bible is the source of divine truth that speaks authoritatively to the believer's faith and practice. All believers need to know the content and message of the Bible as well as to master basic Bible study skills. A basic knowledge of theology is also important.

Along with a knowledge of the Bible and theology you need a knowledge of people for competent ministry to take place. You can accomplish this by becoming a student of people and pursuing studies on temperament. I suggest you begin by reading books on temperament and people skills.

Finally, you will need a knowledge of the ministry essentials for your specific ministry direction. First, you will need to become aware of what the ministry essentials are in general, and then you will need to refine those that are essential and unique to your ministry vision. For example, a second grade Sunday school teacher will profit by having a knowledge of Christian education in general, but even more from a knowledge of how to disciple second graders in particular. A leader of a small group should know something about the small-group process. A church planter should know something about the principles and process of church planting.

Acquiring Ministry Skills

The ministry plan includes the acquisition and development of the skills necessary to accomplish ministry. The skills question is, What do I need to do? Many fail to realize that the inability to exercise certain skills has as great a potential to knock us out of ministry as a lack of character or insufficient knowledge of the Bible. A pastor or lay leader in the church who lacks interpersonal skills may fail at ministry because so much of it is people-related.

A variety of skills will need the constant attention and development of Christ's servants: Bible study, communication (reading, writing, speaking, and listening), conflict resolution, problem solving, consensus building, planning and goal setting, meetings management, risk taking, role clarification, rewards and recognition, vision casting, networking, team building, group process, evaluation, time management, and values clarification.

Addressing Your Emotions

Leaders' emotions are their heart work, reflecting what they feel. In ministry you must ask, What do I need to feel? Scripture has much to say about emotions, beginning in Genesis when Adam and Eve experienced shame due to their sin (Gen. 3:11–12, when they felt shame, compared to Gen. 2:24, when they didn't) and extending through Revelation where John, describing the New Jerusalem, writes: "He will wipe every tear from their eyes. There will be no more death or mourning or crying or pain, for the old order of things has passed away" (Rev. 21:4).

A leader's emotions affect his or her mood. And research as well as ministry experience tell us that the leader's mood is most contagious, spreading quickly throughout a ministry. A good mood characterized by optimism and inspiration affects people positively. However, a bad mood characterized by negativity and pessimism will cripple the ministry and damage people.

Key questions are: What emotions are liabilities for your ministry? What emotions must you deal with to create a better climate for ministry? Again, it's beyond the scope of this book to go into great detail regarding the emotions. However, the following overview should help catalyze your thinking in this area.

To develop emotional well-being and establish a spiritually healthy climate for ministry, servers must cultivate two primary areas: their emotions and those of the people with and to whom they minister. The first area relates to their emotions and is twofold.

Area 1: Professional and lay ministers must understand and then manage their own emotions. Understanding their emotions involves taking four steps:

Step 1: They must learn to recognize their own emotions.

Step 2: They should identify their emotions. Look for anger, anxiety, sadness, fear, shame, discouragement, surprise, joy, and love.

Step 3: They must begin to deal with the emotions that are hurtful, such as anger, anxiety, and fear.

Step 4: They will want to explore why they're experiencing certain emotions.

Once leaders and laypeople in ministry begin to understand their emotions, they must learn to manage their emotions. To accomplish this, they need to remember two things.

1. They can't control being swept by their emotions. The reason is that the emotional mind often overrides the rational mind, such as when we lose our temper.
2. However, they can control how they respond to or handle their emotions when they occur. They can recognize them and deal biblically with them in the power of the Holy Spirit.

Area 2: Leaders must not only be aware of and work on their own emotions but also recognize others' emotions and help them manage them as well. This is commonly referred to as empathy. Most of us have been in situations where an emotionally unhealthy person, whether in a leadership or other ministry position, affects a ministry context negatively. It's imperative that leaders and any others involved in a ministry deal with these people for the sake of the ministry as well as the individual. This can be done by helping such people go through the four steps above and then encouraging them to manage their emotions. Helping them deal biblically with their emotions can be accomplished through example and by working one-on-one with them.

The assumption is that the people in or under our ministries want help. When a person needing help is emotionally and spiritually dysfunctional and not willing to work on the issues, the leader may need to get them professional help.

Leader's Developed Competencies

Character (being)	Soul Work
Knowledge (knowing)	Headwork
Skills (doing)	Handwork
Emotions (feeling)	Heart Work

The Design Format

What does the ministry plan look like? You have gathered your information and are ready to use it to write out your ministry plan—the final product. You may be tempted to skip this step, especially if you favor a verbal approach over a written one. However, writing out your plan helps you think through and articulate it in a way that is not possible if you verbalize it only. You will select one of two possible formats—the short-answer format or the prose format.

The short-answer format may best fit your style. It is for those who do not like to write and involves composing short, precise answers to the questions, *Who? What? Where? When?* and *How?*

The answer to the question *Who?* draws heavily from your life circumstances and considers the people primarily involved in your ministry plan, such as your family and relatives. The answer to the question *What?* includes a brief summary of your design (including learning style) and direction followed by your competencies for ministry (character, knowledge, skills, and emotions) as determined above in the design process. The answer to the question *Where?* focuses on your training contexts (learner-driven, content-driven, mentor-driven, and experience-driven), also determined above in the design process. The answer to the question *When?* introduces the time factor, asking you to plan when you will begin the development process and includes any other pertinent time factors. The answer to the question *How?* focuses primarily on finances, asking how you plan to cover any costs involved in your ministry plan.

The term *prose* describes the common, ordinary language found in speaking or writing, in contrast to other language forms such as poetry. I use it here to describe the approach favored by those who enjoy writing in depth. Rather than write brief answers to the five questions, it allows you to write extensively on each and include any other factors important to your plan. You may compose as little as a page or as much as ten pages. You have the freedom to write as much as you desire and include as many details as you wish.

At this point you should have a good idea about the process of developing a ministry plan and what goes into the final product. However, several sample plans will serve to clarify these even further. What would Carol's, Tom's, and David's plans look like first in the short-answer format and then in the prose format?

The Short-Answer Format

If we applied the short answer format to Carol's circumstances, it would look like this:

1. *Who?* I am a thirty-two-year-old practicing attorney. I am married to my childhood sweetheart, and we have no children. We are in excellent health. Both of his parents are alive and self-supporting. My mom is a widow and occasionally needs some financial help.
2. *What?* My divine design includes the spiritual gifts of leadership, mercy, and pastor. I have a passion for shepherding women. My temperament is a high I (Influencer) with a secondary D (Doer), and my Myers-Briggs score is ENTJ. My learning style is dynamic and commonsense. My ministry direction is twofold: to direct as a layperson the church's small-group ministry program and to lead my own small group of women in the church.

   To develop my character I have a quiet time every other day and have invested heavily in my small-group ministry, which meets once a week. To broaden my knowledge base, I study my Bible regularly during my quiet time and with my husband before we go to bed at night. I am beginning to understand people better through my work with small groups and my training for this ministry. I confess I need a better working knowledge of certain ministry essentials, such as counseling and the small-group process. I hope to gain this in time by taking a course offered at the local community college. To enhance my skills, I have taken a skills inventory offered by my pastor. I know where I am weak and where I am strong. In particular I need to work on my skills in the areas of conflict resolution and team building. I sense that in general I am emotionally mature, but I struggle at times with anger and anxiety. I plan to address these with the help of my small group.
3. *Where?* I have decided that any formal, content-driven training in a classroom is a low priority at this time. I have spent a lot of time in school over the years. I am currently involved in learner-driven training, but what I really need is some experience-driven training in overseeing a small-group program and in leading a small group. So experience-driven training is a very high priority. I have also

given high priority to informal, content-driven training because there is an excellent seminar available on the small-group process as well as several books and periodicals on conflict resolution and team building.

I have a confession. Sometimes I wonder if anyone in the church will be upset that I—a woman—am directing this program!

4. *When?* The church desires to get the small-group program in place as soon as possible, so I've begun to work on it already. I have carved out some time to visit several churches in our community that have recently implemented small-group programs. I have already begun to meet with a small group comprised of women from my church and neighborhood.

5. *How?* The church has set aside a small amount of money to help me cover some expenses. However, I am willing to spend money out of my own pocket to get this program up and running.

The short-answer format applied to Tom's situation could look like this:

1. *Who?* I am a twenty-six-year-old recent graduate from college. Considering my blue-collar background, graduation has been the major accomplishment in my life next to accepting Christ. I am not married, but I am looking. And since I come from a large family with several brothers and sisters, I want to have lots of kids some day. My dad is about to retire due to ill health. He presently owns and operates a gas station in our rural community back home. He and Mom have saved some money for retirement over the last few years, so they should be okay without my help.

2. *What?* My divine design consists of the spiritual gifts of leadership, administration, evangelism, faith, and teaching. My passion is for unchurched, lost people and Christians who are spiritually "treading water." My temperament is high D with a secondary I, and my score on the Myers-Briggs is ENFP. My learning style is commonsense and dynamic. My ministry direction is to spend the rest of my life pastoring the same church, either in a church planting or a renewal context.

To develop my character I attempt a daily quiet time. I will also be involved in a spiritual formation group required of all seminary students for three semesters. After that I plan to enter an accountability relationship with another seminarian in which we will encourage one another to Christlikeness and hold one another accountable for our spiritual goals.

To expand my knowledge base, especially in the Bible, I am depending primarily on seminary and the classes I am required to take, along with the teaching in my church. I also hope to learn much about ministry essentials from my pastor over the next few years.

To acquire and enhance my ministry skills, I am depending on seminary and training for ministry in the church. I must confess that I struggle with emotional immaturity. I plan to address this with the help of my spiritual formation group and an accountability partner.

3. *Where?* Because I have been a Christian for only a short time, formal content-driven training in a classroom context is a high priority, so I plan to enroll in seminary this fall. I have two years of evangelism and discipleship experience with Campus Crusade. However, I will make it a high priority to invest my life in a good church while at seminary and during the summers because I desperately need to get some experience-driven training in the local church. I also plan to take several seminars on church planting and leadership that will be offered in the community while I am at seminary. I have already read several books on pastoral leadership and church growth, and I subscribe to *Leadership Journal*. I have also given some thought to finding a mentor in my church, possibly one of the staff.

4. *When?* I start seminary in the fall. I have also located an excellent church in the area where I will lead a group of laymen in evangelism and discipleship during the first year. The pastor indicated that if things go well, I might be able to do an internship with him during the summer months. Regardless, he plans to help me with the various ministry essentials and my skills development. Also I have registered for a seminar in October on preaching to the unchurched.

5. *How?* I have raised enough support to cover my first year at seminary. Several Crusade staff members taught me how to raise funds and helped me in the process. Some college friends have also indicated a desire to help after they are established in their careers. My desire is to raise enough funds to cover all my expenses so that I can devote all my time to seminary and the church (and to looking for a wife!).

Finally, the short answer format for David could look like this:

1. *Who?* I am twenty-eight years old and recently the pastor of a small church in a sleepy little town located in the suburbs of a midsized

city. I am married, and my wife and I have chosen not to have any children until I have finished all my schooling. We have recently returned to seminary for more training. She is solidly behind my desire to serve the Lord, and she is willing to work until I finish a doctoral program.

2. *What?* My design consists of the spiritual gifts of administration, teaching, and possibly preaching. I have a passion for teaching the Bible to people who are deeply interested in its truths and desire to explore them in depth. My temperament is high T (Thinker) with a secondary D (Doer), and the Myers-Briggs indicated I am an ISTJ. Until recently I thought I was to be a pastor. My learning style is analytical and commonsense. However, in light of my assessment, I now believe I should pursue a teaching ministry on a college or seminary level as my direction. I plan to teach in a school on the mission field because there are few teaching positions available in North America.

To develop my character I am good about having a quiet time every day. I am also in a mentor relationship with one of my professors, and we are studying the life of Christ. To expand my knowledge base I continue to study the Bible on my own to supplement my doctoral studies in the department of Bible exposition.

Where I need more work is in knowing and understanding people. I have already enrolled in temperament training that will qualify me to administer the Biblical and Personal Profiles to people. I also sense that I need more knowledge of certain ministry essentials, such as the training of leaders. They never taught me how to do this in seminary.

Finally, due to my limited ministry experience, I believe I am weak in many of the skills critical to ministry, especially in teaching. I hope to develop these while in the doctoral program. I struggle with emotional maturity, and my professor who has agreed to mentor me desires to address this issue.

3. *Where?* With a personal vision focused on a teaching ministry, formal, content-driven training in the classroom is a very high priority. I will need a doctorate to teach in most institutions overseas, and I would like to take some education courses that will orient me to the world of education in general and help me with the art of teaching in particular. A missionary friend suggested that once I know the country where I will teach, I should begin language studies. I have also placed a medium to high priority on experience-driven, ministry-based training. While I now have two years of ministry experience in the pastorate, I do not have any

ministry-based experience teaching in the classroom. I hope to get this kind of experience while pursuing my doctorate. Finally, I place a lower priority on supplementary training. However, I do plan to attend some meetings (the Evangelical Theological Society and the Society for Biblical Literature) sponsored by some organizations in my academic field as well as read a number of books and articles in periodicals.

4. *When?* My wife and I are presently living in seminary housing, and I have just begun to work on my doctorate, which should take four years to complete. I am currently in the process of writing and interviewing with several mission boards and representatives who sponsor colleges and seminaries in other countries. I hope to have this nailed down by the end of this year or the middle of my second year of studies, so we can begin our language preparation. I plan to finish all my classroom work by the end of my third year and complete the dissertation in time to graduate by the end of the fourth year. I have allowed two years to raise support, so I hope to be on the field in six years.

5. *How?* The company where my wife worked during my prior seminary studies has hired her back with a substantial increase in salary. Both sets of parents are committed Christians, and they are supporting us as well. With my wife's job and the additional parental support, we should be able to meet all our expenses for the next four years.

The Prose Format

If Carol had opted for the prose format, it would have looked something like this:

I am thirty-two years old and have been practicing law for the last two years. I enjoy the legal profession and believe it is where I can best serve the Lord. Being an attorney is not easy work, but it gives me the freedom to take some time off to pursue what I believe will be a significant ministry at the church.

I married Bob shortly after we both graduated from high school. Presently we have no children. We have tried to have a family, but the doctors say we both have an infertility problem. Otherwise we are in excellent health. For now we have given up on children; perhaps someday we will adopt.

Bob and I both have parents who are living. Bob's dad is nearing retirement from an engineering company in south Texas, and his mother has always been a homemaker. Because of his dad's retirement income and benefits, they will both live comfortably. My father died several years ago and left my mom with just enough income to meet her basic living expenses. Bob and I and my brother try to help her financially from time to time. Our parents, however, pose no problems for my ministry plans.

I am delighted with how God has designed me. He has blessed me with the gifts of leadership, mercy, and pastor. I have a passion to work with women, especially those who need someone to listen to them and show them care and concern. My temperament is high I and a secondary D, and according to the Myers-Briggs I am an ENTJ. And my learning style is mostly commonsense with some dynamic influence. My leadership role is a leader-manager, and my style is a combination of Inspirational and Director. My evangelistic style is relational, although at times I may confront a lost person. I am not completely sure of all my natural gifts. I do have a talent for art, which comes from my dad, but I have not sought to develop it to any degree. Lay consultant Bruce Smith suggested that in time I should think about how this could be used for the Lord.

In light of my design and with Bruce Smith's help, I have determined that my personal ministry direction is to lead the church's small-group ministry program and lead a small group consisting mostly of women in the church and a few lost women in my neighborhood. If I think about this ministry at night before I go to bed, I get so excited I cannot fall asleep. In time I may have to give up the leadership of the small-group program. The church is growing rapidly, and eventually it will need to bring in a full-time person to direct the ministry. At that time I will either move to direct another program or assist the new director. I enjoy the shepherding of the women in my small group. They have so many spiritual and emotional problems, and the women from my neighborhood are not yet Christians. They look to me for my leadership and personal counsel—in fact the group is growing.

I am convinced the development of my character is essential to any ministry I pursue in the church. Thus I make sure I have a quiet time every other day, in spite of my busy schedule. My small group has also served to enhance my character development. They constantly pray for and encourage me and have on a few occasions confronted me over certain spiritual glitches in my life. I do not know how I survived spiritually without them.

I desperately need a better knowledge of the Scriptures, so I study them during my quiet time, but I learn the most when my husband and I study the Bible together in the evenings. We both have a voracious appetite for the Scriptures and study them as much as possible. We also soak in the Bible teaching at our church. I am gaining a better understanding of people through my training for the small-group ministry—I am studying the various temperaments and how they relate to one another. I need work in some of the ministry essentials for my unique ministry. In particular I need more knowledge about counseling and the small-group process. I have found a book on each topic at the public library, and I plan to work through the exercises at the back of each book over the next month. Also I plan to take some courses in these areas offered at the local community college in the next year.

I am convinced of the importance of developing skills for my ministry. I have taken a skills inventory and know that I need to develop skills in the areas of conflict resolution and team building. I scored low in these two areas and realize their importance to my ministry. I am not sure yet how I will accomplish this.

Most have told me that they sense that I am an emotionally mature person, and in all honesty, I feel that this is one of my strengths. However, I do struggle from time to time with anger and anxiety. I think that I developed some anger toward my father while growing up. I also find that I tend to worry too much. I have shared this with my small group, and they are helping me address these two emotions.

Much of my professional training has taken place in both an undergraduate and graduate context. My degrees are in American history and law; thus I have experienced a lot of formal, content-driven, classroom-based learning over the past few years. While I am open to more of this kind of training, I do not see it as a high priority for my ministry vision. In time I may take a class or two as mentioned above at a nearby community college. For now I place high priority on experience-driven, ministry-based training along with my learner-driven approach. I have scheduled meetings with some lay and professional directors of small-group programs at churches in the area. My plan is to learn as much as I can from them. And if I can find the time, I may try to gain some expertise working with the programs in their churches. In two months I will attend a small-group seminar that will be conducted in our town. I have also subscribed to a magazine that focuses on small-group ministries and have purchased several books on the subject.

I am told some people in the church believe that women should not be in any leadership roles. I wonder how they will feel about my position as the leader of the small-group program. I have read most of the biblical texts on the subject of the woman's role in ministry, and I do not see any problems with what I am doing. I also have the full support of the pastoral staff and the church board.

When I asked the pastor how soon he wanted the small-group ministry up and running, he replied, "Yesterday!" So I dropped several minor projects and have been working on the program ever since. While several small groups have already formed on their own, I hope to have the formal program in place in less than a year.

The pastor and board are behind this nonbudgeted ministry to the extent that they have given money from their own pockets. Presently I have two thousand dollars to work with. For now this amount should be sufficient to cover my travel costs, the seminar, and the books and magazines. I so believe in what I am doing that I will gladly take money out of my own pocket to implement the program.

If Tom had chosen the prose format, it might have resembled the following longer plan:

I am twenty-six years old and could have graduated from college at twenty-three, but I had to work a couple of years at my dad's gas station to save up enough money to go to school. We are what some call a blue-collar family, and I am the first one in my family to graduate from college, which I consider a major accomplishment. My dad has worked most of his life in a local gas station. He began as a young boy pumping gas. Eventually he learned how to be a mechanic. Finally, he was able to save enough money to purchase the station when it came up for sale. He has worked hard all his life but never had enough money to send any of his five kids to college. He and Mom are proud that I have a college degree even though they never emphasized school when we were growing up. He is about to retire due to a mild heart attack and rheumatoid arthritis. He wants his college-graduate son to take over the operation of the station, but he has accepted the fact that my oldest brother will have to do that.

I am fascinated with how God has designed me. He has chosen to give me the spiritual gifts of leadership, administration, evangelism, faith, and teaching. I have a passion to reach out to and spend time with unchurched, lost people. I also have a passion to help Christians who seem to be "stuck in neutral" in their spiritual growth. My temperament is high D and secondary I, and I am an ENFP on the Myers-Briggs Inventory. My learning style is commonsense and dynamic. My leadership role is leader-manager, and my style is a combination of Director and Inspirational. After two years of heavy evangelistic ministry with Campus Crusade, it is obvious to everyone that my evangelistic style is confrontational. I even walked up to the college president one day and to everyone's surprise spoke with him about his salvation. I think I have a natural gift for leadership; I play the guitar, and some people tell me I sing well, although I have had no formal training in music or voice.

Several Crusade staff members and the ministry consultant who taught our dorm Bible studies agree that my personal ministry vision or direction is to pastor a new paradigm, cutting-edge church with a Great Commission vision. They had hoped I would come on staff with Crusade but realized that God was directing me away from parachurch to local church ministry. I find the thought of leading and pastoring a church exciting, though I am not sure yet whether I should go into church planting or church renewal. Since I see the need for and prefer new paradigm ministries, I suspect I may be a church planter. Also my gift and experience in evangelism are well suited for church planting.

I know all too well the importance of developing my character. Campus Crusade did an excellent job of driving this into my thick skull, so I attempt to have a quiet time every day. I say "attempt" because I do miss once or twice a week when I get real busy. In addition to my quiet time, the seminary requires that all seminary students involve themselves in spiritual formation groups for three semesters. These groups will help me focus on my depravity in the context of my dignity as a Christian. When I finish the spiritual formation requirements, I hope to become a leader of a group the last year. I also plan to form an accountability relationship with another seminary student. We will meet once a week and hold each other accountable for our walk with Christ and the accomplishment of the spiritual goals we set for ourselves each month.

I need to expand my knowledge of the Bible and doctrine. In fact that is one reason why I have enrolled in seminary. Though I have been involved in parachurch ministry and have studied the Bible, I want to work systematically through the Scriptures and theology with professors who are thoroughly trained in their areas of expertise. If the seminary curriculum delivers on its promises, I should accomplish this goal. Due to my parachurch training, I have found I have a good knowledge of many of the ministry essentials. I hope to gain some help in ministry essentials that relate specifically to the local church from a pastor or someone in the church I attend while in seminary. In particular I see a need to know more about church planting and church renewal. The seminary offers electives in these two areas that should give me the essential knowledge base critical to my future.

What I have said about my knowledge of the ministry essentials also applies to my ministry skills. The more I work on my ministry plan, the more I appreciate my parachurch ministry experience. I am amazed at the skills I have developed while working with Crusade on the college campus as a student. I feel strong in my communication, problem-solving, and conflict-resolution skills. My goal is to discover where I am weak in the skills necessary to pastor a church. I hope to get help with these in the church I attend while in seminary.

I must confess that I struggle with emotional and spiritual immaturity. I tend to struggle in particular with shame, anger, and fear. Having graduated from college, I feel somewhat ashamed about my blue-collar roots and sometimes I feel inferior to others around me. I tend to get angry over little things that really do not matter all that much. For some reason they matter too much to me. I also find that I fear that if others really get to know me, they will reject me. A pastor has agreed to mentor me, and he has agreed to address these issues with me.

My professional training has taken place in college on an undergraduate level in the school of business. My degree is in business administration. Though I have completed four years of classroom-based training, I have only been saved for two years and need more training in Bible, theology, and church history. Thus I place a high priority on formal, content-driven, classroom-based education. I have already decided to pursue either the church planting or church renewal tracks in the pastoral ministries department at seminary.

I place high priority on experience-driven, ministry-based training as well as classroom-based. I have met the pastor in an excellent church not far from the seminary who has agreed to allow me to lead a group of laymen in the areas of evangelism and discipleship and indicates that he might be available to mentor me through several summer internships. He is the one that I mentioned above. He is also interested in using his church to plant a daughter church in the next county in two or three years. Perhaps I will play a significant role in birthing that new church.

I have discovered that a ministry organization will conduct two weekend seminars in the city, one during the fall and the other during the spring semester. I have already mailed in the tuition for the seminar on leadership to take advantage of their "early bird" special. In addition to reading books on pastoral ministry, leadership, and church growth, I have a four-year subscription to *Leadership Journal*—a graduation gift from my sister.

For a while I debated whether I should try to work my way through seminary to cover my expenses. Then several of the Crusade staff took me aside and taught me how to raise funds. They said I was a natural. In a period of six months I raised enough money to cover one year of expenses while at seminary. A significant portion came from several people whom I won to Christ and then discipled. Others have indicated a desire to involve themselves financially with me when they become more established in the marketplace. My parents said they wanted to help, but Dad's retirement will not allow it.

Finally, I suspect that David, who likes to write, will opt for the prose format. His plan will look something like this:

I am twenty-eight years old and have just completed two years in the pastorate of a small church that proved to be a disaster. They were the most frustrating years of my life. Had it not been for my wonderful wife, I might not have survived as well as I have. I am convinced that God used these two years to show me that I am not cut out to be a pastor, as our parents once thought. He also used this opportunity to provide me with valuable ministry experience and insight.

Obviously I am married. In fact we just celebrated our fourth anniversary. We have chosen not to begin a family until I complete my doctoral studies. This will prove hard on my wife since she is from a large family and loves kids. But we both agree that I should be in school, and she is fully committed to work and support us until I finish.

God has blessed us with two wonderful sets of parents. Both fathers are pastors who love the Lord and are serving him in their churches. My mom works while my wife's mom is a homemaker. They pray for us regularly and have always given us wise counsel—except when they advised me to become a pastor. I think both were blinded by their desire to see someone else in the family, a son or at least a son-in-law, become a minister.

I am amazed how God has designed me. I only wish I had discovered it earlier in life. He has given me the spiritual gifts of administration, teaching, and possibly a cross-cultural gift of some sort (I am fascinated with people from other cultures). Of the three, teaching is my strong suit and is at the center of my gift-cluster. While my last congregation questioned my people skills, many times they complimented me on my ministry of teaching—they learned a lot of Bible over the last two years. I believe one reason for this is my passion for teaching the Bible to those who want to probe deeply into its spiritual truths. My temperament is high T (Thinker) with a secondary D (Doer). My learning styles are analytical and commonsense. The Myers-Briggs indicates I am an ISTJ. My leadership role is manager, and my style is Analytical. I must confess I am weak in the area of evangelism, but I think my style is intellectual. I have several natural gifts, such as acting, speaking, cooking, and auto mechanics, which could serve me well on the mission field.

My personal direction or vision is to pursue teaching on a college or seminary level with a mission organization in a foreign culture. Most missions organizations prefer a doctorate for those who teach in their schools. This gives the organization more credibility in the eyes of foreign governments. Consequently I place a high priority on formal, content-driven, classroom-based education. I would also like to pursue studies in the field of education. I am not really aware of what takes place in an educational institution, and I need to take some courses in the methodology of teaching. With my gift of administration I plan also to take one or two courses in educational administration. Most likely, God will use me in an administrative position in addition to teaching. A missionary friend suggested that once I know the country where I will minister, I should begin formal or informal language preparation. This is excellent advice.

I realize now the importance of developing my character. I say "now" because while I was in seminary everybody talked about it, but not many students were doing something about it. There were no spiritual formation groups when I went through seminary, and I failed to see the importance of a regular quiet time with God. Instead, I managed to convince myself that I could accomplish spiritual formation by doing my homework devotionally. It did not work, and I paid dearly for it in the first year of my pastorate. Now I take advantage of my obsessive-compulsiveness, and I rarely miss my daily quiet time, even on holidays! I have also developed a close friendship with one of my profs. We meet once a week for lunch and are presently studying the life of Christ together with an emphasis on applying the truths to our lives.

I have a good knowledge base in the Scriptures (my problem, like so many, is applying the truths to my life). I majored in theology in seminary, and I am working on my doctorate in the same area. I continue to expand my knowledge through personal study and through my doctoral courses. After two rough years in the ministry,

I have discovered I need a better knowledge of people. I really don't understand why people do some of the things they do. I plan to take the professional training that prepares people to administer both the Personal and the Biblical Profile. This will thoroughly orient me to the four temperaments. I have also agreed to listen more carefully to my wife, who understands people well.

My ministry experience also showed me that I am weak in my knowledge of some ministry essentials and critical ministry skills. I do not know how to train leaders, and I do not know enough about leadership, as they hardly touched on these issues in my seminary training. Due to my limited ministry experience (somehow I got out of my internship in seminary), I have not adequately developed the skills important to ministry. I plan to get some of this in my church. This inadequacy applies specifically to teaching. I hope this information is covered somewhere in the doctoral program. While the program does not require any classwork in teaching or education (which seems strange), I plan to take a teaching internship under my professor friend.

I do struggle at times with my emotions or seeming lack thereof. I come across to people as a little distant and aloof. It is not that I do not like people. I just struggle in knowing how to relate to them. In particular I want to work on empathy. I have a professor friend at the school who has agreed not only to mentor me, but to help me focus on addressing these emotions and others.

For a while I placed a low priority on experience-driven, ministry-based education. I thought I only needed it for the pastorate or some other practical ministry. However, having observed a number of excellent teachers at the seminary, I am convinced I would benefit from an internship with one of them. After all, the best way to learn to teach is to teach. As already mentioned, I have asked one professor, and he has consented to work with me. Along with this opportunity, we are attending and ministering in a Hispanic church to gain exposure to people of another culture. This is for my wife's benefit as well as my own. She is open to the mission field but wants and needs more exposure to cross-cultural contexts.

I plan to finish my studies and assume a teaching position on the mission field in six years. Normally the doctorate takes four years to complete, which includes three years of classroom preparation and one year to research and write the dissertation. I hope to select and be accepted by an appropriate mission agency at the end of my second year. My wife and I also plan to determine our country for ministry and begin to learn its language and culture by the end of the third year. My personal goal is to have a working knowledge of the language by graduation.

During the last two years we will travel to various churches and meet with people to raise our support. I know the value of networking and plan to meet a lot of Christian people over the next four years both in and beyond the seminary community. Some have already expressed an interest in our future, specifically our parents' churches. I am presently making a list of people we have ministered to or recently met who might become involved in our support. We have committed this timetable to the Lord and believe he will direct us according to his marvelous sovereign will (James 4:13–15).

My wife has agreed to work for the next four years as our primary means of support. As soon as her old boss heard she was coming back to town, he called and offered to increase her salary and benefits significantly. When we arrived in town, he took us to a fashionable restaurant and confessed he did not realize her value to the company until she was gone. She was delighted and agreed to return to work.

Another source of income is our parents. They supported us during our prior time in seminary and want to do so again. In fact their churches, which have served as our home churches, recently agreed to support a limited number of students involved in ministry preparation. They (along with most churches in North America) have never done this before. I suspect that pressure from our parents and those of other students preparing for ministry had a lot to do with the change of heart.

Designing Your Personal Ministry Plan

1. What are your life circumstances?
   a. Age:
   b. Marital and family status:
   c. Prior education:
   d. Gender:
   e. Health and disabilities:

   f. Finances:

   g. Other:

2. Briefly jot down the main ingredients of your divine design.
   a. Spiritual gifts:

   b. Passion:

   c. Temperament:

   d. Leadership role and style:

   e. Evangelism style:

   f. Natural talents and gifts:

3. Identify your learning style(s)—commonsense, dynamic, imaginative, analytical:

4. What is your personal ministry direction?
   a. Ministry mission:

   b. Ministry vision:

5. For the sake of your competence for ministry, what are you doing to grow and develop in the following areas?
   a. Your character:

   b. Your knowledge base (Bible, people, ministry essentials, and other areas):

   c. Your ministry skills:

   d. Your emotions:

6. What are the training contexts for your vision?
   a. Learner-driven training
      A requirement?
      Priority?
         High___
         Medium___
         Low___
      Where and how?

   b. Content-driven training
      A requirement?
      Priority?
         High___
         Medium___
         Low___
      Where and how?

   c. Mentor-driven training
      A requirement?
      Priority?
         High___
         Medium___
         Low___
      Where and how?

   d. Experience-driven training
      A requirement?
      Priority?
         High___
         Medium___
         Low___
      Where and how?

7. In light of the information above, write out your ministry plan using either the short-answer format or the prose format. Be sure to consider the following:

  a. *Who* is involved in your plan (spouse, children, parents, relatives)?

  b. *What* is involved in your plan (design, direction, learning style, and competencies)?

  c. *Where* will you realize this plan (contexts)?

  d. *When* do you hope to implement this plan (timing)?

  e. *How* will you implement this plan (finances)?

9

WORKING THE MINISTRY PLAN

When we left David, Tom, and Carol in the last chapter, they had designed a lifetime personal training plan tailor-made for their individual ministry situations. Now it is time to move from where they are to where they believe God wants them to be. It is time to work the plan.

Working the plan involves implementing the personal ministry plan. You must place a premium on getting it done. You can come up with the best plan to get you to where you think God wants you to be, but if you do not execute the plan, all is for naught. It has been a fascinating, fulfilling process that has consumed your time and perhaps some expense but it has taken you nowhere.

The difference between your success and failure is working your plan. Implementation is the great unaddressed issue in the ministry world today. I believe that its absence is the major cause of most disappointments that are often mistakenly attributed to other causes.

The problem is that most assume that implementation will just happen. Quite to the contrary, you must intentionally work the plan for the plan to work. How do you work your plan? In this chapter I will present the problem of implementation and then provide a solution, consisting of four aspects that will guide and enable you to carry out your plan: practice, focus, persistence, and assistance.

The Problem

The problem that we face in executing our plans is our old ways and habits of doing things that we have become accustomed to over time. They are highly change resistant. Depending on your age, you have been practicing certain behaviors over a significant period of time and they have become wired in your brain circuitry. It is natural for you to do these things in certain ways.

This has much to do with how our brains are wired. An example would be riding a bicycle. Think of what it was like the first time you tried to ride a bicycle. It was not a natural experience to you, so you pursued it with fear and trepidation. Most likely you were not in any hurry. However, today when you go on a bike ride, you simply jump on and take off, without thinking about the mechanics of how to ride the bike. This is due to constant practice and repetition that has been encoded in your brain. Working your plan will be like learning how to ride your bicycle or drive a car. You will have to reconfigure your brain.

The Solution

So how might you handle breaking up some of the old ways and habits, especially when it comes to executing your plan? The answer is the same as learning how to ride your bicycle. You will have to work at it, creating new neural pathways, until these new ways are firmly encoded in your brain. The four aspects of the solution that follow—practice, focus, persistence, and assistance—will aid you in the process.

Practice

To begin with, you have to take action. You must get started. For example, before actually writing this book, I had to plan it. However, in time I reached a point where I had to start pounding the keys on my computer or you would not have this book in front of you. I found that the longer I delayed, the more difficult it became to actually get this work down on paper. We see the same in Scripture. The apostle Paul carefully and strategically planned his missionary journeys. However, he came to a point where it was time to stop planning and get going (Acts

13:1–21:16). The same holds true for you. You can get caught up in the design phase and never quite get to the working part.

If you find yourself struggling with getting started, it may be because you have missed your passion. Remember that your passion is what you care deeply and feel strongly about. It affects your emotions deeply and should drive and motivate your working the plan. If this is not the case, then revisit the section in chapter 4 on passion and see if there is a problem.

Another reason that you may be delaying getting started is that you may have failed to determine your priorities, and the mountain looks too big to climb. There is no way you can do everything at once. If this is the case, return to chapter 7 and reread the section on setting priorities.

A third reason for stalling may be spiritual in nature. In the busyness of life, you may have forgotten to trust God and the work of his Spirit to enable the process of working your plan, and you may be operating on your own power (see Zech. 4:6). If that is the case, then address this issue now before reading any further. It is essential to bathe your plan and its execution in prayer and then to step out in faith, depending on the Holy Spirit to empower you.

There are at least three guidelines for taking action on your plan. First, intentionally and consciously choose to practice the components of the plan. For example, when you assessed your emotional competencies, you may have discovered that you had a problem with anxiety, and that has become a priority item to be dealt with up front. The answer to this problem is found in Philippians 4:6–7 where Paul counsels us to stop being anxious and then tells us to take our requests to God in prayer and thanksgiving, and he will give us a peace that will tranquilize our worries.

A second guideline is to intentionally take advantage of the many daily opportunities to work your plan. You can intentionally work your plan at work or in your ministry. Let your workmates or ministry teammates know what you are doing and enlist their help. You can work your plan with your family. Make sure your spouse knows what you are doing, and enlist his or her help. And include your kids in the process. You can work your plan with your friends and those you spend time with, enlisting their help as well.

A third guideline is what some refer to as mental rehearsal. Researcher Daniel Goleman writes: "Brain studies have shown that imagining something in vivid detail can fire the same brain cells that are actually involved in that activity."[1] Thus he suggests that you first visualize your priority components because it will have the same benefit as if you were actually doing the components, and you will feel less awkward when you attempt to do them. A great example is Olympic divers who think through the entire dive, every move, before even getting on the board. The same is true for ice skaters, gymnasts, and others. So if you were going to teach a class of sixth graders a lesson on sanctification, you would first work through in your mind how you would accomplish this before you actually encountered the class. Think through the situation and what you would do. Anticipate certain questions and think through how you would respond.

Focus

Next is focus. As you practice your plan, you must be focused. Again, determining your planning priorities will be a great aid in focusing on your plan. The point is you are not trying to do all the plan at the same time, but you are focused on those parts that when implemented will have the greatest impact for you, your ministry, and the Savior.

You must keep in mind that your time and energy are limited. You have only twenty-four hours and so much energy each day to invest in your ministry plan. Focus will enable you to use your time and energy wisely.

The problem will be distractions, especially concerns that flare up and call for your time and energy. Some find that they spend most of their time putting out fires and little time accomplishing what is really important. Distractions may also consist of opportunities to pursue other directions in life that can seem more exciting than executing your plan.

So what should you do with distractions? First, you have to determine if an interruption is serious. Some things will legitimately call for immediate attention, such as a medical emergency. Most, however, will not. Once you have determined that it is not a real emergency, you must discipline yourself to say no. You must realize that to say yes to one thing means that you will have to say no to something else. So do it. The problem, especially for those in ministry, is they do not like to disappoint people. I have observed that this is most true of leaders with the Influencer temperament. What you must realize is that you cannot make everyone happy or please them all.

Another problem is your current daily routine. If you are like most people, your day is filled with all kinds of activities—some more important than others. And it is the ones that are not important that can sap your time and energy. So what can you do? The answer is to create a "stop doing" list. Review a typical day and identify your time wasters. Then place them on your "stop doing" list and keep it with you.

Persistence

The third guideline in working your plan is persistence—sticking to the plan. A great biblical example of persistence is the apostle Paul. He writes: "Not that I have already obtained all this, or have already been made perfect, but I press on to take hold of that for which Christ Jesus took hold of me. Brothers, I do not consider myself yet to have taken hold of it. But one thing I do: Forgetting what is behind and straining toward what is ahead, I press on toward the goal to win the prize for which God has called me heavenward in Christ Jesus" (Phil. 3:12–14). For Paul, persistence was "pressing on toward the goal."

This might be a problem because you will encounter disappointment and failure as you pursue your training plan. And these can discourage you and make you want to give up the process entirely. Paul certainly experienced failure and disappointments in his ministry. If you are not convinced of this, read 2 Timothy 4:9–18 as one example. However, note how he handled disappointments: "But one thing I do: Forgetting what is behind and straining toward what is ahead, I press on . . ."

Paul forgot what was behind him. I do not think that he is saying that he simply walked away from his past. I believe that he is saying he did not get caught up in the past to the extent that it discouraged him from his pursuit of Christ and his plan for Paul. The key is to learn from the past, not live in the past. Living in the past is like trying to drive somewhere by looking in the rearview mirror. It is nearly impossible. The key then to overcoming failure is not to be overwhelmed by your mistakes but to treat them as learning opportunities.

Paul moved or pressed on. He had a goal that he wanted to accomplish and he was passionate about it. His goal was to win the prize for which God had called him. I believe it was to accomplish his purpose for being here in the first place—to serve Christ and accomplish his mission (v. 10; Acts 20:24) and then to die and go to be with him (his goal is similar to that of David in Acts 13:36). If in your ministry plan you have truly discovered and tapped into your passion, then it will motivate you to strain and press on as well. Your vision of what you could be and do will grab hold and not let go of you.

Often it is helpful to have a hero—someone you admire who inspires you—when attempting to accomplish some goal. I suggest that you make Paul your training hero and that you memorize Acts 20:24 and Philippians 3:12–14. Let God bring them to mind so that you may persist in your development.

Assistance

A fourth aspect of the process is getting some assistance in the pursuit of working your plan. Going it alone is difficult even for the extreme introvert and loner. You need to cultivate supportive relationships with people who will be on your side while you work your plan. What does this kind of support look like? How would you recognize such a person if you saw him or her? Here are several ways to identify people who will be supportive:

- They are people who understand you and can be counted on to encourage you in the process. You will know who they are, most likely your immediate family and your closest friends. Sometimes we kid ourselves and believe wrongly that some people are our friends, but in reality a relationship with them is toxic. Not only do such people tend to be down on themselves, but they purposely try to discourage us because they are jealous of us, are competing with us, and so on. You do not need friends like that.
- They are people who will provide you with what I refer to as "safety zones," where you can address the unthinkable, even questions that challenge our faith. These zones are also places where we can let off steam and get a hearing.
- These people will give you honest, candid feedback. They will tell you not necessarily what you want to know, but what you need to hear. They do this because they love you and care very much about you and who you are. And it is the fact that they love you and have your best intentions at heart that helps you listen to what they have to say, even if you do not like it.
- Perhaps most important, these people will hold you accountable for working your ministry plan. You know that if you attempt for some reason to scuttle the process, they will be there to "get in your face" and challenge you. You may walk away from the process, but they will not make it easy.
- These people can be a group of fellow learners who are also pursuing a training plan and understand what you are doing. They could be peers or even mentors who may or may not be involved in your church.

Worksheet

1. Do you find it difficult to implement things once you have planned them? Why?

2. Do you find it easy or difficult to take action after you have made plans? If difficult, have you missed your passion? Did you prioritize

the various components of your plan? Have you been operating in the flesh and not the Spirit?

3. Will you intentionally and consciously choose to carry out your ministry plan? Why or why not? Do you take advantage of the many daily opportunities to work your plan? Why or why not? Have you tried mental rehearsal? Why or why not?

4. Are you a very focused person? Do you face a lot of distractions in your work and/or ministry? How do you handle them? Are you good at telling people no? Why or why not? Would it help you to create a "stop doing" list? If so, will you?

5. Would you and others consider you to be a persistent person? Why or why not? How hard will it be for you to stick to the plan? How do you normally handle disappointments and failures? Do you learn from your mistakes? Why or why not? How might these affect your planning? Do you have any heroes? If so, who are they and how might they serve to encourage you to accomplish your planning goals?

6. Do you prefer to work alone or do you like to be around people? Who really understands you and can be counted on to encourage you? Do you have anyone in your life who will provide for you a "safety zone"? Do you have any friends whom you can trust to give you honest, candid feedback? Whom do you have in your life who can and will hold you accountable to carry out your plan? What will you do if you do not have people like this in your life?

APPENDIX A

SPIRITUAL GIFTS INVENTORY

Instructions for Responding

1. Work through each of the following 110 statements on spiritual gifts. After each, check the appropriate box that best describes to what extent the statement accurately describes you.
2. Do not answer on the basis of what you wish were true or what another says might be true, but on the basis of what, to the best of your knowledge, is true of you.

Questions

	Never	Rarely	Sometimes	Often	Always
	1	2	3	4	5
1. I enjoy working with others in determining ministry goals and objectives.	☐	☐	☐	☐	☐
2. I have a strong desire to start or be involved in a new ministry.	☐	☐	☐	☐	☐
3. I delight in telling lost people about what Christ has done for them.	☐	☐	☐	☐	☐

	Never	Rarely	Sometimes	Often	Always
	1	2	3	4	5
4. It bothers me that some people are hurting and discouraged.	☐	☐	☐	☐	☐
5. I have a strong ability to see what needs to be done and believe that God will do it.	☐	☐	☐	☐	☐
6. I love to give a significant proportion of my resources to God's work.	☐	☐	☐	☐	☐
7. I have a strong capacity to recognize practical needs and to do something about them.	☐	☐	☐	☐	☐
8. I have a clear vision for the direction of a ministry.	☐	☐	☐	☐	☐
9. I always feel strong compassion for those in difficult situations.	☐	☐	☐	☐	☐
10. I have a strong desire to nurture God's people.	☐	☐	☐	☐	☐
11. I spend a significant portion of my time each week studying the Bible.	☐	☐	☐	☐	☐
12. I am motivated to design plans to accomplish ministry goals.	☐	☐	☐	☐	☐
13. I prefer to create my own ministry problems than to inherit others.	☐	☐	☐	☐	☐
14. I have a strong attraction to lost people.	☐	☐	☐	☐	☐
15. I am very concerned that more people are not serving the Lord.	☐	☐	☐	☐	☐
16. I have a strong capacity to trust God for the difficult things in life.	☐	☐	☐	☐	☐
17. I am eager to financially support ministries that are accomplishing significant things for God.	☐	☐	☐	☐	☐
18. I enjoy helping people meet their practical needs.	☐	☐	☐	☐	☐
19. I find that I have a strong capacity to attract followers in my ministry.	☐	☐	☐	☐	☐
20. I am always motivated to sympathize with those in the midst of a crisis.	☐	☐	☐	☐	☐
21. I am at my best when leading and shepherding a small group of believers.	☐	☐	☐	☐	☐
22. I have strong insight into the Bible and how it applies to people's lives.	☐	☐	☐	☐	☐
23. I feel significant when developing budgets to accomplish a good plan.	☐	☐	☐	☐	☐

	Never	Rarely	Sometimes	Often	Always
	1	2	3	4	5
24. I am motivated to minister in places where no one else has ministered.	☐	☐	☐	☐	☐
25. I find that unsaved people enjoy spending time with me.	☐	☐	☐	☐	☐
26. I have a strong desire to encourage Christians to mature in Christ.	☐	☐	☐	☐	☐
27. I delight in the truth that God accomplishes things that seem impossible to most people.	☐	☐	☐	☐	☐
28. God has greatly blessed me with life's provisions in order to help others.	☐	☐	☐	☐	☐
29. I enjoy making personal sacrifices to help others.	☐	☐	☐	☐	☐
30. I prefer to lead people more than to follow them.	☐	☐	☐	☐	☐
31. I delight in extending a hand to those in difficulty.	☐	☐	☐	☐	☐
32. I enjoy showing attention to those who are in need of care and concern.	☐	☐	☐	☐	☐
33. I am motivated to present God's truth to people so that they better understand the Bible.	☐	☐	☐	☐	☐
34. I am at my best when creating an organizational structure for a plan.	☐	☐	☐	☐	☐
35. I am definitely a self-starter with a pioneer spirit.	☐	☐	☐	☐	☐
36. I derive extreme satisfaction when lost people accept Christ.	☐	☐	☐	☐	☐
37. I have been effective at inspiring believers to a stronger faith.	☐	☐	☐	☐	☐
38. I am convinced that God is going to accomplish something special through me or my ministry.	☐	☐	☐	☐	☐
39. I am convinced that all I have belongs to God, and I am willing to use it for his purposes.	☐	☐	☐	☐	☐
40. I work best when I serve others behind the scenes.	☐	☐	☐	☐	☐
41. If I am not careful, I have a tendency to dominate people and situations.	☐	☐	☐	☐	☐
42. I am a born burden-bearer.	☐	☐	☐	☐	☐
43. I have a deep desire to protect Christians from people and beliefs that may harm them.	☐	☐	☐	☐	☐
44. I am deeply committed to biblical truth and people's need to know and understand it.	☐	☐	☐	☐	☐

	Never	Rarely	Sometimes	Often	Always
	1	2	3	4	5
45. I delight in staffing a particular ministry structure.	☐	☐	☐	☐	☐
46. I am challenged by a big vision to accomplish what some believe is impossible.	☐	☐	☐	☐	☐
47. I feel a deep compassion for people who are without Christ.	☐	☐	☐	☐	☐
48. I have the ability to say the right things to people who are experiencing discouragement.	☐	☐	☐	☐	☐
49. I am rarely surprised when God turns seeming obstacles into opportunities for ministry.	☐	☐	☐	☐	☐
50. I feel good when I have opportunity to give from my abundance to people with genuine needs.	☐	☐	☐	☐	☐
51. I have a strong capacity to serve people.	☐	☐	☐	☐	☐
52. I am motivated to be proactive, not passive, in my ministry for Christ.	☐	☐	☐	☐	☐
53. I have the ability to feel the pain of others who are suffering.	☐	☐	☐	☐	☐
54. I get excited about helping new Christians grow to maturity in Christ.	☐	☐	☐	☐	☐
55. Whenever I teach a Bible class, the size of the group increases in number.	☐	☐	☐	☐	☐
56. I am good at using a ministry's resources in solving its problems.	☐	☐	☐	☐	☐
57. I gain deep satisfaction from creating something out of nothing.	☐	☐	☐	☐	☐
58. Training and helping others to share their faith is high on my list of priorities.	☐	☐	☐	☐	☐
59. People who are struggling emotionally or spiritually say I am an excellent listener.	☐	☐	☐	☐	☐
60. I delight in trusting God in the most difficult of circumstances.	☐	☐	☐	☐	☐
61. I have the capacity to give of myself as well as my possessions to help others.	☐	☐	☐	☐	☐
62. I am good at doing seemingly insignificant tasks to free people up for vital ministries.	☐	☐	☐	☐	☐
63. Most people place a lot of trust in me and my leadership.	☐	☐	☐	☐	☐
64. I have a desire to make a significant difference in the lives of troubled people.	☐	☐	☐	☐	☐

	Never	Rarely	Sometimes	Often	Always
	1	2	3	4	5
65. I enjoy being around believers and encouraging them to trust Christ for their circumstances.	☐	☐	☐	☐	☐
66. I have a desire to search the Bible for truths that apply to my life and the lives of others.	☐	☐	☐	☐	☐
67. I like monitoring plans that accomplish ministry goals.	☐	☐	☐	☐	☐
68. I am a risk-taker when it comes to developing new ministries.	☐	☐	☐	☐	☐
69. Over the years I have prayed much for my non-Christian friends.	☐	☐	☐	☐	☐
70. I spend a significant amount of time exhorting believers to make Christ Lord of their lives.	☐	☐	☐	☐	☐
71. I am able to trust God in situations when most others have lost all hope.	☐	☐	☐	☐	☐
72. Friends worry that some people take advantage of my generosity with my possessions.	☐	☐	☐	☐	☐
73. I am motivated to accomplish tasks that most people consider insignificant.	☐	☐	☐	☐	☐
74. People are confident in my abilities to help them accomplish their ministry goals.	☐	☐	☐	☐	☐
75. Suffering people are attracted to me and find me comforting to be around.	☐	☐	☐	☐	☐
76. I have the ability and courage to confront Christians about sin in their lives.	☐	☐	☐	☐	☐
77. God has given me unusual ability to explain deep biblical truths to his people.	☐	☐	☐	☐	☐
78. I prefer that a ministry's affairs be conducted in an orderly and efficient manner.	☐	☐	☐	☐	☐
79. I want to accomplish great things for God but in my own way.	☐	☐	☐	☐	☐
80. I am deeply motivated to address the doubts and questions of lost people.	☐	☐	☐	☐	☐
81. I have the ability to confront disobedient Christians and see them change.	☐	☐	☐	☐	☐
82. I am motivated by people who dream big dreams for God.	☐	☐	☐	☐	☐
83. People regularly come to me with requests for help in meeting their financial needs.	☐	☐	☐	☐	☐
84. I look for opportunities to serve the practical needs of God's ministries.	☐	☐	☐	☐	☐
85. I am happiest in a ministry when I am able to exert a strong influence in the group.	☐	☐	☐	☐	☐

	Never	Rarely	Sometimes	Often	Always
	1	2	3	4	5
86. People close to me believe that I allow "down and outers" to take advantage of me.	☐	☐	☐	☐	☐
87. Christians often seek me out for counsel regarding important decisions in their lives.	☐	☐	☐	☐	☐
88. I have a strong desire to study and explain the truths of the Bible in depth.	☐	☐	☐	☐	☐
89. I am convinced that paying attention to details is very important.	☐	☐	☐	☐	☐
90. I believe we must create new ministry structures for the new ministries we start.	☐	☐	☐	☐	☐
91. I feel a strong attraction toward evangelistic ministries.	☐	☐	☐	☐	☐
92. I could easily spend much of my time encouraging people in their walk with Christ.	☐	☐	☐	☐	☐
93. I am frustrated by people who never take risks.	☐	☐	☐	☐	☐
94. I find it difficult to understand why Christians do not give more help to those with real needs.	☐	☐	☐	☐	☐
95. I prefer to remain behind the scenes helping people with practical matters.	☐	☐	☐	☐	☐
96. I have a strong desire to take charge in most situations.	☐	☐	☐	☐	☐
97. I delight in visiting people in hospitals or nursing homes.	☐	☐	☐	☐	☐
98. I pray constantly for people who look to me for care.	☐	☐	☐	☐	☐
99. I have observed that people who sit under my teaching experience changed lives.	☐	☐	☐	☐	☐
100. I have a strong desire to see people work together to accomplish their goals.	☐	☐	☐	☐	☐
101. I am convinced that the future of any country lies in starting fresh ministries.	☐	☐	☐	☐	☐
102. I get extremely frustrated when I cannot share my faith.	☐	☐	☐	☐	☐
103. I find great satisfaction in reassuring Christians of their need to walk with Christ.	☐	☐	☐	☐	☐
104. People are amazed at my ability to trust God to provide in the most difficult situations.	☐	☐	☐	☐	☐
105. When I give significantly to help others, I do not expect anything in return.	☐	☐	☐	☐	☐
106. I am convinced that no job is too menial if it truly helps people.	☐	☐	☐	☐	☐

	Never	Rarely	Sometimes	Often	Always
	1	2	3	4	5
107. In meetings, people look to me for the final opinion regarding a matter.	☐	☐	☐	☐	☐
108. I believe strongly in giving those who fail a second and even a third chance.	☐	☐	☐	☐	☐
109. I enjoy visiting people in their homes and when they are in the hospital.	☐	☐	☐	☐	☐
110. I am greatly challenged by people's questions about the Bible.	☐	☐	☐	☐	☐

Instructions for Scoring

1. Place the number from each of your answers on the line corresponding to the question number.
2. Add the numbers horizontally and place the total for each row in the space before each gift.

1.___	12.___	23.___	34.___	45.___	56.___	67.___	78.___	89.___	100.___	___ Administration
2.___	13.___	24.___	35.___	46.___	57.___	68.___	79.___	90.___	101.___	___ Apostleship
3.___	14.___	25.___	36.___	47.___	58.___	69.___	80.___	91.___	102.___	___ Evangelism
4.___	15.___	26.___	37.___	48.___	59.___	70.___	81.___	92.___	103.___	___ Encouragement
5.___	16.___	27.___	38.___	49.___	60.___	71.___	82.___	93.___	104.___	___ Faith
6.___	17.___	28.___	39.___	50.___	61.___	72.___	83.___	94.___	105.___	___ Giving
7.___	18.___	29.___	40.___	51.___	62.___	73.___	84.___	95.___	106.___	___ Helps
8.___	19.___	30.___	41.___	52.___	63.___	74.___	85.___	96.___	107.___	___ Leadership
9.___	20.___	31.___	42.___	53.___	64.___	75.___	86.___	97.___	108.___	___ Mercy
10.___	21.___	32.___	43.___	54.___	65.___	76.___	87.___	98.___	109.___	___ Pastor
11.___	22.___	33.___	44.___	55.___	66.___	77.___	88.___	99.___	110.___	___ Teacher

Instructions for Determining Your Spiritual Gifts

1. Place the names of your five highest scoring gifts in the spaces below under Spiritual Gifts Inventory.

2. Place the names of any other gifts that are not identified in this inventory yet are present in your life under the title Other Spiritual Gifts.

Spiritual Gifts Inventory   **Other Spiritual Gifts**

1._____   _____
2._____   _____
3._____   _____
4._____   _____
5._____   _____

Instructions for Determining Your Gift-Mix and Gift-Cluster

1. To determine your gift-mix, place the names of your five highest gifts in descending order in the space below titled Gift-Mix.
2. To determine if you have a gift-cluster, decide if the first gift or another gift in your mix is dominant and supported by the other gifts. If this is the case, place it in the center space under the title Gift-Cluster and place the other gifts in the spaces surrounding it.

Gift-Mix

1._____
2._____
3._____
4._____
5._____

Gift-Cluster

_____   _____

_____

_____   _____

APPENDIX B

SPIRITUAL GIFTS INVENTORY

Short Version

Instructions for Responding

1. Work through each of the following fifty-five statements on spiritual gifts. After each, check the appropriate box that best describes to what extent the statement accurately describes you.
2. Do not answer on the basis of what you wish were true or what another says might be true, but on the basis of what, to the best of your knowledge, is true of you.

Questions

	Never	Rarely	Sometimes	Often	Always
	1	2	3	4	5
1. I enjoy working with others in determining ministry goals and objectives.	☐	☐	☐	☑	☐
2. I have a strong desire to start or be involved in a new ministry.	☐	☐	☑	☐	☐

	Never	Rarely	Sometimes	Often	Always
	1	2	3	4	5
3. I delight in telling lost people about what Christ has done for them.	☐	☐	☑	☐	☐
4. It bothers me that some people are hurting and discouraged.	☐	☐	☐	☑	☐
5. I have a strong ability to see what needs to be done and believe that God will do it.	☐	☐	☐	☐	☑
6. I love to give a significant proportion of my resources to God's work.	☐	☐	☐	☐	☑
7. I have a strong capacity to recognize practical needs and to do something about them.	☐	☐	☐	☐	☑
8. I have a clear vision for the direction of a ministry.	☐	☐	☐	☐	☑
9. I always feel strong compassion for those in difficult situations.	☐	☐	☐	☑	☐
10. I have a strong desire to nurture God's people.	☐	☐	☐	☐	☑
11. I spend a significant portion of my time each week studying the Bible.	☐	☐	☐	☐	☑
12. I am motivated to design plans to accomplish ministry goals.	☐	☐	☐	☑	☐
13. I prefer to create my own ministry problems than to inherit others.	☐	☑	☐	☐	☐
14. I have a strong attraction to lost people.	☐	☑	☑	☐	☐
15. I am very concerned that more people are not serving the Lord.	☐	☐	☑	☐	☐
16. I have a strong capacity to trust God for the difficult things in life.	☐	☐	☐	☐	☑
17. I am eager to financially support ministries that are accomplishing significant things for God.	☐	☐	☐	☐	☑
18. I enjoy helping people meet their practical needs.	☐	☐	☐	☐	☑
19. I find that I have a strong capacity to attract followers in my ministry.	☐	☐	☐	☐	☑
20. I am always motivated to sympathize with those in the midst of a crisis.	☐	☐	☑	☐	☐
21. I am at my best when leading and shepherding a small group of believers.	☐	☐	☐	☑	☐
22. I have strong insight into the Bible and how it applies to people's lives.	☐	☐	☑	☐	☐
23. I feel significant when developing budgets to accomplish a good plan.	☐	☐	☑	☐	☐

	Never	Rarely	Sometimes	Often	Always
	1	2	3	4	5
24. I am motivated to minister in places where no one else has ministered.	☐	☑	☐	☐	☐
25. I find that unsaved people enjoy spending time with me.	☐	☐	☐	☑	☐
26. I have a strong desire to encourage Christians to mature in Christ.	☐	☐	☐	☑	☐
27. I delight in the truth that God accomplishes things that seem impossible to most people.	☐	☐	☐	☐	☑
28. God has greatly blessed me with life's provisions in order to help others.	☐	☐	☐	☐	☑
29. I enjoy making personal sacrifices to help others.	☐	☐	☐	☑	☐
30. I prefer to lead people more than to follow them.	☐	☐	☐	☐	☑
31. I delight in extending a hand to those in difficulty.	☐	☐	☐	☐	☑
32. I enjoy showing attention to those who are in need of care and concern.	☐	☐	☐	☑	☐
33. I am motivated to present God's truth to people so that they better understand the Bible.	☐	☐	☐	☑	☐
34. I am at my best when creating an organizational structure for a plan.	☐	☐	☐	☐	☑
35. I am definitely a self-starter with a pioneer spirit.	☐	☐	☑	☐	☐
36. I derive extreme satisfaction when lost people accept Christ.	☐	☐	☐	☑	☐
37. I have been effective at inspiring believers to a stronger faith.	☐	☐	☑	☐	☐
38. I am convinced that God is going to accomplish something special through me or my ministry.	☐	☐	☐	☐	☑
39. I am convinced that all I have belongs to God, and I am willing to use it for his purposes.	☐	☐	☐	☐	☑
40. I work best when I serve others behind the scenes.	☐	☑	☐	☐	☐
41. If I am not careful, I have a tendency to dominate people and situations.	☐	☐	☐	☐	☑
42. I am a born burden-bearer.	☐	☐	☐	☑	☐
43. I have a deep desire to protect Christians from people and beliefs that may harm them.	☐	☐	☐	☑	☐
44. I am deeply committed to biblical truth and people's need to know and understand it.	☐	☐	☐	☐	☑
45. I delight in staffing a particular ministry structure.	☐	☐	☐	☑	☐

	Never	Rarely	Sometimes	Often	Always
	1	2	3	4	5
46. I am challenged by a big vision to accomplish what some believe is impossible.	☐	☐	☐	☐	☑
47. I feel a deep compassion for people who are without Christ.	☐	☐	☑	☐	☐
48. I have the ability to say the right things to people who are experiencing discouragement.	☐	☐	☐	☑	☐
49. I am rarely surprised when God turns seeming obstacles into opportunities for ministry.	☐	☐	☐	☐	☑
50. I feel good when I have opportunity to give from my abundance to people with genuine needs.	☐	☐	☐	☐	☑
51. I have a strong capacity to serve people.	☐	☐	☐	☐	☑
52. I am motivated to be proactive, not passive, in my ministry for Christ.	☐	☐	☐	☐	☑
53. I have the ability to feel the pain of others who are suffering.	☐	☐	☑	☑	☐
54. I get excited about helping new Christians grow to maturity in Christ.	☐	☐	☑	☑	☐
55. Whenever I teach a Bible class, the size of the group increases in number.	☐	☐	☐	☐	☑

Instructions for Scoring

1. Place the number from each of your answers on the line corresponding to the question number.
2. Add the numbers horizontally and place the total for each row in the space before each gift.

1. 4	12. 4	23. 3	34. 5	45. 4	20 Administration
2. 3	13. 2	24. 2	35. 3	46. 5	15 Apostleship
3. 3	14. 3	25. 4	36. 4	47. 3	17 Evangelism
4. 4	15. 3	26. 4	37. 3	48. 4	18 Encouragement
5. 5	16. 5	27. 5	38. 5	49. 5	25 Faith —
6. 5	17. 5	28. 5	39. 5	50. 5	25 Giving —
7. 5	18. 5	29. 4	40. 2	51. 5	— 21 Helps
8. 5	19. 5	30. 5	41. 5	52. 5	25 Leadership —
9. 4	20. 3	31. 5	42. 4	53. 3	19 Mercy
10. 5	21. 4	32. 4	43. 4	54. 4	— 21 Pastor
11. 5	22. 3	33. 4	44. 5	55. 5	— 22 Teacher

Instructions for Determining Your Spiritual Gifts

1. Place the names of your five highest scoring gifts in the spaces below under Spiritual Gifts Inventory.
2. Place the names of any other gifts that are not identified in this inventory yet are present in your life under the title Other Spiritual Gifts.

Spiritual Gifts Inventory

1. _____
2. _____
3. _____
4. _____
5. _____

Other Spiritual Gifts

_____
_____
_____
_____
_____

Instructions for Determining Your Gift-Mix and Gift-Cluster

1. To determine your gift-mix, place the names of your five highest gifts in descending order in the space below titled Gift-Mix.
2. To determine if you have a gift-cluster, decide if the first gift or another gift in your mix is dominant and supported by the other gifts. If this is the case, place it in the center space under the title Gift-Cluster and place the other gifts in the spaces surrounding it.

Gift-Mix

1. _____
2. _____
3. _____
4. _____
5. _____

Gift-Cluster

_____   _____

_____

_____   _____

APPENDIX C

TEMPERAMENT INDICATOR 1

Instructions

Read the four terms listed across each row. Then rank each characteristic for how well it describes you in a ministry or work-related environment. Number 4 is most like you, and number 1 is least. In each row use all four numbers.

Sample:

_3_ Direct	_4_ Popular	_1_ Loyal	_2_ Analytical
___ Decisive	___ Outgoing	___ Dependable	___ Logical
___ Controlling	___ Expressive	___ Steady	___ Thorough
___ Competent	___ Influential	___ Responsible	___ Skeptical
___ Blunt	___ Enthusiastic	___ Sensible	___ Compliant
___ Competitive	___ Persuasive	___ Cooperative	___ Serious
___ Callous	___ Impulsive	___ Submissive	___ Accurate
___ Volatile	___ Manipulative	___ Conforming	___ Picky
___ Persistent	___ Personable	___ Harmonious	___ Creative
___ Productive	___ Animated	___ Restrained	___ Fearful
___ Self-reliant	___ Articulate	___ Predictable	___ Diplomatic
___ **Total**	___ **Total**	___ **Total**	___ **Total**

Instructions for Scoring

1. Total the numbers in each column above and place that number in the blank provided at the bottom of each column.
2. On the scale below, circle the number in each column that is closest to the total score for the above column.
3. Connect the circles.
4. The highest number represents your strongest temperament type. The next highest represents your second-strongest temperament type.
5. Have someone who knows you well complete the indicator on you. Compare the scores and discuss any differences.

50	50	50	50
45	45	45	45
40	40	40	40
35	35	35	35
30	30	30	30
25	25	25	25
20	20	20	20
15	15	15	15
10	10	10	10
5	5	5	5
0	0	0	0
Doer	**Influencer**	**Relator**	**Thinker**

Appendix D

Temperament Indicator 2

Instructions

1. As you take this indicator, please keep in mind that there are no correct or incorrect answers.
2. Read each statement and circle the item (a or b) that best represents your preference in a ministry or work-related environment.
3. Do not spend a lot of time thinking about your answers. Go with your first impulse.

Questions

1. When around other people, I am
   a) expressive
   b) quiet
2. I tend to
   a) dislike new problems
   b) like new problems
3. I make decisions based on my
   a) logic
   b) values

4. I prefer to work in a
   a) structured environment
   b) nonstructured environment
5. I feel more energetic after being
   a) around people
   b) away from people
6. I work best with
   a) facts
   b) ideas
7. People say I am
   a) impersonal
   b) a people-pleaser
8. My friends at work say I am very
   a) organized
   b) flexible
9. I get more work accomplished when I am
   a) with people
   b) by myself
10. I like to think about
    a) what is
    b) what could be
11. I admire
    a) strength
    b) compassion
12. I make decisions
    a) quickly
    b) slowly
13. I prefer
    a) variety and action
    b) focus and quiet
14. I like
    a) established ways to do things
    b) new ways to do things
15. I tend to be rather
    a) unemotional
    b) emotional

16. Most often I dislike
    a) carelessness with details
    b) complicated procedures

17. In my relationships I find that over time it is easy to
    a) keep up with people
    b) lose track of people

18. I enjoy skills that
    a) I have already learned and used
    b) are newly learned but unused

19. Sometimes I make decisions that
    a) hurt other people's feelings
    b) are too influenced by other people

20. When my circumstances change, I prefer to
    a) follow a good plan
    b) adapt to each new situation

21. In conversations I communicate
    a) freely and openly
    b) quietly and cautiously

22. In my work I tend to
    a) take time to be precise
    b) dislike taking time to be precise

23. I relate well to
    a) people like me
    b) most people

24. When working on a project, I do not
    a) like interruptions
    b) mind interruptions

25. Sometimes I find that I
    a) act first and ask questions later
    b) ask questions first and act later

26. I would describe my work style as
    a) steady with realistic expectations
    b) periodic with bursts of enthusiasm

27. At work I need
    a) fair treatment
    b) occasional praise

28. In a new job I prefer to know
   a) only what it takes to get it done
   b) all about it

29. In any job I am most interested in
   a) getting it done and the results
   b) the idea behind the job

30. I have found that I am
   a) patient with routine details
   b) impatient with routine details

31. When working with other people, I find it
   a) easy to correct them
   b) difficult to correct them

32. Once I have made a decision, I consider the case
   a) closed
   b) still open

33. I prefer
   a) lots of acquaintances
   b) a few good friends

34. I am more likely to trust my
   a) experiences
   b) inspirations

35. I consistently decide matters based on
   a) the facts in my head
   b) the feelings in my heart

36. I prefer to work
   a) in an established business
   b) as an entrepreneur

Instructions for Scoring

1. Place a check in the a or b space below to indicate how you answered each question.
2. Add the checks down each column and record the total for each column at the bottom.
3. The highest score for each pair indicates your temperament preference.

4. For each pair subtract the lower from the higher score to discover the difference in your preferences. A higher number indicates a clear choice or preference but does not indicate the measure of development. For example, a higher score for extraversion means that you prefer it over introversion. It does not mean that you are a strong extravert.

	a	b		a	b		a	b		a	b
1	✓	__	2	✓	__	3	__	✓	4	✓	__
5	✓	__	6	✓	__	7	__	✓	8	✓	__
9	__	b	10	✓	__	11	__	✓	12	✓	__
13	✓	__	14	__	✓	15	__	✓	16	✓	__
17	✓	__	18	✓	__	19	✓	__	20	✓	__
21	✓	__	22	✓	__	23	✓	__	24	✓	__
25	✓	__	26	✓	__	27	__	✓	28	__	✓
29	__	✓	30	✓	__	31	✓	__	32	__	✓
33	__	✓	34	✓	__	35	✓	__	36	✓	__
Total	6	3	**Total**	8	1	**Total**	4	5	**Total**	7	2

E	I	S	N	T	F	J	P
Extravert	Introvert	Sensing	Intuition	Thinking	Feeling	Judgment	Perception
3		7			1	5	

APPENDIX E

LEADERSHIP ROLE INDICATOR

Instructions

1. There are no correct or incorrect answers to the questions.
2. Read each statement carefully and circle the item (a or b) that *best* represents your leadership role.
3. Do not spend too much time with each question; instead go with your initial impulse.

Questions

1. In my approach to change, I
   a) cope with change
   b) cope with complexity
2. In leading an organization or ministry, I
   a) do the right things
   b) do things right
3. When viewing my work or ministry, I see
   a) the whole
   b) the parts
4. My general outlook on life and ministry is
   a) optimistic
   b) realistic

5. In my work or ministry, I operate on the basis of
    a) faith
    b) facts

6. In my role as a leader, I might be described as
    a) an influencer
    b) a coordinator

7. When I view my work or ministry, I think in terms of
    a) opportunity
    b) accomplishment

8. In my work or ministry, I seek
    a) effectiveness
    b) efficiency

9. In my leadership, I would describe myself as a
    a) visionary
    b) realist

10. In my work or ministry, my focus is on
    a) ideas
    b) functions

11. In my work or ministry, I can be counted on to provide
    a) direction
    b) control

12. In my leadership role, I see myself as
    a) a persuader
    b) an implementer

13. In my work or ministry, I would describe myself as a
    a) risk-taker
    b) stabilizer

14. When communicating to a group, people say that I speak
    a) persuasively
    b) informatively

15. One of my desires for my job or ministry is to see
    a) growth
    b) harmony

16. In my ministry at church, I
    a) take risks
    b) don't take risks

17. I have the spiritual gift(s) of
   a) leadership
   b) administration
18. In my work or ministry, I am
   a) proactive
   b) reactive
19. One of my strengths is
   a) motivating people
   b) organizing people
20. I'm best at
   a) setting direction
   b) solving problems

Instructions for Scoring

1. Place a check in the a or b spaces below to indicate how you answered each question.
2. Add the checks down each column and record the totals at the end.
3. The highest column score indicates your leadership role, whether leader or manager.
4. Most likely you will check both a and b items, meaning that you are a combination of both. However, note the column below that you mark more than the other.

	a	b		a	b		a	b
1	__	✓	9	✓	__	17	✓	__
2	__	✓	10	__	✓	18	✓	__
3	✓	__	11	✓	__	19	__	✓
4	__	✓	12	__	✓	20	__	✓
5	__	✓	13	__	✓			
6	✓	__	14	✓	__	**Total**	11	9
7	✓	__	15	✓	__		**Leader**	**Manager**
8	✓	__	16	✓	__			

APPENDIX F

LEADERSHIP STYLE INVENTORY

Instructions

Of the four statements on leadership style listed for each question (lettered A through D), check the one statement that is "most like me" and the one that is "least like me." You should have only one check in each column per question.

Sample:

	Most like me	Least like me
A. Needs difficult assignments.	**A.** (+2)	**A.** (–2)
B. Makes decisions emotionally.	**B.** (+2)	**B.** (–2)
C. Seeks identity with a group.	**C.** ✓ (+2)	**C.** (–2)
D. Emphasizes quality control.	**D.** (+2)	**D.** ✓ (–2)

Answer on the basis of what you believe is true of you, not on the basis of what you desire or hope is true. As you answer the questions, it will be helpful to consider your past experience as well as how you see yourself leading in your current or a future ministry context (church, parachurch, or ministry). Go with your first impression. Resist the temptation to analyze each or any response in detail.

Suggestions for responding: You should not worry about how you score on this inventory. This is not a test that you pass or fail, and there is no best or preferred leadership style. Sometimes it's helpful to have others who know you well (spouse, parent, team member, good friend) take the inventory about you. You may want to take this inventory to discover what leadership style is best for your church or parachurch ministry. Should this be the case, change "most like me" to "most like us" and "least like me" to "least like us."

Check the reason you're taking this inventory:

____ To discover my leadership style

____ To help another discover his or her leadership style

____ To discover the best leadership style for my ministry's context (church, parachurch, or ministry)

		Most like me	Least like me
Q1	A. Loves a challenge.	A. ✓ (+2)	A. (−2)
	B. Spends time with people.	B. (+2)	B. (−2)
	C. Behaves in a predictable manner.	C. (+2)	C. ✓ (−2)
	D. Sets high ministry standards.	D. (+2)	D. (−2)
		Most like me	Least like me
Q2	A. Focuses on the details.	A. (+2)	A. (−2)
	B. Likes to start things.	B. (+2)	B. ✓ (−2)
	C. Motivates people.	C. ✓ (+2)	C. (−2)
	D. Shows patience with people.	D. (+2)	D. (−2)
		Most like me	Least like me
Q3	A. Develops deep friendships.	A. ✓ (+2)	A. (−2)
	B. Desires that people do quality work.	B. (+2)	B. (−2)
	C. Makes decisions quickly.	C. (+2)	C. ✓ (−2)
	D. Has lots of friends.	D. (+2)	D. (−2)
		Most like me	Least like me
Q4	A. Communicates with enthusiasm.	A. (+2)	A. (−2)
	B. Enjoys helping people.	B. ✓ (+2)	B. (−2)
	C. Thinks analytically.	C. (+2)	C. ✓ (−2)
	D. Challenges the status quo.	D. (+2)	D. (−2)
		Most like me	Least like me
Q5	A. Leads with authority.	A. ✓ (+2)	A. (−2)
	B. Displays optimism in ministry.	B. (+2)	B. ✓ (−2)
	C. Helps others feel comfortable in a group.	C. (+2)	C. (−2)
	D. Insists on accuracy of facts.	D. (+2)	D. (−2)
		Most like me	Least like me
Q6	A. Thinks systematically.	A. (+2)	A. (−2)
	B. Sets lofty goals.	B. (+2)	B. ✓ (−2)
	C. Treats others fairly.	C. ✓ (+2)	C. (−2)
	D. Prefers to minister with a team.	D. (+2)	D. (−2)

		Most like me	Least like me
Q7	**A.** Prefers a predictable routine.	**A.** ✓ (+2)	**A.** (−2)
	B. Evaluates programs well.	**B.** (+2)	**B.** ✓ (−2)
	C. Likes direct answers to questions.	**C.** (+2)	**C.** (−2)
	D. Loves to entertain people.	**D.** (+2)	**D.** (−2)
		Most like me	Least like me
Q8	**A.** Expresses self freely.	**A.** ✓ (+2)	**A.** (−2)
	B. Delights in sincere appreciation.	**B.** (+2)	**B.** (−2)
	C. Values quality and accuracy.	**C.** (+2)	**C.** (−2)
	D. Looks for new and varied activities.	**D.** (+2)	**D.** ✓ (−2)
		Most like me	Least like me
Q9	**A.** Solves problems well.	**A.** (+2)	**A.** (−2)
	B. Likes to "think out loud."	**B.** (+2)	**B.** (−2)
	C. Places a premium on keeping promises.	**C.** (+2)	**C.** ✓ (−2)
	D. Enjoys opportunities to display expertise.	**D.** ✓ (+2)	**D.** (−2)
		Most like me	Least like me
Q10	**A.** Needs to know what's expected.	**A.** ✓ (+2)	**A.** (−2)
	B. Pursues variety in ministry.	**B.** (+2)	**B.** ✓ (−2)
	C. Enjoys inspiring people to do great things.	**C.** (+2)	**C.** (−2)
	D. Listens well to others.	**D.** (+2)	**D.** (−2)
		Most like me	Least like me
Q11	**A.** Demonstrates great patience with people.	**A.** (+2)	**A.** (−2)
	B. Shows displeasure over poor performance.	**B.** (+2)	**B.** ✓ (−2)
	C. Makes his/her perspective clear to others.	**C.** ✓ (+2)	**C.** (−2)
	D. Expects good things from people.	**D.** (+2)	**D.** (−2)
		Most like me	Least like me
Q12	**A.** Presents ideas in compelling ways.	**A.** (+2)	**A.** (−2)
	B. Shows loyalty to those over him/her.	**B.** (+2)	**B.** (−2)
	C. Displays strong self-discipline in work.	**C.** ✓ (+2)	**C.** (−2)
	D. Believes in individual accomplishment.	**D.** (+2)	**D.** ✓ (−2)
		Most like me	Least like me
Q13	**A.** Is direct with people.	**A.** ✓ (+2)	**A.** (−2)
	B. Enjoys being with people.	**B.** (+2)	**B.** (−2)
	C. Has a calming influence on others.	**C.** (+2)	**C.** ✓ (−2)
	D. Relates to people intellectually.	**D.** (+2)	**D.** (−2)
		Most like me	Least like me
Q14	**A.** Asks "why" questions.	**A.** ✓ (+2)	**A.** (−2)
	B. Likes to get results.	**B.** (+2)	**B.** (−2)
	C. Is a persuasive communicator.	**C.** (+2)	**C.** (−2)
	D. Exhibits a strong empathy for others.	**D.** (+2)	**D.** ✓ (−2)
		Most like me	Least like me
Q15	**A.** Helps group members get along.	**A.** (+2)	**A.** (−2)
	B. Encourages others to think deeply.	**B.** (+2)	**B.** ✓ (−2)
	C. Shows persistence in pursuing goals.	**C.** (+2)	**C.** (−2)
	D. Relates well to people emotionally.	**D.** ✓ (+2)	**D.** (−2)
		Most like me	Least like me
Q16	**A.** Enjoys expressing himself/herself.	**A.** (+2)	**A.** (−2)
	B. Cooperates well to accomplish tasks.	**B.** (+2)	**B.** ✓ (−2)
	C. Utilizes strong problem-solving skills.	**C.** (+2)	**C.** (−2)
	D. Takes the initiative with people.	**D.** ✓ (+2)	**D.** (−2)

		Most like me	Least like me
Q17	A. Leads with strength.	A. ✓ (+2)	A. (−2)
	B. Enjoys interacting with people.	B. (+2)	B. (−2)
	C. Helps others feel comfortable.	C. (+2)	C. (−2)
	D. Follows directions carefully.	D. (+2)	D. ✓ (−2)
		Most like me	Least like me
Q18	A. Wants explanations and answers.	A. (+2)	A. ✓ (−2)
	B. Prefers practical experience.	B. (+2)	B. ✓ (−2)
	C. Relates well to other people.	C. ✓ (+2)	C. (−2)
	D. Enjoys serving other people.	D. (+2)	D. (−2)
		Most like me	Least like me
Q19	A. Supports group decisions.	A. (+2)	A. (−2)
	B. Strives to improve situations.	B. (+2)	B. (−2)
	C. Gravitates naturally to leadership positions.	C. ✓ (+2)	C. (−2)
	D. Exhibits an ability to speak spontaneously.	D. (+2)	D. ✓ (−2)
		Most like me	Least like me
Q20	A. Encourages people's ideas.	A. (+2)	A. (−2)
	B. Cares about how change affects people.	B. (+2)	B. ✓ (−2)
	C. Provides lots of facts and data.	C. (+2)	C. (−2)
	D. States convictions firmly.	D. ✓ (+2)	D. (−2)
		Most like me	Least like me
Q21	A. Confronts dissenters directly.	A. ✓ (+2)	A. (−2)
	B. Cultivates commitment in others.	B. (+2)	B. ✓ (−2)
	C. Strives diligently to get along with others.	C. (+2)	C. (−2)
	D. Emphasizes working conscientiously.	D. (+2)	D. (−2)
		Most like me	Least like me
Q22	A. Focuses attention on the finer points.	A. (+2)	A. (−2)
	B. Pursues high personal performance.	B. ✓ (+2)	B. (−2)
	C. Stimulates people around him/her.	C. (+2)	C. ✓ (−2)
	D. Is easy to work with.	D. (+2)	D. (−2)
		Most like me	Least like me
Q23	A. Avoids conflict.	A. (+2)	A. (−2)
	B. Values good regulations.	B. (+2)	B. ✓ (−2)
	C. Overcomes opposition.	C. (+2)	C. (−2)
	D. Influences people naturally.	D. ✓ (+2)	D. (−2)
		Most like me	Least like me
Q24	A. Generates much enthusiasm.	A. (+2)	A. (−2)
	B. Shows sensitivity toward people.	B. (+2)	B. ✓ (−2)
	C. Prefers to probe a matter deeply.	C. ✓ (+2)	C. (−2)
	D. Finds difficult tasks challenging.	D. (+2)	D. (−2)
		Most like me	Least like me
Q25	A. Takes charge instinctively.	A. ✓ (+2)	A. (−2)
	B. Works best through other people.	B. (+2)	B. ✓ (−2)
	C. Displays care for others.	C. (+2)	C. (−2)
	D. Provides expertise in a particular area.	D. (+2)	D. (−2)

Leadership Style Inventory Scoring

Instructions for Scoring the Inventory

1. Transfer the appropriate score for each checked statement on the Leadership Style Inventory to the scoring sheet below.

   For example: If on question **Q1** you checked that statement **A** was "least like me," transfer the point value of **–2** to the appropriate blank on the scoring sheet, marked **A** beside question **Q1**. Likewise, transfer the point value of **+2** for the statement that was "most like me" to the appropriate blank on the scoring sheet.

2. Once all scoring information has been transferred from the Inventory to the scoring sheet, add up each column and place the total at the bottom of the sheet in the row marked Column Totals.

3. Note that adding the four column totals together should result in a sum of zero. If this is not the case, then either data has been inaccurately transferred from the Inventory to the scoring sheet or an error in addition has occurred. Please check your work.

Sample Inventory Questions

		Most like me		Least like me	
Q1	**A.** Loves a challenge.	**A.**	(+2)	**A.** ✓	(–2)
	B. Spends time with people.	**B.**	(+2)	**B.**	(–2)
	C. Behaves in a predictable manner.	**C.** ✓	(+2)	**C.**	(–2)
	D. Sets high ministry standards.	**D.**	(+2)	**D.**	(–2)
		Most like me		Least like me	
Q2	**A.** Focuses on the details.	**A.**	(+2)	**A.**	(–2)
	B. Likes to start things.	**B.**	(+2)	**B.** ✓	(–2)
	C. Motivates people.	**C.**	(+2)	**C.**	(–2)
	D. Shows patience with people.	**D.** ✓	(+2)	**D.**	(–2)

Sample Scoring Sheet

Q1	A. −2	B.	C. +2	D.	
Q2	A.	B. −2	C.	D. +2	
Column Totals	−2	−2	+2	+2	= 0
	Director	Inspirational	Diplomat	Analytical	

Q1	A. +	B.	C. −	D.	
Q1	A. +	B.	C. −	D.	
Q2	B. −	C. +	D.	A.	
Q3	C. −	D.	A. +	B.	
Q4	D.	A.	B. +	C. −	
Q5	A. +	B. −	C.	D.	
Q6	B. −	C. +	D.	A.	
Q7	C.	D.	A. +	B. −	
Q8	D. −	A. +	B.	C.	
Q9	A.	B.	C. −	D. +	
Q10	B. −	C.	D.	A. +	
Q11	C. +	D.	A.	B. −	
Q12	D. −	A.	B.	C. +	
Q13	A. +	B.	C. −	D.	
Q14	B.	C.	D. −	A. +	
Q15	C.	D. +	A.	B. −	
Q16	D. +	A.	B. −	C.	
Q17	A. +	B.	C.	D. −	
Q18	B. −	C. +	D.	A.	
Q19	C. +	D. ↯ −	A.	B.	
Q20	D. +	A.	B. −	C.	
Q21	A. +	B. −	C.	D.	
Q22	B. +	C. −	D.	A.	
Q23	C.	D. +	A.	B. −	
Q24	D. ↯	A.	B. −	C. +	
Q25	A. +	B. −	C.	D.	
Column Totals	8	2	−8	−2	= 0
	Director	Inspirational	Diplomat	Analytical	

Identification of Leadership Style

Answer the following questions to identify your leadership style.

1. What is your primary or dominant style (the one with the highest score)? _Director_
2. What is your secondary style? _Insp._
3. Does one of the two remaining styles also exert a noticeable impact on you? If so, which one? _____
4. According to this information, circle your leadership style in the following list (it will be the combination of your primary and secondary styles).

Director
(Director-Inspirational)
Director-Diplomat
Director-Analytical

Inspirational
Inspirational-Director
Inspirational-Diplomat
Inspirational-Analytical

Diplomat
Diplomat-Director
Diplomat-Inspirational
Diplomat-Analytical

Analytical
Analytical-Director
Analytical-Inspirational
Analytical-Diplomat

Complete the following:
My leadership style is _____.

Note: If a third style has a noticeable impact, you may want to place it in parentheses after your style. For example: Director-Inspirational (Analytical).

You will find it helpful to write a short composite that summarizes what you have discovered about your leadership style. Using the information in chapter 4, describe in several sentences your best leadership context. Summarize your strengths based on your primary and secondary styles. Do the same for your weaknesses. What will you do with this information? The section What Difference Does All This Make? in chapter 4 will help you answer this question.

Appendix G

Natural Gifts and Talents Inventory

Instructions

1. Look over the following list of potential church and parachurch ministries. Circle any you have enjoyed doing in the past or think you might enjoy doing in the future.
2. For each circled item, indicate the degree of your interest by placing a letter in front of it from the following scale:

   A. Passionate interest
   B. Strong interest
   C. Slight interest

____ accounting	____ hospitality
____ administration	____ leadership
____ adolescents	____ library
____ adults	____ lighting
____ advertising and publicity	____ marketing
____ art	____ ministry assessment
____ audiovisual	____ parking
____ bookkeeping	____ playing a musical instrument
____ building and grounds	____ preaching

____ children

____ coaching

____ cooking

____ custodial

____ directing traffic

____ drama

____ evangelism

____ facilities maintenance

____ finances

____ graphic design

____ greeting

____ helps

____ shepherding

____ singing

____ small groups

____ sound control

____ stage production

____ teaching

____ telephoning

____ typing

____ visitation

____ word processing

____ worship

____ writing

APPENDIX H

NATURAL GIFTS AND ABILITIES INDICATOR

Instructions

1. Look over the following list of occupations and vocational topics. Circle any you have enjoyed doing in the past or think you would enjoy pursuing in the future.
2. For each circled item, indicate the degree of your interest by placing a letter in front of it from the following scale:

   A. Passionate interest
   B. Strong interest
   C. Slight interest

Vocational Topics

___ accounting	___ management
___ advertising	___ marketing
___ agriculture	___ mathematics
___ architecture	___ medicine
___ armed services	___ ministry
___ art	___ music
___ automotive services	___ politics

___ business   ___ psychiatry
___ computer science   ___ psychology
___ cooking   ___ real estate
___ electronics   ___ sales
___ engineering   ___ science
___ industrial arts   ___ social work
___ insurance   ___ teaching
___ law enforcement   ___ theater

Occupations

___ accountant   ___ mathematician
___ actor/actress   ___ mechanic
___ appraiser   ___ minister
___ architect   ___ musician
___ artist   ___ nurse
___ athlete   ___ nutritionist
___ carpenter   ___ physical therapist
___ chef   ___ physician
___ coach   ___ pilot
___ comedian   ___ policeman
___ computer specialist   ___ politician
___ construction worker   ___ professor
___ contractor   ___ psychiatrist
___ counselor   ___ psychologist
___ dancer   ___ real estate agent
___ designer   ___ reporter
___ detective   ___ sailor
___ driver   ___ salesperson
___ economist   ___ schoolteacher
___ electrician   ___ scientist
___ engineer   ___ secretary
___ entertainer   ___ singer
___ farmer   ___ social worker
___ hair specialist   ___ soldier
___ homemaker   ___ stockbroker
___ inventor   ___ welder
___ investor   ___ writer
___ marketer

Appendix I

Training Venues

Process-Oriented Venues

Classroom

The classroom is a staple training venue for many churches. The obvious features of the classroom are its limited size—usually three to fifty people—and the one-way communication environment—usually driven by seating configured in rows. The most important consideration with the classroom is a caution: Do not overly rely on classroom training. Because it is the easiest to provide, many churches rely exclusively on it. The downside of classroom training is the inherent limits on relationship building, interaction, and ministry exposure.

An example of classroom training is a class I (Will) attended at Dallas Theological Seminary, taught by Howard Hendricks. There were approximately thirty students who met for thirteen weeks, and each class lasted seventy-five minutes. The class was content-driven (I did receive some fantastic content!); however, thirteen weeks later, I had not developed any significant relationships with other students or with the teacher. Even though this class served my professional training well, it did not provide for the relationship building and ministry exposure I also needed.

When is the classroom format appropriate? Use it when there is a need to cover a large amount of information. For some people, in certain seasons in life, it may be more convenient to meet in a series of weekly classes. Also, a classroom can be a nonthreatening entry point for beginners. Remember, if you rely on the classroom, try to make it conducive to interaction and make sure you provide complementary training venues that will promote relationship building.

Small Group

The second venue is the small group of three to twelve individuals meeting in a relational environment for training. The small group can meet for any length of time—four weeks or an entire year or more—and on average each meeting lasts for an hour and a half to two hours. A small group will usually meet in a home or in a classroom with seating arranged in a circle (for discussion and interaction).

The obvious strength of the small group is that it provides the opportunity to build relationships. While this strength limits the amount of information covered, the information that is taught tends to make more of an impact because the application of ideas can be discussed and debated during the meeting. The key aspects of character and emotional development are possible because of the sharing, accountability, and prayer that can take place in a small group. Also, if the leader-in-training plans to lead a small group in the future, valuable modeling is taking place as well.

There are a number of downsides to the small group. One, of course, is its time-intensive nature, especially if it continues for more than eight weeks. Often the leadership responsibilities for existing leaders preclude their investing their time in a small-group community just for the leadership development of emerging leaders. Also as relationships flourish and as special needs in the group arise, it is more difficult to stay on task when covering content. Finally, keep in mind that a small-group environment is a little more intimidating as an entry point for prospective leaders.

An illustration of small-group leadership training is a group of seven group leaders I (Will) led for a year. We met weekly either in a restaurant, where there were minimum distractions, or in a home for about two hours a meeting. Three of the men were existing group leaders, and four were emerging leaders. The content of the group was focused on personal spiritual formation, with significant time provided to discuss issues occurring in each leader's group. Several lifelong relationships developed in that group, even though many of the men have since moved geographically.

A small-group format is particularly good when leaders have a need for emotional support because of their personal life or the season of the ministry they are leading. A small group works well for leaders who are taking a break from their leadership post for a short time. In general we have found short-term groups (four to eight weeks) to be the best for training, especially if the members of the group are concurrently active in leadership.

Turbo Group

A turbo group is a specialized small group of three to twelve individuals meeting short-term in a relational environment. The purpose is focused training with the goal of launching group members into leadership. A typical duration for a turbo group is eight to twelve weeks. The turbo format emphasizes focused content on leadership and modeling. The goal is to impart all of the critical information that the individual needs to get started in leadership. Usually, there is a launch date or deadline that makes the quick learning of the necessary information essential. Typically, a portion of the group time is dedicated to the leader's modeling the kind of leadership the members will be exercising. Also it's common for the group members to practice leading the group. This allows a unique feedback dynamic as everyone gets the chance to evaluate everybody else as they take a turn practicing group leadership. Because group members will be leading in the near future, there is a heightened responsiveness to feedback and skills development.

There are two primary limitations to the turbo group. The first is that the shorter duration and the modeling focus limit the amount of content covered. The second limitation is that a skilled, experienced leader is needed for the group to function well. Because modeling is taking place, the strengths and weaknesses of the group leader will be duplicated.

An illustration of a turbo group is a gathering of six emerging coaches (leaders of small-group leaders) that I (Will) led for eight weeks. Each meeting lasted two hours. The content included specific information that each person needed to function as a coach. There was also a significant focus on skills development. One of the key functions of a coach is to visit a group meeting and to evaluate the leader in a debriefing session after the meeting. Observation and evaluation skills are critical. During the turbo-group sessions, over the course of the eight weeks, each group member took a turn leading the group. During the last thirty minutes of each group meeting, the entire group evaluated the performance of the group leader. The group evaluation led to exponential learning and skill development for this key skill set.

The turbo group is a strong option for leadership development. It is particularly useful in high-growth environments or any time a group of leaders launches at one time. For example, a church that is launching a small-group ministry for the first time should consider turbo groups. In one setting in which I (Will) worked, the church launched five new discussion groups that corresponded to the Sunday morning teaching series. In this case, the church prepared five new leaders through the turbo-group process.

Apprenticing

Apprenticing is when an individual performs a ministry leadership function, in a learning role, under the direct supervision of an experienced leader. This venue is especially effective because the on-the-job nature provides experience-driven learning, and the supervision of an experienced leader provides mentor-driven learning. Most professions or avocations that require specialized skill development require some form of apprenticeship. Think for a minute of the diverse arenas that use apprenticeships—music, cuisine, martial arts, academics, trades—the list could go on and on.

The word *apprenticeship* shares a common root with the term *apprehend* and conveys the meaning of seizing new understanding and ability. The effectiveness of the apprenticeship is directly related to the close proximity of the teacher and learner. In fact one dictionary definition highlighted this close relationship with the definition "binding to or putting under the care of a master."

Every church should seriously consider apprenticing as a training venue. The great thing about apprenticing is that it can take place any time ministry is occurring. In other words, every event and activity that your church is currently doing provides a built-in opportunity for apprenticing. Therefore no extra time or cost commitment is required. Also apprenticing is unique in its ability to touch on all four levels of learning (knowledge, skills, character, and emotions) as a result of the life-on-life context. It is particularly effective for learning skills. In fact for every significant skill we have learned, we can picture corresponding faces of the men and women who provided training and modeling.

Another strength of apprenticing is the high motivation of the learner. If you teach an emerging leader "five keys to leading small-group prayer" in a classroom setting, he or she is liable to fall asleep. But if you share the same content the evening before the person is scheduled to actually lead a small-group prayer time, he or she will be completely attentive.

You may wonder, if apprenticing is so effective, why don't more churches use it? The difficulty of apprenticing is the intentionality it takes to do it well. It requires planning and patience in the ministry setting itself, as well as a long-term, intensive time commitment on the part of both the apprentice and the master. When churches do have apprenticing venues in place, one of the greatest challenges is connecting leaders with apprentices. We have found that the recruiting of the apprentice is best driven by each individual leader.

Many churches use apprenticing throughout their small-group structure, and the primary benefit is that every small-group meeting becomes a training session. One important limitation in this instance is that both the strengths and weaknesses of the leader get duplicated in the apprentice. As a result, a church should be careful not to rely solely on apprenticing for training, even though it has such clear and unique benefits.

An illustration of this venue is a church that strongly encourages small-group leaders or Sunday morning Bible fellowships to have apprentices as a part of the group leadership team. One church I (Will) work with has approximately forty small groups. About 50 percent of the groups have a clearly identified apprentice. During training events, group leaders are encouraged to bring apprentices, even to the point that special tickets are provided as tools for invitation. Individual coaching and one-on-one meetings always keep the recruiting of an apprentice at the top of the discussion list. When a group grows and is ready to multiply, a new group is formed and the apprentice leader launches into his or her own ministry. One of the first responsibilities of the emerging group leader is to repeat the process by finding an apprentice for the newly birthed group.

One-on-One

A one-on-one venue is simply two individuals meeting in a relational environment, not in the ministry context, for training. The primary benefit of the one-on-one venue is the extreme flexibility for two individuals to meet. They can meet anywhere at any time in a formal or informal learning setting. Because one-on-one is relationship intensive, the opportunity for character and emotional development is also present.

The primary limitations of a one-on-one venue are the time commitment and the relative "inefficiency" of the trainer's time, because it does not multiply the time, knowledge, and experience of the trainer beyond one person at a time.

The beauty of one-on-one meetings is the opportunity for unstructured and informal training initiatives at the discretion of the trainer. In my training role in the local church, I (Will) look for leaders who need special support and attention and schedule one-on-ones with them. The one-on-one meeting is a great tool for capturing teaching moments. At other times, I use a one-on-one approach in a more structured manner, encouraging every leader to meet one-on-one every month with the leader above him or her in the organization. This helps to provide a regular connection through listening, training, and support with every frontline leader in the church.

Coaching

While *coaching* is a broad term, we are referring here specifically to an outside professional who focuses on the personal and leadership development of a higher level church leader. The coaching process is unique in how it accomplishes leadership development. The coach works not by providing answers per se but by asking questions through which the leader gains new insight and takes new actions.

Howard Hendricks defines coaching as "helping people do what they don't want to do, so they can become what they want to become." This is a great definition, especially in an athletic context. But for a church leadership context, we would tweak the definition to be: "helping people discover what they could not discover on their own, so they can become what they want to become."

While executive coaching has continued to flourish in corporate settings in the last decade, we see surprisingly little occurring in the church. This is unfortunate, because if the point leaders in the local church stop growing, leadership development at every level is stifled. We would encourage every senior pastor reading these words to seriously consider finding a coach. There are several ways to do this: Ask other pastors who may have used coaches, ask business leaders in the congregation, call The Malphurs Group (see contact information at the end of this book).

Coaching as a specialized one-on-one meeting is very flexible. In fact much coaching takes place over the phone (usually in an hour or less) and can be accomplished through a long-distance relationship. Coaching can be structured as frequently as desired and for as long as the leader needs it. For example, a coach can meet on a quarterly basis in a relationship that lasts for years or on a weekly basis in a relationship that lasts for several months.

The primary limitation of coaching is the cost involved, as professional coaching comes with a wide range of fees. However, the church could include this as a line item in the budget under the pastor's professional development. Also the church might consider using a coach before hiring the next staff person. In helping or advising the leader in better carrying out ministry, the coach would actually be relieving some of the workload. Also the coach could help clarify what position the next staff hire should fill. Compared to the costs of another staff person (salary, benefits, and so on), a coach is much less expensive. We address this further under the next venue—consulting.

Consulting

Consulting is when an outside individual immerses himself or herself in the church culture to bring specialized knowledge for organizational and leadership development. The distinction between a coach and a consultant is that the consultant brings expertise in a certain arena. For example, this expertise may be in strategic planning and mapping, marketing and communications, leadership development, capital campaign fundraising, or some other skill. We believe that the effectiveness of the consultant comes when he or she is willing to commit the time needed to know and understand the organization.

A consultant can play a vital role, especially at critical seasons in the life of the church. These seasons include confronting growth barriers, navigating high-growth rates, facility changes, relocation, pastoral leadership changes, and directional changes. Having the right knowledge during these times will significantly impact the scope of the church's ministry for decades.

In some cases a consultant can augment church staffing. The primary benefits are that the consultant works only on important, nonurgent issues, unlike other pastoral staff; the consultant incurs no overhead cost, such as health insurance and other benefits; and the length of the consulting contract is flexible. We believe that both professional coaching and consulting will play increasingly vital roles in the future of church staffing, especially in leading-edge churches with strategic thinking, because churches are recognizing that objective consultants see the issues more clearly and they bring insights from diverse experiences. Their counsel shortens the learning curve for churches as they go through the critical seasons mentioned above.

The primary limitation of consulting is the cost, which is highly variable. But today's leaders and their churches must ask if they can afford *not* to bring in a consultant. Check references on consultants before hiring them and don't be afraid to pay more for the right kind of expertise. As with many things, you get what you pay for. In addition, make sure the consultant is theologically trained. What you and they do together is deeply theological, and the typical corporate consultant comes up short here. Of course, we recommend that you consult with The Malphurs Group in these areas (www.malphursgroup.com).

Self-Led

Self-led venues are those in which a potential leader trains himself or herself. In chapter 8 we describe this under the learner-driven training type. The primary tools are books, audiocassettes or CDs, and the Internet.

The best part of using self-led venues is the flexibility. For example, a leader can listen to a tape while driving to work. This is very significant, because it is a way for the church to deliver pertinent information to leaders, without having another meeting or adding another time commitment.

An illustration of a self-led venue is a cassette tape that a church produces in-house for quarterly leadership training. The church staff plan the content of the training, which focuses on the skills for leading people into biblical community. While the conversation is recorded, the pastors discuss the training topic with one another. The product is a thirty-five-minute tape of fun and informal conversation that brings practical leadership training to each group leader—at his or her own time and convenience. Along with the training, leaders get to know their pastors better while hearing stories from their experiences.

There are few limitations with self-led training. Even if your church doesn't have the resources to make its own audio training (highly unlikely in developed countries today), you can create a leadership library of books and cassette tapes for leaders to check out. Another option is a leadership newsletter that leaders can read on their own time. One drawback is that the leader who is self-led may not be receiving feedback concerning his or her ideas and practices. This venue should be used with another venue in which there is give-and-take with a more experienced leader.

While we have not personally developed web training, there is no question that it is a key tool for the future. Last month I (Will) took a six-hour defensive driving course on the Internet. Rather than going to a six-hour class, I completed the course in the evenings over five or six days at my own convenience.

Event-Oriented Venues

We now turn to the event-oriented venues.

Huddle

A huddle is a specialized small group of three to twelve individuals with common ministry responsibilities that meets in an interactive environment for training. The distinguishing feature of the huddle is the gathering of leaders who share similar ministry responsibilities. A huddle, for example, may consist of a group of children's Sunday school teachers or student small-group leaders or finance committee members. Meeting once or at periodic intervals, a huddle is useful because it allows for training, sharing, discussion, and problem solving around ministry-specific issues. A huddle can be a time for encouragement and celebration among the leadership community. It can also serve as a skills-development time for ministry-specific skills.

An example of a huddle is a gathering of small-group hosts—the people in small groups who provide an environment, usually their home, in which the small groups meet. During this huddle there was training and discussion about creating an ideal small-group environment in the home. Child care was the most significant challenge for the hosts, so they developed several child-care strategies. As they shared their favorite horror stories of wild pets and coffee-stained sofas, the hosts connected with one another. It was a very valuable equipping time for this specific group of leaders.

Seminar

The seminar is a relatively large group of individuals who meet in a one-way communication environment for one time of focused instruction. The seminar differs from the class in two primary ways. The seminar services a larger group, and the seminar is a one-time event. As a one-time event, it is usually more time-intensive than a class, lasting anywhere from three hours to an entire day.

A seminar may be a venue either that the church provides for itself or that an outside organization offers in the area. For example, churches and denominations invite us to do a number of seminars each year on various topics, such as strategic planning, church planting, and other vital areas of leadership.

Seminars have many benefits. They are relatively easy for a church to plan and are low cost. If your church does not have an adequate room to host the seminar, you could hold it at a local hotel or other public meeting place. Through a seminar, a church is able to provide focused content to many people at one time. This maximizes the time of the trainer and allows the ministry to target individual topics effectively. The seminar is also a very good entry point for emerging leaders. The low level of interaction makes it less threatening, and the one-time nature makes it easier to schedule than some other training venues. Because seminars are commonly used in the business world, the *seminar* label itself has an appealing ring to people.

Use seminars when your goal is to deliver content to a large number of people. You might use a seminar in a large church for new leaders training. A three-hour introductory seminar for potential leaders could be called Leadership 101 or New Leaders Training.

Also a church should take advantage of seminars sponsored by outside organizations that come to your area. One church that I (Will) worked with sends all its leaders to a time-management seminar every year.

Conference

A conference is a large group of individuals who meet in a one-way communication environment for instruction from a teacher, usually a notable leader. Conferences are larger than seminars and involve multiple days of training.

Conferences have popped up everywhere over the past few decades. Several of the prominent megachurches have led the way by hosting leadership-training conferences. Two of these are Willow Creek Community Church and Saddleback Community Church. However, a host of other churches all over the country offer church-based conferences that may attract three thousand to fifteen thousand people in weekend attendance.

There are numerous benefits to using this venue.

- A local church-based conference provides a wonderful vision-casting opportunity. Leaders can see the giant potential of their local church.
- Leaders can network with those from other churches.
- The opportunity for leaders to spend several days off-site usually brings refreshment and new insight.
- Traveling together provides special team-building opportunities for a church's leaders. Traveling and eating together, going to entertainment, and just hanging out can be special times for leaders who attend conferences with their colleagues.
- Many conferences provide very useful, focused training in small, breakout seminars.

We highly recommend conferences for leadership development, because no event can catalyze the commitment of an emerging leader as a conference can. Recognizing the value of conferences, some church staffs will take forty or fifty volunteer leaders across the country to attend a church conference. In one case, the church paid five hundred dollars of the seven-hundred-fifty-dollar total trip cost for leaders who wanted to go. The church was convinced that it was the best investment it could make in the life of its leaders. We agree.

The limitations of conferences include scheduling, necessary travel, and cost. We recommend that a pastor or other leader attend conferences first to discover which one will work best for his church. Once you select a conference, you must recruit people early to attend and you must decide if the church is going to offset the cost for lay leaders.

Getaway

A getaway is a group of individuals who meet off-site for one day of training. The site should be between forty-five and sixty minutes away (close enough to drive round-trip in one day, yet far enough to be a true getaway).

The getaway has many advantages.

- It allows for a diversity of training types and venues. You can literally use any of the other venues mentioned in this chapter. For example, imagine a day consisting of an hour-long large-group seminar, which then divides into multiple, forty-five-minute small-group sessions. Then, after lunch and free time for one-on-one discussion, the last two hours of the day are spent in several workshop options.
- A getaway can help forge leadership community. Something happens when leaders "rub minds" together with one another in a daylong event. There is the cross-pollination of ideas, and new relational chemistry develops. Much of this happens through relationship building during the informal and in-between times.

  During one getaway that I (Will) led, I remember feeling humbled by this observation. I realized that the primary benefit of the getaway was not my prepared teaching but the spontaneous sharing and learning that happened leader-to-leader after my talk was over. (In fact this motivated me to provide less one-way communication in getaways and to create more interactive learning environments.)
- A getaway is an excellent venue to train new leaders and potential leaders. New leaders assimilate into the leadership culture quickly in a getaway environment (for the reasons mentioned above). A new leader track can be planned for this purpose.
- A getaway can be downright fun. Prepare team-building activities or recreation (appropriate to the gender and age) for your leaders. The hour after lunch is a good time for activity.

The three limitations of a getaway are planning, expense, and time. A daylong event like this takes considerable logistics planning (facility selection, registration, travel, meals, training materials, child care, and so on). It also incurs expense that will vary depending on location.

The other limitation is the fixed time. The schedules of some leaders will mean they will miss it. Therefore, plan in advance and recruit early. Provide early registration incentives if you are charging something for the getaway. We recommend charging people to attend because it creates commitment and raises expectations as well as helping to pay for the facility and food.

Retreat

A retreat is a group of individuals who meet off-site for training over multiple days. A retreat differs from a getaway by adding the overnight experience. This effectively amplifies the strengths and limitations of the getaway—increased relationship building and increased preparation logistics and cost.

Many churches use an annual retreat effectively in the leadership-development process, because the strength of this venue is its ability to accommodate a variety of training experiences. If you choose this venue, the selection of facilities is critical. Never book a facility without doing an on-site visit or receiving a recommendation from a trusted individual.

Workshop

A workshop is a relatively small group of individuals meeting over a period of time in a skills-focused, interactive environment for training. A workshop will usually last a half-day to a day and will focus on a specific ministry skill. Some examples of workshops are those emphasizing life-application teaching, church marketing, and leading from a personal mission statement.

The key difference between a workshop and other training venues is that the participants of a workshop move beyond hearing something to actually doing something. For example, in the life-application teaching workshop, those attending would actually work as a group to craft a teaching series. There is a high degree of interaction with others in the workshop and with the instructor. Because of this, I (Aubrey) prefer the workshop to the seminar and conference venues when training leaders.

I (Will) am currently planning a workshop with leaders involved in the welcoming system or "first impressions" ministry of their church. During the workshop, we will look at the facility maps of the different churches and chart where parking attendants and greeters should stand. We will discuss and work on role descriptions for the various team members and role-play and practice the type of interaction that should happen when a guest walks through the doors of the church.

In the local church, short workshops for leaders can be very effective. You can do workshops on a wide variety of topics, such as inductive Bible study, preparing a Bible lesson, mentoring, conflict resolution, recruiting, and vision casting. When planning a workshop, make sure the topic is an issue your leaders are currently confronting.

The first challenge of having a workshop is finding an experienced trainer. Because the trainer will be modeling behavior as well as providing skill-based training, he or she must have more to offer than knowledge. The trainer must be good at what he or she does. The second challenge is time. Taking a day to learn a specific skill is a big commitment for busy lay leaders. Consequently it may be wise to bring in a well-known person, who is a recognized expert in the particular skill, to do the training for you.

Rally

A rally is a group of individuals meeting in a one-way communication environment for celebration-based training that is focused on past accomplishments or future expectations. This venue may seem a little unusual, but it is a critical type of training that often gets overlooked.

The distinction of this venue is that it targets the heart—the goal being motivation and inspiration. The primary role of the trainer is to champion the cause and cast the vision, and the primary benefit of a rally is that it reminds leaders why they sacrifice. Day in and day out, our lay leaders make an enormous commitment, often with little thanks. The leadership-development process must take leaders' morale into consideration and plan intentional venues that will serve to fill the leaders' emotional tanks.

A rally could be a "vision night." Bill Hybels practices this venue at Willow Creek Community Church. Once a year there is a special gathering when the pastor opens his heart about the future direction of the church. Many other churches hold a very effective vision night.

Another example of a rally is one that I (Will) recently led. We had just finished a semester-long training of five turbo groups for coaches. At the end of the semester we leaders planned a final event of which the trainees were unaware. We set up a room to look like the stage of a television game show that was popular at the time—*Who Wants to Be a Millionaire*—even with lighting and sound effects. When the turbo group members arrived, they realized they were contestants on the game as we asked review questions about the coaches' training. Afterward we cast the vision of the essential role of the coach and thanked them for their commitment to the training. The bottom line is that we filled their emotional tank with a fun and motivating time together.

There was a time when I (Will) would have secretly heaped negative judgment on a training venue like this. Through experience, however, I have learned that touching the heart and providing laughter are vital aspects of the leadership experience. Don't overlook your leader's heart.

Benchmarking

Benchmarking is taking a small group of individuals to visit another ministry context for learning and modeling. Benchmarking is one of the easiest and yet most underutilized training venues. Basically, every church within an hour's drive provides a potential benchmarking opportunity. Usually churches are more than willing to allow another church's leadership team to observe their ministries and will share what they know in an effort to multiply their strengths for the kingdom.

The advantages of benchmarking are numerous. It is a no-lose proposition. The stronger points of the church you are visiting provide vision and modeling for your leaders, and the weaker points can bring affirmation to what your ministry is already doing better. On one occasion I (Will) took a children's ministry leadership team to visit the children's ministry at another church. It was effective modeling because they learned some simple and creative ideas that were new and easily transferable. The event was also affirming to the leaders.

The church we visited had a similar-size ministry to that of our church with almost twice the paid staff. Consequently our leaders felt like real champions for having "done more with less" over the years. It was a fantastic win-win trip.

The other advantages of benchmarking are the low cost, the team-building dynamic, and the opportunity to take some downtime from the leader's own ministry. For example, it was a great Sunday break for the children's ministry team when we visited another church.

Of course, this leads us to the greatest challenge of benchmarking—having all of your leaders absent while visiting another ministry. This will usually require some creative problem solving, but the extra effort to pull this off will yield much fruit.

NOTES

Chapter 1 The Concept of Your Divine Design

1. Ralph Mattson and Arthur Miller, *Finding a Job You Can Love* (Nashville: Thomas Nelson, 1982), 123.

2. Ibid.

3. A variety of models exist as based on the physiological, cognitive, behavioral, psycho-analytic, humanistic, or genetic perspectives of psychology. See Rod Plotnik and Sandra Mollenauer, *Introduction to Psychology* (New York: Random House, 1986), 5–10. The deterministic model is often referred to today as the behavioral model; the developmental as the humanist model.

4. See the brief discussion on this in Gerald Corey, *Theory and Practice of Counseling and Psychotherapy,* 4th ed. (Pacific Grove, CA: Brooks/Cole, 1991), 293.

5. Whereas Skinner ruled out the possibility of any self-determination and freedom, the current trend allows that an individual has some ability to choose.

6. Plotnik and Mollenauer, *Introduction to Psychology*, 9.

7. Mattson and Miller, *Finding a Job You Can Love*, 123.

8. Lyle Schaller, *Activating the Passive Church: Diagnosis and Treatment* (Nashville: Abingdon Press, 1981), 11.

9. Source unknown.

10. In Frank Tillapaugh's *Unleashing the Church* (Ventura, CA: Regal, 1982), 20.

Chapter 2 The Importance of Your Divine Design

1. Every Christian should explore both his dignity and his depravity in that order. We are able to deal with our depravity best when we consider it in the context of our dignity. To focus on one without considering the other leads to an extreme. For example, to focus on our depravity alone, as Christians are prone to do, results in a low view of ourselves that is not biblical and leads to discouragement, depression, and low self-esteem. To focus only on our dignity can produce spiritual pride.

2. A part of knowing who we are includes all that has taken place spiritually as the result of being in Christ. This includes such divine blessings as forgiveness, redemption, reconciliation, justification, propitiation, and many others.

3. I first heard this from Bruce Bugbee, who is the founder and president of Network Ministries International, which provides training and support for volunteer and staff identification and placement according to one's divine design. This excellent organization also provides tapes, seminars, and written materials as well as comprehensive training through Networking University. For more information see http://www.brucebugbee.com.

4. Mattson and Miller, *Finding a Job You Can Love*, 119.

5. Donald A. McGavran, *Understanding Church Growth* (Grand Rapids: Eerdmans, 1970), 223.

6. For further discussion of the homogeneous principle see Aubrey Malphurs, *Planting Growing Churches for the 21st Century* (Grand Rapids: Baker, 1992), 168–71.

7. A definition used by Brad Smith in a brochure for the Center for Christian Leadership on the theme of authenticity published by Dallas Theological Seminary, summer 1992.

8. A definition used by Dr. William Lawrence in "Vision for Personal and Leadership Development" (a paper presented to the National Association of Professors of Christian Education, October 1992), 9.

9. Ibid.

10. An excellent book that is designed to help teams function well together is Glenn Parker, *Team Players and Teamwork* (San Francisco: Jossey-Bass, 1990).

Chapter 3 The Components of Your Divine Design

1. Charles C. Ryrie, *The Holy Spirit* (Chicago: Moody, 1965), 83.

2. Each question is preceded by a negative Greek particle that implies that the expected answer is no. See H. E. Dana and Julius R. Mantey, *A Manual Grammar of the Greek New Testament* (New York: Macmillan, 1955), 265.

3. Robert Clinton, *The Making of a Leader* (Colorado Springs: Navpress, 1988), 92.

4. Bruce Bugbee, an assistant pastor at Willow Creek Community Church near Chicago, includes the gifts of counseling, craftsmanship, and creative communication in his list of gifts. Bruce L. Bugbee, *Networking: Participants Manual* (The Charles E. Fuller Institute of Evangelism and Church Growth, P.O. Box 91990, Pasadena, CA 91109-1990), 51.

5. Some argue that these gifts were limited in their use to the first century during the foundational period of the church. See William McRae, *The Dynamics of Spiritual Gifts* (Grand Rapids: Zondervan, 1976), 64–75, 90–99; and Joseph C. Dillow, *Speaking in Tongues* (Grand Rapids: Zondervan, 1975).

6. See my thesis for the Department of New Testament Literature and Exegesis, "The Relationship of Pastors and Teachers in Ephesians 4:11" (Th.M. thesis, Dallas Theological Seminary, 1978).

7. Kevin W. McCarthy, *The On-Purpose Person* (Colorado Springs: Pinion Press, 1992), 108.

8. Bill Hybels, *Honest to God?* (Grand Rapids: Zondervan, 1990), 112.

9. Fergus P. Hughes and Lloyd D. Noppe, *Human Development: Across the Life Span* (St. Paul, MN: West, 1985), 378.

10. Ibid.

11. James C. Dobson, *Parenting Isn't for Cowards* (Waco, TX: Word, 1987), 24.

12. Ken Voges and Ron Braund, *Understanding How Others Misunderstand You* (Chicago: Moody, 1990), 39.

13. I develop these preferences in more detail in chapter 4.

14. Hybels, *Honest to God?*, 114.

15. Ibid., 73.

16. As Christians, we must not forget that many people who may not profess Christ are just as concerned with accuracy and arriving at truth as we are.

17. Sylvan J. Kaplan and Barbara E. W. Kaplan, *The Kaplan Report: A Study of the Validity of the Personal Profile System* (Chevy Chase, MD: Performax Systems, 1983).

18. Isabel Briggs Myers and Mary H. McCaulley, *Manual: A Guide to the Development and Use of the Myers-Briggs Type Indicator* (Palo Alto, CA: Consulting Psychologists Press, 1985), ch. 11.

19. Roland Kenneth Harrison, *Introduction to the Old Testament* (Grand Rapids: Eerdmans, 1969), 1004.

20. Ibid., 1007–8.

21. Ibid., 1006.

22. Ibid., 1007.

23. Derek Kidner, *Proverbs: An Introduction and Commentary* (Downers Grove, IL: InterVarsity, 1964), 17.

24. David Ward, "Theologically Justifying Personality Type Training" (a student paper presented at Dallas Theological Seminary, Dallas, TX, 1992), 3.

25. Mels Carbonell covers nine spiritual gifts and how they combine with the D, I, S, and C temperaments in his booklet "Uniquely You in Christ: Combination—Personalities and Spiritual Gifts Profile." You may purchase this tool by writing to 255 Bellevue Loop, Fayetteville, GA 30214, or calling 404-461-4243.

26. While some distinctions probably exist between management and administration depending on the area of study (education, military, government, or business), for purposes of simplicity, this book will treat them as fundamentally the same.

27. John P. Kotter, "What Leaders Really Do," *Harvard Business Review* (May–June 1990), 103.

28. See the following on leadership: Ted W. Engstrom, *The Making of a Christian Leader* (Grand Rapids: Zondervan, 1976), 23; Abraham Zaleznik, "Managers and Leaders: Are They Different?" *Harvard Business Review* (May–June 1977), 67–78; Bruce W. Jones, *Ministerial Leadership in a Managerial World* (Wheaton, IL: Tyndale, 1988), 39–52; Mary E. Tramel and Helen Reynolds, *Executive Leadership* (Englewood Cliffs, NJ: Prentice-Hall, 1981), 59–60.

29. Kotter, "What Leaders Really Do," 104.

30. Ibid.

31. Warren Bennis and Burt Nanus, *Leaders: The Strategies for Taking Charge* (New York: Harper and Row, 1985), 21.

32. Peter R. Drucker, *The Effective Executive* (New York: Harper and Row, 1967), 4.

33. C. Peter Wagner, *Leading Your Church to Growth* (Ventura, CA: Regal, 1984), 89.

34. David W. Bennett, *Metaphors of Ministry* (Grand Rapids: Baker, 1993), 121.

35. Hybels, *Honest to God?*, 126.

36. Ibid., 127.

37. Ibid., 128–29.

38. Ibid., 129.

39. Ibid., 130.

40. Ibid., 131.

41. Ibid.

42. Ibid., 132.

43. Exploring these in more detail is beyond the purpose of this book. However, if you desire to pursue your design in any of these areas, several of the articles I have cited in the footnotes contain quizzes and explanations.

44. Mattson and Miller, *Finding a Job You Can Love*, 98–99.

45. Penny Zeitler, "Not Everyone Learns Alike," *Leadership* (Summer 1987), 28–33. See also Bernice McCarthy, *The 4MAT System* (EXCEL, Inc., 200 West Station Street, Barrington, IL 60010).

46. Knowing our learning style can be very useful. Students could decide on class projects and select their teachers based on learning style. Teachers could base their instructional methodology as well as their assignments on their students' learning styles.

47. Norman Shawchuck, *How to Manage Conflict in the Church: Understanding and Managing Conflict* (Glendale Heights, IL: Spiritual Growth Resources, 1983), 23–27.

48. Robert M. Bramson and Susan Bramson, "What Kind of Thinker Are You?" *Reader's Digest* (December 1987), 149–52.

49. Glenn M. Parker, *Team Players and Teamwork* (San Francisco: Jossey-Bass Publishers, 1990), ch. 3.

50. Parker includes a survey on pages 159–64 to help you determine your team-player style.

Chapter 4 The Discovery of Your Divine Design

1. William McRae, *The Dynamics of Spiritual Gifts* (Grand Rapids: Zondervan, 1976), 114.

2. This inventory does not include all the gifts, such as the sign gifts.

3. J. Robert Clinton, *The Making of a Leader* (Colorado Springs: NavPress, 1988), 92.

4. Ibid.

5. Ibid.

6. I have designed these two instruments specifically for this book. They are aids only to help you get started in the discovery process. You should follow these with the other, more sophisticated instruments of high validity.

7. You can purchase both profiles from the Charles E. Fuller Institute of Evangelism and Church Growth, P.O. Box 91990, Pasadena, CA 91109-1990, 800-999-9578. You may also be able to purchase them from a counseling organization in your area. For a name or address contact the Carlson Learning Company, P.O. Box 59159, Minneapolis, MN 55459-8247 or call 612-449-2856.

8. Bob Phillips, *The Delicate Art of Dancing with Porcupines* (Ventura, CA: Regal, 1989).

9. For information as to the availability of the MBTI in your area, contact the Center for Applications of Psychological Type, 2815 N.W. 13th Street, Suite 401, Gainesville, FL 32609, 904-375-0160. This inventory is not available to the general public. You must take it through a professional counseling center, a consulting organization, or the departments of education or psychology at a nearby college or university.

10. The Keirsey Temperament Sorter costs only 25 cents. You can order copies from Prometheus Nemesis Book Company, Box 2748, Del Mar, CA 92014 or call 619-632-1575.

11. David Keirsey and Marilyn Bates, *Please Understand Me* (Del Mar, CA: Promethean Books, 1978).

12. Roy M. Oswald and Otto Kroeger, *Personality Type and Religious Leadership* (Washington, DC: The Alban Institute, 1988).

13. Ken R. Voges, *Biblical Personal Profile* (Minneapolis: Performax Systems International, 1985), 21.

14. Ibid.

15. Ibid.

16. I have designed this tool to get you started in the process of determining your leadership role. It has not been validated and may not accurately reflect your leadership role. I am not aware of any other tool that helps determine leadership role, however.

17. Mels Carbonell demonstrates how the gift of evangelism combines with the four temperaments in his booklet "Uniquely You in Christ."

18. You may order the Campbell Interest and Skills Survey from National Computer Systems, Inc., P.O. Box 1294, Minneapolis, MN 55440.

19. Herbert A. Shepard and Jack A. Hawley, *Life Planning: Personal and Organizational* (Washington, DC: National Training and Development Service Press, 1974).

20. James M. Kouzes and Barry Z. Posner, *The Leadership Challenge: How to Get Extraordinary Things Done in Organizations* (San Francisco: Jossey-Bass, 1987), 101.

Chapter 5 The Concept of Ministry Direction

1. Tillapaugh, *Unleashing the Church*, 20.

2. Aubrey Malphurs, *Advanced Strategic Planning*, 2nd. ed. (Grand Rapids: Baker, 2005), ch. 5.

3. Kent and Barbara Hughes, *Liberating Ministry from the Success Syndrome* (Wheaton, IL: Tyndale, 1988), 125.

4. Ibid., 126.

5. Ibid.

6. Ibid., 129–31.

7. Arthur J. DeJong, *Reclaiming a Mission* (Grand Rapids: Eerdmans, 1990), 63.

8. In fact, some old paradigm churches are hostile toward them.

9. Jerry White, *The Church and the Parachurch: An Uneasy Marriage* (Portland: Multnomah, 1983), 36.

10. Ibid., 54.

11. Leith Anderson, *Dying for Change* (Minneapolis: Bethany, 1990), 10.

12. Ibid.

13. White, *The Church and the Parachurch*, 106–10.

14. Ibid., 89–93.

15. William McRae, *The Principles of the New Testament Church* (Dallas: Believers Chapel, 1974), 17.

16. The topic of women serving as pastors and elders is hotly debated among evangelicals today. I believe that 1 Timothy 2:11–15 and 1 Corinthians 11:3 teach that they are not to be in the position of pastor or elder.

Chapter 6 The Discovery of Your Ministry Direction

1. For more information see Aubrey Malphurs, *Planting Growing Churches for the 21st Century* (Grand Rapids: Baker, 1992), 152–54.

2. Robert W. Thomas, "Personality Characteristics of Effective Revitalization Pastors in Small, Passive, Baptist General Conference Churches" (D.Min. Dissertation, Talbot School of Theology, 1989), 1. Some might object to his use of trait theory as an approach to assessment. Thomas defends this practice on pages 26–32.

3. Ibid.

4. This profile consists of a high I temperament combined with a secondary D. It is a combination of the temperaments of two biblical characters, Peter and Paul.

5. John G. Geier and Dorothy E. Downey, *Personal Profile System* (Minneapolis: Performax Systems International, 1977), 17.

6. In *Pouring New Wine into Old Wineskins: How to Change a Church without Destroying It* (Grand Rapids: Baker, 1993), ch. 4, I bring other divine design elements to bear on the issue of who makes good renewal pastors.

7. Ken R. Voges, *Workbook: Level 1 Part A*. The Biblical Behavioral Series (Minneapolis: Performax Systems International, 1986), 6. Italics mine.

8. Malphurs, *Planting Growing Churches for the 21st Century*, ch. 5.

9. Ibid., 91.

10. For more information, contact Mr. Paul Williams at P.O. Box 9, East Islip, NY 11730-0009.

11. Malphurs, *Planting Growing Churches for the 21st Century*, 99–100.

12. Thomas, "Personality Characteristics," 113–14.

13. Paul D. Tieger and Barbara Barron-Tieger, *Do What You Are* (Boston: Little, Brown, 1992), 90.

14. Ibid., 89.

Chapter 7 Initiating the Ministry Plan

1. David P. Ludeker, "Training for Ministry: A Life-Time Experience," *American Baptist Quarterly* (June 1984), 116.

Chapter 8 Designing the Ministry Plan

1. David A. Kolb, *Experiential Learning: Experience as the Source of Learning and Development* (Englewood Cliffs, NJ: Prentice-Hall, 1984).

2. Kouzes and Posner, *The Leadership Challenge*, 284.

3. Ibid.

4. Ibid., 285.

Chapter 9 Working the Ministry Plan

1. Daniel Goleman, Richard Boyatzis, and Annie McKee, *Primal Leadership: Realizing the Power of Emotional Intelligence* (Boston: Harvard Business School Press, 2002), 161.

INDEX

New Age movement, 21
Noppe, Lloyd, 55

Oswald, Roy, 81

Palau, Luis, 54, 58
parachurch, 111–13
paradigm, 110–11
Parenting Isn't for Cowards, 55
passion, 52, 175, 177
   definition of, 52–53
   discovering, 78–79
   examples of, 54
   importance of, 53–54
pastoring, 51–52
Perkins, John, 53, 54, 58
Personal Profile, 56–57, 59, 80, 81, 123, 124, 140–42
personality, 55, 56
Personality Type and Religious Leadership, 81
Phillips, Bob, 80
Planting Growing Churches for the 21st Century, 123
Please Understand Me, 80–81
Posner, Barry, 96, 146
prayer, 75, 175
preaching, 47, 54

race, 35–36
recruiting, 104, 220, 228
relators, 82
revelation, general and special, 58–59
Reynolds, Helen, 62
Richards, Larry, 26, 103

Saddleback Valley Community Church, 14, 225
Schaller, Lyle, 22
Shawchuck, Norman, 70
Shepard, Herbert, 96
shepherding, 108, 114
   skills, 25, 91, 143–46
   conflict resolution, 153
   consensus building, 153
   development of, 21–22, 218
   ministry, 86, 89, 133, 153
   and roles clarification, 153
   task-oriented, 88
Skinner, B. F., 20
spiritual gifts, 13, 15, 26, 28, 44, 53–54, 69, 94, 113–14, 123
   definition of, 44–46

description of, 47–52
direction of, 46–47
discovering, 74–78
and temperament, 60–61
Spiritual Gifts Inventory, 76
spiritual growth, 70, 163
Sproul, R. C., 54, 58
Swindoll, Chuck, 121

teaching, 19, 45–46, 51, 52, 61, 77, 89, 103, 141–42
temperament, 54–55, 92–93, 117, 118, 122, 134, 140
   definition of, 55–56
   description of, 56–58
   discovering, 80–84
   examples of, 58
   importance of, 56
   and spiritual gifts, 60–61
   theological justification for, 58–60
Temperament Indicator, 80, 92, 140
temperament inventory, 80. *See also* Myers-Briggs Type (Temperament) Indicator
thinkers, 82, 138
Thomas, Robert, 122–24
training, 128, 134–36
   classroom-based, 148–49
   and life circumstances, 147–50
   methods, 142–47
   ministry-based, 148, 159, 162, 165
   supplementary, 160
Tramel, Mary, 62
truth, God's, 40, 52, 59, 60

Understanding How Others Misunderstand You, 80

Voges, Ken, 57, 80, 123
vulnerability, 39

Wagner, Peter, 63–64
Wagner-Modified Houts Questionnaire, 76
Ward, David, 60
Warren, Rick, 14
White, Jerry, 112–13
Willow Creek Community Church, 14, 58, 118, 225, 228
wisdom tradition, 60
women in ministry, 36–37, 51, 103, 113–14, 149, 162–63

Zaleznik, Abraham, 62

Aubrey Malphurs is the president of The Malphurs Group, a church consulting and training service, and serves as professor of pastoral ministries at Dallas Theological Seminary. He is also the author of several books on leadership, including the trilogy *Being Leaders*, *Building Leaders*, and *Leading Leaders*.

Malphurs is available for training and consulting on various topics related to leadership. You may contact him through

The Malphurs Group
7916 Briar Brook Ct.
Dallas, TX 75218
214-327-1752
email: aubrey@malphursgroup.com
website: www.malphursgroup.com

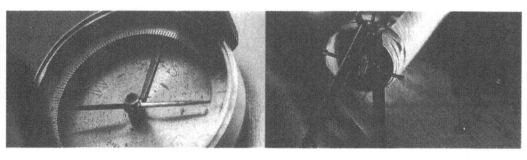

Made in the USA
Lexington, KY
28 December 2014